CONTENTS

RĀMA PĀṆIVĀDA'S

KAṀSAVAHO

(A Prākrit Poem in Classical Style)

Text and Chāyā critically edited for the first time with various Readings, Introduction, Translation, Notes, etc.

DR. A.N. UPADHYE

MOTILAL BANARSIDASS
Delhi Mumbai Chennai Kolkata
Bangalore Varanasi Pune Patna

Edition : 2002

First Edition: 1940
Second Edition: 1966

Also available at:

MOTILAL BANARSIDASS

41 U.A. Bungalow Road, Jawahar Nagar, Delhi 110 007
8 Mahalaxmi Chamber, 22 Bhulabhai Desai Road, Mumbai 400 026
236, 9th Main III Block, Jayanagar, Bangalore 560 011
120 Royapettah High Road, Mylapore, Chennai 600 004
Sanas Plaza, 1302 Baji Rao Road, Pune 411 002
8 Camac Street, Kolkata 700 017
Ashok Rajpath, Patna 800 004
Chowk, Varanasi 221 001

Printed in India

BY JAINENDRA PRAKASH JAIN AT SHRI JAINENDRA PRESS,
A-45 NARAINA, PHASE-I, NEW DELHI 110 028
AND PUBLISHED BY NARENDRA PRAKASH JAIN FOR
MOTILAL BANARSIDASS PUBLISHERS PRIVATE LIMITED,
BUNGALOW ROAD, DELHI 110 007

PREFACE

Kaṁsavaho of Rāma Pāṇivāda, though listed by OPPERT and mentioned by AUFRECHT at the close of the last century, did not attract the attention of Prākrit scholars till a Ms. of it from the Madras Oriental Library was lately described in the *Triennial Catalogue of Mss.*, Volume VI—Part I. Sanskrit, Madras 1935.

Rāma Pāṇivāda is a genuine poet with a confident grip over his expression ; he has inherited the spirit of classical Sanskrit authors whose models he closely follows ; though he belongs to the closing period of Prākrit literature, his work can be creditably ranked with the mediæval Prākrit poems ; and his language is a fine specimen of literary Prākrit handled after closely studying the Sūtras of Prākrit grammars.

The detailed results of my study of the two Mss. that were accessible to me I have presented here. The constitution of the text was attended with many difficulties, but I have faithfully handled the material and never trespassed its limits. This limited material almost forced me to offer some emendations which are marked with asterisks in the text ; and my suggestions on the Chāyā are put in the foot-notes within square brackets. The inclusion of the Chāyā and the addition of the English Translation and the critical and explanatory Notes, I hope, would go a long way to facilitate the understanding of the text. The Introduction is occupied with a critical study of the various aspects of *Kaṁsavaho* after describing the Ms. material and the method of text-constitution. The details about Rāma Pāṇivāda are critically set forth ; and the source and model, the Prākrit dialect and the style of *Kaṁsavaho* are thoroughly scrutinised. With all modesty the Introduction aims at enlightening the readers on the position of *Kaṁsavaho* in the realm of Prākrit literature in particular and Indian literature in general.

The Syndicate of the University of Bombay have been pleased to select me as the Springer Research Scholar to conduct research in Prākrit literature, and here I record my sense of gratitude to the Syndicate for enabling me to make my study about Rāma Pāṇivāda and his *Kaṁsavaho* so exhaustive.

I offer my thanks to various scholars who helped me in the preparation of this edition. Pt. K. SAMBASHIVA SHASTRI, Trivandrum, kindly made the Travancore Ms. accessible to me ; Prof. M. R. BALAKRISHNA WARRIER, M.A., Trivandrum, favoured me with a valuable summary of his Malayālam articles about Rāma Pāṇivada and his activities ; Rao Saheb Mahākavi Ullur S. PARAMESVARA AIYAR, M.A., B.L., and Mr. C. K. NARAYANA KURUP, Trivandrum, kindly sent to me some notes about Rāma Pāṇivāda and his compositions ; my friend Dr. V. RAGHAVAN, M.A., Ph.D., Madras, helped me with important references about our author's works ; and my friend Prof. M. V. PATWARDHAN, M.A., Sangli, spared his valuable time and made important suggestions in the Translation and Notes : to all these scholars I offer my sincere thanks. My thanks are also due to my pupil and friend Mr. J. N. DANI, B.A., B.T., Kolhapur, who helped me in arranging the Glossary.

I record my sense of gratitude to the Prime Minister, Kolhapur Government, Kolhapur, for the help given towards the publication of this book.

I feel much obliged to Pt. NATHURAM PREMI, Bombay, for his valuable assistance in the publication of this book. I should also note with satisfaction the kind cooperation that I received from the New Bharat Press and the Karnatak Press which have ably discharged their responsibility.

I have to acknowledge my indebtedness to the University of Bombay for the substantial financial help it has granted towards the cost of the publication of this book.

karmaṇyevādhikāras te

Rajaram College,
Kolhapur :
June 1940.

A. N. UPADHYE.

BY THE SAME AUTHOR

1. PAṀCASUTTAṀ of an Unknown ancient writer : Prākrit Text edited with Introduction, Translation, Notes with Copious extracts from Haribhadra's Commentary, and a Glossary. Second Ed., revised and enlarged, Crown pp. 96, Kolhapur 1934.

2. PRAVACANASĀRA of Kundakunda, an authoritative work on Jaina ontology, epistemology etc. : Prākrit text, the Sanskrit commentaries of Amṛtacandra and Jayasena, Hindī exposition by Pāṅḍe Hemarāja : edited with an English Translation and a critical elaborate Introduction etc. New Edition, Published in the Rāyachandra Jaina Śāstramālā vol. 9, Royal 8vo pp. 16 + 132 + 376+ 64, Bombay 1935.

3. PARAMĀTMA-PRAKĀŚA of Yogīndudeva. An Apabhraṁśa work on Jaina Mysticism : Apabhraṁśa text with various readings, Sanskrit Ṭīkā of Brahmadeva and Hindī exposition of Daulatarāma, also the critical Text of YOGASĀRA with Hindī paraphrase : edited with a critical Introduction in English. New Ed., Published in the Rāyachandra Jaina Śāstramālā vol. 10, Royal 8vo. pp. 12 + 124 + 396, Bombay 1937.

4. VARĀṄGACARITA of Jaṭāsiṁhanandi. A Sanskrit Purāṇic kāvya of A.D. 7th century : Edited for the first time from two palm-leaf Mss. with various readings, a critical Introduction, Notes, etc. Published in the Māṇikachandra D. Jaina Granthamālā No. 40, Crown pp. 16 + 88 + 396, Bombay 1938.

INTRODUCTION

1. Critical Apparatus

This *editio princeps* of *Kaṁsavaho* is based on the following Ms. material :

M—This is a Devanāgarī transcript on bluish ledger paper, 8½ × 13″ in size, and belongs to the Rajaram College Library, Kolhapur (R. No. 19201). It is a recent copy made from a Ms. in the Government Oriental Mss. Library, Madras. In the *Triennial Catalogue* (Madras 1935), Vol. VI, Part I, Sanskrit, the Madras Ms. (R. No. 5190) is thus described : 'Paper. 10½ × 9½ inches. Foll. 38. Lines 20 in a page. Devanāgarī. Good. Transcribed in 1925-26 from a Ms. of M. R. Ry. Kṛṣṇa Variyar, Nelinattur Variyam, Shoranore, Malabar District.' It is complete in four Sargas and contains both text and Chāyā. I have personally seen this Ms. Though written in Devanāgarī characters, the double consonants are represented by *nŏlli*, i.e., a fat zero the following consonant of which is to be pronounced as a double consonant. I learn from the Curator that the original of it was a palm-leaf Ms. My conjecture is that it might have been written either in Malayālam or Grantha characters. I tried to put myself in communication with the owner of the Ms., but I was not successful. All my readings are taken from the transcript (in the Rajaram College Library) which contains both the Prākrit Text and the Sanskrit Chāyā. There are certain lacunae in the text, and the Ms. bristles with scribal errors here and there. On the whole the Sk. Chāyā is better preserved.

T—Three other Mss. of *Kaṁsavaho* with Sk. Chāyā are known from Travancore. Two of them belong to the Palace Library of His Highness the Maharaja of Travancore, but they are incomplete. The third, which contains the text and the Chāyā of all the four cantos, belongs to a private library in Travancore. It is a palm-leaf Ms. written in Malayālam script. I have seen it personally in the Exhibition of Mss. arranged at the time of the All-India Oriental Conference, Trivandrum, 1937. Its description was given thus : 'No. 2533, Substance : Palm-leaf, Size : 9″ × 1½″, Leaves : 57 with 8 lines per page and 20 words per line, Script : Malayalam, No. of Granths 600, Owner : the same as that of No. 2533A (i.e., Vasudeva Sarma Avl. of Vattapalli Mattom, Śucīndram). Through the kindness of the Curator, Govt. Oriental Mss. Library, Trivandrum, I have received a Devanāgarī transcript, containing text and Chāyā, which I have designated as T in this Edition. This is now presented by me to the Rajaram College Library, and its R. No. is 24619. There is another Devanāgarī transcript of the palm-leaf Ms. in the Oriental Library, Trivandrum, and through the kindness of Pt. K. SAMBASHIVA SHASTRI I had noted down the readings from it during my short stay at Trivandrum; but as these readings substantially agree with those of T, I have not recorded them separately.

The Prākrit Text preserved in both the transcripts, M and T, is very unsatisfactory. The number of lacunae, scribal errors and other irregularities is greater in T than in M. So far as the Prākrit verses are concerned, both these transcripts use *ḷ* for *l*. They constantly confuse between *p* & *v*, *d* & *dh*, *p* & *ph*, *kh* & *gh*, *k* & *t*, between *a*, *i* & *u*, between *aṁ* & *ā*, *u* & *ḷ* and between a long vowel and a vowel followed by an *anusvāra*. Very often consonants expected to be double stand single preceded by an *anusvāra* ; and when we want the *anusvāra*, we find the subsequent consonant a double one instead : the number of such errors is very great in both the transcripts. Some of these scribal errors have their origin in the Malayālam script itself in which *v* & *p* are quite similar and *u*, *ḷ* & *i* are much alike; and the copyists, being ignorant of Prākrit, were likely to misread the original. In reproducing the Sanskrit Chāyā, the copyists are more careful and their performance is not so bad as in the Prākrit portion. The interchange between a double consonant and a consonant preceded by an *anusvara* is due to the device of Nŏlli, a fat zero, used in Grantha, Kannada, Malayalam and Telugu scripts when Prākrit was being written. The difference between the sign which indicates *anusvara* and the Nŏlli which indicates that the following consonant is to be doubled is very little: the former is a small zero and the latter a fat one; and the scribes who were ignorant of Prakrit were sure to confuse these two signs. Even the Madras Ms., though written in Devanāgarī, uses some Nŏllis on the top of the letters now and then; and, if I remember right, the local Devanāgarī transcript at Trivandrum used something like the sign of equality on the heads of letters to indicate that the following letter is to be doubled. This Nŏlli device gives duplicates like *khkh, ghgh* etc., but I have uniformly adopted the standard convention of writing *kkh, ggh* etc. Anunāsika is unknown to these Mss. I have used *l* for *ḷ* throughout.

2. Presentation of the Text and Chāyā

When I first read the Text, the scribal errors simply bewildered me. But a close study of the work with the help of both the transcripts enabled me to fill the gaps, to correct the scribal errors and to hit on the right reading. The fact that Rāma Pāṇivāda has written a commentary on the *Prākṛta Prakāśa* of Vararuci was enough to indicate that he might have been following the Sūtras of Vararuci, and this was further confirmed by the fact that he uses many Prākrit words specially illustrated in the Sūtras and the commentaries of that grammar. So I could conveniently check some of the meaningless scribal errors of the copyists in the light of the Sūtras of Vararuci. In so eliminating the errors I had always in view the possibility of misreading the original Malayālam, especially in the case of some letters, already noted above, which are written almost alike in the Malayālam script. When the grammatical standard was well-nigh settled and the possible orthographical errors were deleted, the Sanskrit Chāyā helped me, more than once, to lay my finger on the possible original reading. In discarding, discriminating and ascertaining the various readings, I have taken utmost precaution to see that I am not violating the limits of the material supplied by the Mss. After eliminating the scribal errors, if I found that the two Mss. differed, I have adopted one reading and given the other in the foot-notes. When both the Mss. agreed on a suspicious reading, which could not be called a scribal error, I have usually adopted it in view of the metrical necessities etc. When certain forms do not agree with the recognised conventions of the Prākrit language, though both the Mss. concur, I have followed this method : I have put the expected form in the Text with an asterisk to indicate that I have gone beyond the material supplied by the Mss. ; and the available readings are given in the foot-notes. I do not claim that my suggestions are final, and the asterisk will immediately attract the attention of the intelligent reader who may have something to say for or against my suggestion.

Following the lead of GOLDSCHMIDT[1] and PANDIT[2] I have

---

1 *Rāvaṇavaho*, Prākṛt und Deutsch Herausgegeben von Seigfried GOLDSCHMIDT, Strassburg 1880.

2 *Gaüḍavaho*, A Historical Poem in Prākrit by Vākpati, ed. by S. P. PANDIT, Bombay 1887.

added hyphens to indicate the separate members of a compound expression with the hope that this might facilitate the understanding of the text. I have not introduced them meticulously but only as far as practicable. I do agree with PANDIT[3] that *pi, tti* etc. are all used and are to be pronounced as enclitics in Prākrit ; but when he insists that they should be printed without being separated from the words to which they cling, I fear that he is carrying the principle to a logical extreme which results into a practical disadvantage that some of the combinations not only present a difficulty but also assume a misleading form. The convention of writing them separately has been established now through the efforts of eminent editors of Prākrit texts. Really speaking *avagraha* has no legitimate place in Prākrit Phonology, especially because there is no rigour of Sandhi in Prākrit as in Sanskrit. But remembering that Rāma Pāṇivāda is writing under strong Sanskrit influence I have introduced the *avagraha* here and there. If it was not to be introduced, there were two alternatives before me : either the two words should be written in combination or written separately without *avagraha*. The former would have created some difficulty in understanding and the latter would have given rise to quite awkward words which have never been current in Prākrit in earlier literature. So to avoid these disadvantages I have introduced *avagraha* which should not be quite objectionable in the work of an author writing under the strong influence of Sanskrit.

The transcripts are quite reliable so far as the Sanskrit Chāyā is concerned. The Chāyā in both the Mss. is in perfect agreement : there is only one solitary case where there is a different reading with a corresponding difference in the Prākrit text (i. 38). There are minor different readings on the common

3 Ibidem, Critical Notice p. x.

Prākrit original ; and only a few important ones are noted by me in the foot-notes. The Chaya ought to be as literal as possible ; but, almost as a rule, the Chaya of our Text substitutes the forms of the past tense, Imperfect and Perfect, when the corresponding form in the Prakrit text is that of the Present tense. It is difficult to gauge the reason of this change. In such cases and in others where a literal paraphrase was needed I have added my suggestions in the square brackets in the foot-notes without disturbing the Chayā found in both the Mss. The Chaya is presented by me in the prose form, and at the beginning of each verse I have put a few words of the Prākrit verse in square brackets. For the convenience of reference, a comma is put to indicate where the second line of the Prākrit verse stops, and the Sandhi rules are not strictly observed. In the Mss. the Sanskrit rendering is given immediately after every verse ; but in this edition it is printed continuously at the end of the Text.

3. RĀMA PĀṆIVĀDA AND HIS WORKS

The name of the author is mentioned as Rāma Pāṇivāda in the various colophons of *Kaṁsavaho*. From the researches of Mahakavi ULLUR S. PARAMESWARA AIYAR, Prof. M. R. BALKRISHNA WARRIER and other scholars it is quite plain that our author is identical with the famous Keraḷa poet of that name. Prof. WARRIER has already published in the Malayālam language an extensive critical biography of Rāma Pāṇivāda, and he has also contributed many articles in Malayālam about this poet. He has kindly sent to me a summary of his researches, and this section about the author is based mainly on his notes.

Pāṇivādas or Nambiārs formed a caste of Malabar. It

was their hereditary profession to help the Cākkiārs or the traditional actors of Keraḷa in the staging of Sanskrit plays. There are two types of performances staged by the Cākkiārs (Sūtas) : Kūttu and Kūṭiyāṭṭam. In the former the Pāṇivāda or Nambiār was to play on the drum called 'Mizhāvu or Muruja-vādya ; and in the latter, which consisted in enacting scenes from classical Sanskrit dramas, he played on the drum. It is from this drum (pāṇi-vādya) that the caste-name Pāṇivāda appears to be derived. The women of the Nambiār caste generally took the female parts in these plays. As a result of this, the members of this caste, as a whole, were well versed in Sanskrit ; and the tradition of Sanskrit scholarship was deep-rooted in their community. These Nambiārs enacted the dramatic narrations of Purāṇic stories as well.

Rāma Pāṇivāda,[4] as his name indicates, belonged to the Pāṇivāda or the Nambiār community, a section of the Ambalavāsi community of Keraḷa. He was born about the year A. D. 1707 at Kalakkathu house, Kiḷḷikuriśi Maṅgalam, a village near the present railway station Lekkidi in South Malabar. Before it was ceded to the British, the village was included in the Cochin State. His father is believed to have been a Nampūdiri Brahmin of Kumāranallūr in central Travancore who was a priest in the temple of Kiḷḷikuriśi Maṅgalam, the famous Śaiva temple of the locality.

Rāma Pāṇivāda began his studies first under his father and then under an eminent teacher Nārāyaṇa Bhaṭṭatiri, a learned Nampūdiri Brahmin of Thrikkārimoṇ Illam. In his different works Rāma refers in glowing and respectful terms

---

4 M. KRISHNAMACHARIAR : *Classical Sanskrit Literature* § 177 ; the name of our author is given as Ramapaninada. There are some references to Rāma Pāṇivāda in T. K. K. MENON's *Landmarks in Malayalam Literature*, Ernakulam, 1937.

to his teacher at whose auspicious hands were laid the very foundations of his profound erudition and wide knowledge. From the way in which Nārāyaṇa Bhaṭṭatiri is mentioned in different works it appears that the statement *saā gurūṇaṁ caraṇe samallio* (i. 2) and the concluding salutation *siriguru-pāāṇaṁ ṇamo* at the close of the fourth canto have in view this Nārāyaṇa Bhaṭṭapāda. It appears from Pāṇivāda's tributes that Nārāyaṇa Bhaṭṭa was a great scholar and an eminent teacher. Unfortunately none of his works has come down to us. His place Thrikkārimoṇ Illaṁ was situated only at a distance of seven miles from the birth-place of Rāma Pāṇivāda. Nārāyaṇa's family was one of hereditary Tāntrins in the famous Śaiva temple at Kiḷḷikuriśi Maṅgalaṃ, and Rāma Pāṇivāda tells us in his *Śrīkṛṣṇavilāsam* how his Guru performed the Pratiṣṭhā ceremony at the time of the renovation of that temple. This Nārāyaṇa Bhaṭṭa Pāda should be distinguished from another Nārāyaṇa Bhaṭṭa (A. D. 1560-1646), the author of *Nārāyaṇīya, Prakriyā-sarvasvam, Mānameyodaya* and other works. Some scholars have confused these two authors on account of the similarity of names.[5]

Rāma Pāṇivāda had the necessary education and training; but in order to continue a literary career he needed the patronage of some munificent king or nobleman. He left home and first approached Kolatiri Rāja of North Malabar. Kolatiri, being engaged in a war against his neighbour, could not offer a cordial welcome and patronage at his court to our author who consequently recorded his sad experiences in the following well-known verse :

कोलभूपस्य नगरे वासरा हरिवासराः ।
मषकैर्मत्कुणैश्चापि रात्रयः शिवरात्रयः ॥

5 For instance, K. Sāmbaśiva Śāstri in his Preface to *Vṛtta-vārtikam* Trivandrum Sanskrit Series No. cxxxi.

Then he lived for some time at the court of king Vīrarāya of Veṭṭatu Nāḍu. It was at the request of this king (but according to another Ms., of Rāmavarman) that he composed *Candrikā-vīthī* to be staged at the Śaiva temple at Triprangoṭu on the Śivarātri day. Further he found a temporary patron in Muriyanāṭṭu Nambiār, a local chieftain of the Mukundapuram Taluk of the Cochin State. During his short stay there he composed a couple of Stotras, *Mukunda-śatakam* and *Śiva-śatakam*, for his patron. Manakoṭṭu Achan was another patron whom Rāma Pāṇivāda mentions in his Malayālam work *Śivapurāṇam*. About A.D. 1735 this patron passed away, the family became extinct, and the estates passed into the possession of Pāliyatu Achans, the traditional ministers of the Rājā of Cochin. Our author became a dependant of Pāliyatu Achan with whom he lived at Jayanta- or Chenna-mangalam for some time and received his generous support. It is here that he composed his *Viṣṇu-vilāsam* and its Malayālam version *Viṣṇugīta* at the instance of Śrī-Kubera, the Pāliyam chief.

Rāma Pāṇivāda had spent some time in the neighbourhood of Kumāranallūr, to which place his Brahmin father belonged. During his stay here he came into contact with Thekkeṭathu Bhaṭṭatiri of Kuṭamāḷūr Maṭom and through him with the Rājā of Ampalapuzha or Chempakaśśeri. The Nampūdiri kings of Chempakaśśeri were liberal patrons of poets and scholars from times immemorial ; and many of the Keraḷa poets enjoyed their proverbial patronage. Rāma Pāṇivāda spent some years of his life at the court of the then ruling king Deva Nārāyaṇa. On his request Pāṇivāda wrote many works the chief of which was the Mahākāvya *Rāghavīyam*, the magnum opus of the poet, along with a commentary on it. Deva Nārāyaṇa's patronage appears to have been quite fruitful since it was at his court that our author wrote *Pañcapadī* which is written on the model of *Aṣṭapadī* of Jayadeva and it appears to have been inspired by the study of *Mahānāṭakam* and *Bhagavadajjukīyam* of Bodhāyana. It was followed by *Līlāvatī-vīthī* and the Prahasana *Madanaketucaritam* which was staged in the temple of Raṅganātha. In honour of the family deity of Deva Nārāyaṇa he composed *Ambaranadīśa-stotram.*[6]

With the conquest of the kingdom of Chempakaśśeri by Vīra Mārtaṇḍa Varman, the founder of modern Travancore, about the middle of the 18th century A. D., Rāma Pāṇivāda became a dependant of this illustrious monarch who was a liberal patron of men of letters and under whose benevolence many Sanskrit and Malayālam poets flourished. On the request of this patron our author wrote *Sītārāghavam* that was staged at the Śrī Padmanābha temple at Trivandrum. Later on he enjoyed the patronage of Kārtika Tirunāl Mahārāja who was a nephew and successor of Mārtaṇḍa Varman. He received a decent grant from this patron which he spent on the renovation of the Maṇḍapam of the temple at Kiḷḷikuriśi Maṅgalam. He accompanied the Mahārāja during the royal visits to Śucīndram, Thiruvaṭṭār, Kanyākumārī, Padmanābhapuram and other famous temples of South Travancore. He left Trivandrum and settled for some time at Ampalapuzha. It is believed that he died (about A. D. 1775) as the result of the bite of a rabid dog. Rāma Pāṇivāda seems to have remained a bachelor throughout his life.

Though Rāma Pānivāda had to change his patrons now and then, his literary career appears to have been quite unbroken and rigorous. Patrons he sought, not to praise them and to get prizes, but to have better opportunities to toil in the fields of learning and scholarship. New circumstances and novel

---

6 Ambaranadīśa is the god at Ampalapuzha, the family deity of the Rājā of Chempakaśśeri.

opportunities only inspired him to work in new moulds and on novel models with the result that Rāma Pāṇivāda has left to posterity a vast amount of literature varying in taste and varied in form.

The works of Rāma Pāṇivāda are found in three languages Sanskrit, Malayālam and Prākrit. To start with his Sanskrit works, he has composed four dramas : *Candrikā*,[7] a Vīthī ; *Līlāvatī*,[8] a Vīthī ; *Madanaketucaritam*,[9] a Prahasana ; and *Sītārāghavam*,[10] a Nāṭaka. He wrote the following Kāvyas : *Viṣṇuvilāsakāvyam*,[11] which has eight cantos and deals with the first nine Avatāras or incarnations of Viṣṇu and on which he himself has written a svopajña-ṭīkā called *Viṣṇupriyā* ; *Bhāgavatacampū*,[12] which is a campū-kāvya dealing with the story of the Daśamaskandha of *Bhāgavata*, of which only seven Stabakas have been discovered and the story runs upto Mucukunda-mokṣa, and which is said to contain numerous Prākrit passages; *Rāghavīyam*,[13] with a svopajña commentary called *Bālapāṭhyā* which is the greatest of Pāṇivāda's works consisting of twenty

---

7 *Candrikā*, a Vīthī : Trivandrum Curator's Office Collection for Kollam 1093-94, p. 13, No. 96.

8 *Līlāvatī*, a Vīthī, Ibidem No. 99.

9 *Madanaketucaritam* : three Mss. in Paliyam Library, Cochin State ; Govt. Oriental Mss. Library Madras R. No. 5163.

10 *Sītārāghavam* : Govt. O. Mss. Library Madras D. No. 12721 and R. No. 5135 ; Trivandrum Palace Library Catalogue No. 1600 ; Trivandrum Curator's Office Collection for Kollam 1104, p. 27, No. 148.

11 *Viṣṇuvilāsam* : Govt. O. Mss. Library Madras No. 3442 ; Paliyam Library, Cochin State.

12 Not less than nine *Bhāgavatacampūs* by different authors are mentioned by KRISHṆAMACHARIAR in his *Classical Sanskrit Literature*. He does not, however, attribute one to Rāma Pāṇivāda.

13 *Rāghavīyam* : Govt. O. Mss. Library Madras D. No. 11706 and R. No. 3397 ; Trivandrum Curator's Office Collection for Kollam 1104, p. 29, No. 162 ; Ibid. for Kollam 1087, p. 29, No. 282 also Paliyam Library Cochin State.

cantos and covering 1576 verses. Some of his important Stotras are : *Mukundaśatakam*,[14] *Śivaśatakam, Pañcapadī, Ambaranadīśa-stavam, Sūryaśatakam.* He has some scientific works also to his credit : *Vṛttavārtikam*,[15] which deals with classical Vṛttas or metres ; *Rāsakrīḍā*, a work in four Paricchedas illustrating different metres ; *Tālaprastāra*, which deals with the subject of Tāla and is written in Anuṣṭubh metre. Besides his Svopajña glosses noted above, he has written a commentary called *Vilāsinī*[16] on *Śrī-Kṛṣṇavilāsakāvya* of Sukumāra and another called *Vivaraṇa* on the *Dhātukāvya*[17] of Nārāyaṇa Bhaṭṭapāda. The latter appears to have remained incomplete.

Rāma Pāṇivāda has written a large number of works in Malayālam,[18] and only some important ones may be noted here: *Śrī-Kṛṣṇacaritam* in the maṇi-pravāḷa style ; *Śivapurāṇam* (kiḷippāṭṭu) ; *Pañcatantram* (kiḷippāṭṭu) which is an adaptation of the Sanskrit work in Malayālam ; *Rukmāṅgadacaritam* (kiḷippāṭṭu) ; etc. It is a point of great controversy among the Malayālam scholars whether Rāma Pāṇivāda and Kuñjan Nambiār were identical or two independent authors of the Keraḷa country. Eminent scholars like Mahākavi Ullur S. Parameswara AIYAR, Prof. WARRIER, Dr. GODAVARMA and others have discussed this subject in great details. Those who accept

---

14 *Mukundaśataka* with a commentary by his fellow-pupil : Govt. O. Mss. Library Madras, No. 3403.

15 *Vṛttavārtikam* and *Rāsakrīḍā* ed. by K. Sāmbaśiva Śāstri, Trivandrum Sanskrit Series No. cxxxi, Trivandrum 1937.

16. *Vilāsinī* : M. KRISHNAMACHARIAR'S *Classical Sanskrit Literature* § 169 ; the first four cantos are published at Palghat with the commentary of Rāma Pāṇivāda.

17. *Dhātukāvya-vyākhyā* : Govt. O. Mss. Library Madras No. 3656.

18. Those who are interested in other Malayālam compositions of our author should kindly read the various contributions on the subject by Prof. WARRIER of Trivandrum.

the identity naturally attribute the authorship of the Tuḷḷal pāṭṭus, about seventy in number, to Rāma Pāṇivāda. They are like ballads which are extremely popular in the Keraḷa country.

Rāma Pāṇivāda has not stopped with Sanskrit and Malayālam, but he has tried his hand at Prākrits as well. For this, he had already some background. As a Sanskrit playwright the study of Prākrits was indispensable to him. Ancient conventions require that specific characters should speak particular dialects. It is this need that kept the study of Prākrits quite alive in the Keraḷa country. It is reported that the *Prākṛta-prakāśa* of Vararuci and the *Setubandha* or *Rāvaṇavaho* of Pravarasena formed a part of the course of study of the Keraḷa Paṇḍitas who have made their own contributions to Prākrit literature. Bilvamaṅgala, also known as Kṛṣṇalīlāśuka, composed a Prākrit kāvya *Govindābhiṣeka*[19] or *Śrīcihnakāvya* to illustrate the rules of Vararuci's Prākrit grammar after the model of *Bhaṭṭikāvya*. It contains twelve cantos of which the first eight were composed by Bilvamaṅgala and the rest by Durgāprasādayati, also a Keraḷīya, who was his disciple and commentator. Both of them flourished in the 13th century A.D.[20] Among other Prākrit works written by Keraḷa authors may be mentioned *Śauricarita*,[21] a Yamaka-kāvya, of Śrīkaṇṭha and *Candralekhā*,[22] a drama of the Saṭṭaka type, of Rudradāsa, both of whom lived before Rāma Pāṇivāda.

As to Rāma Pāṇivāda's contribution to Prākrit literature we find Prākrit passages in his dramas like *Madanaketucaritam* and *Sītārāghavam*. It is also reported that his *Bhāgavata-*

---

19 *Govindābhiṣeka* : Govt. O. Mss. Library Madras Nos. 4156, 5156B.

20. There are different opinions about his age which is put between 11th and 15th century A.D.

21 *Śauricarita* : Govt. O. Mss. Library Madras No. 4321.

22 *Candralekhā* : Govt. O. Mss. L. Madras No. 3207(a).

campū contains some Prākrit passages. His more important works in Prākrit however are: *Prākṛta-vṛttiḥ*,[23] *Uṣāniruddham*[24] and *Kaṁsavaho*.

I have personally seen a palm-leaf Ms. of *Prākṛta-vṛttiḥ* in the exhibition of Mss., arranged at Trivandrum, at the time of the session of the All-India Oriental Conference in 1937. The description of the Ms. was given thus: G. O. L. No. 2533A, Substance: palm-leaf, Size: 9″ × 1½″, Leaves 58 with 8-9 lines per page and about 28 letters in a line, Script: Malayālam, Number of Granthas 900, Owner: Vasudeva Sarma Avl. of Vattapalli Mattom Śucīndram, Subject: the grammar of Prākrit languages. This Ms. contains the Prākrit Sūtras at the end. The Ms. opens thus:

सुकृतिभिरेव गृहीतो बहुविधरूपावतारगम्भीरः ।
जयति स भगवान्विष्णुः प्राकृतशास्त्रप्रपञ्च इव ॥
प्रणिपत्य विघ्नराजं श्रीगुरुपादान् मुनित्रयं वाणीम् ।
शङ्करमद्रिसुतां च प्राकृतवृत्तिर्मया क्रियते ॥
तत्रादौ लिपिविन्यासस‍ङ्केतः क्रियते—बिन्दुर्विधीयते etc.

The Ms ends thus:

पैशाचेऽपि 'शषसां सः' 'रडलानां ळः' इत्येतावन्मात्रमेव विशेषः, इति तावदत्रैवान्तर्भूतोऽयमपि विशेषः ।

प्राकृतलक्षणमेतत्प्रायेणोक्तं प्रयोगमनुसृत्य ।
अपरमपभ्रंशादेर्लक्षणमन्यत्र विज्ञेयम् ॥

The colophon runs thus: इति रामपाणिवादविरचितायां प्राकृतवृत्तावष्टमः परिच्छेदः । समाप्ता चेयं प्राकृतवृत्तिः ॥

Through the kindness of the Curator, Government Oriental Mss. Library, Trivandrum, I have received a Devanāgarī transcript

---

23. *Prākṛtavṛttiḥ*: Govt. O. Mss. Library Madras No. 5209; The Trivandrum Maharaja's Palace Library No. 764; Paliyam Library, Cochin State.

24. *Uṣāniruddham*: Govt. O. Mss. Library Madras No. 2817.

of the Sūtras from this Ms. Ignoring all sorts of desperate errors of copyists I have compared this Sūtrapātha with the one edited by COWELL, and I have the following observations to make. There is, however, no doubt that Rāma Pāṇivāda is commenting on the Sūtras of the *Prākṛta-prakāśa* of Vararuci. Here and there some Sūtras are differently worded. Some sūtras from chap. 3 are transferred to chap. 4 which may be a scribal blunder. The 5th chapter covers chaps. 5 & 6 of COWELL'S edition. Our Ms. has in all only eight chapters which cover the matter of the nine chapters of COWELL'S text. A careful study of the recension of Vararuci's Sūtras on which Rāma Pāṇivāda has commented would be interesting especially when the authenticity of some of the chapters of Vararuci's grammar is still an open question.

Uṣāniruddham is the next Prākrit work attributed to Rāma Pāṇivāda. The Madras Ms. does not mention the name of the author. There are four cantos, and the story is based on the famous episode of the marriage of Uṣā and Aniruddha as we get it in the *Bhāgavata*. Through the kindness of my friend Dr. RAGHAVAN I have received some excerpts from the Madras Ms. which contains the Prākrit text and the Sanskrit Chāyā. I shall reproduce here some Prakrit verses with minor emendations here and there. The opening Prākrit line stands thus: सिरिगणवइणो णमो अविग्घो होदु । Then there are these verses:

1 भद्दस्स वो भत्तिगुणल्लिआणं भवेज्ज णिच्चं भअवं गणेसो ।
दाणेण जो पीणइ माणसाइं वणीवआणं व महुव्वआणं ॥
2 अबोधणिद्दाविहलो वि लोओ जीसे पसाए सइ संपबुद्धो ।
सच्छंददो बज्झइ कव्वगुंफं चित्तम्मि णो भासउ भारई सा ॥
6 अत्थावबोहम्मि पहाणभूदे गोणत्तणेणोवअरंति सद्दा ।
दे सक्कआ वा उण पाअडा वा बुहाण को तत्थ विसेससंगो ॥
8 उसाणिरुद्धं ति मए णिबद्धं जं किं पि कव्वं जदुणाहदेव्वं ।
सुदं सुणंताण वि जं ण तत्ती जहिं क्खु वाण्णिज्जइ वासुदेवो ॥

The colophon of the First canto stands thus :

इअ उसाणिरुद्धे पढमो सग्गो ।

The concluding verse, at the close of the Fourth canto, reads thus :

इत्थं सुत्थिअपुत्तपोत्तणिअरो वित्थिण्णकित्तिच्छडा–
जोण्हापण्हुअवेरिविक्कमतमो उब्भासिआसामुहो ।
आणंदण्णवपुण्णम[illegible]सहरो सव्वाण णिव्वाणदो
देवो देवइणंदणो दिसदु वो णिस्सेसणिस्सेअसं ॥

Even these stray extracts are enough to show how the author is indebted to Rājaśekhara : the first verse reminds us of the Nāndī of *Karpūramañjarī* and the sixth closely agrees with *K.-mañjarī* I. 8.

4. KAṀSAVAHO[25] : A CRITICAL STUDY

i) EARLIER ACQUAINTANCE WITH THE WORK.

In the *Catalogus Catalogorum* (Parts I-III, Leipzig 1891-1903) of Theodor AUFRECHT we have an entry about *Kaṁsvadha* which is described as a Prākṛta-kāvya (p. 77). AUFRECHT gives reference to OPPERT 5918 which stands for 'Lists of Sanskrit Mss. in Private Libraries of Southern India' by Gustav Oppert, Vol. I, Madras 1880-4 and Vol. II, Madras 1885-8. Though noted by AUFRECHT, somehow this work has not attracted the attention of Prākrit scholars. That was quite natural in view of the meagre information given by AUFRECHT.

---

25 I wished I read the name as *Kaṁsavahaṁ* ; but out of regard for my predecessors, GOLDSCHMIDT and PANDIT, and to maintain uniformity with *Rāvaṇavaho* and *Gaüḍavaho* I have regularly written *Kaṁsavaho*.

Lately a Ms. of *Kaṁsavaho* is described in the *Triennial Catalogue* of Mss. in the Govt. Oriental Mss. Library, Vol. VI—Part I Sanskrit, Madras 1935. One of the transcripts used for this edition is copied from the Madras Ms.

ii) THE THEME AND THE TITLE.

Rāma Pāṇivāda has composed *Kaṁsavaho* (in 233 Prākrit verses divided into four cantos) to celebrate the incident of the slaying of Kaṁsa by Kṛṣṇa. This event, which is described at length in *Śrīmad-Bhāgavatam*, has something dramatic and thrilling about it. As such it has engrossed the attention of many a literary genius in India from pretty early times; and if the author happens to be a devotee of Viṣṇu-Kṛṣṇa he is all the more eloquent in glorifying the destruction of that cruel Kaṁsa at the hands of boy Kṛṣṇa. Tradition attributes a play Kaṁsavadha to Pāṇini. Patañjali[26] discusses the dramatic representation of the slaying of Kaṁsa, one party painting their faces red and the other black. Among the plays attributed to Bhāsa, there is *Bālacarita* which depicts in a lively and vivid manner the various feats of Kṛṣṇa culminating in the slaying of Kaṁsa. Among other Sanskrit plays dealing with this incident we might mention *Kaṁsavadham*,[27] in seven Acts, of Śeṣakṛṣṇa who was a contemporary of Akbar; then the *Kaṁsavadham* of Dāmodara;[28] and lastly *Kaṁsavadham* of Haridāsa[29] who is a modern author from East Bengal and who, it is said, composed this work at the age of fourteen. Dharma-

---

26 KEITH: *Sanskrit Drama* p. 32, 36 etc.: M KRISHNAMACHARIAR: *Classical Sanskrit Literature*, p. 535.

27 Published in Kāvyamālā, No. 6, Bombay 1888; See *Classical Sanskrit Literature*, p. 654.

28 Ibidem, p. 641, foot-note 2.

29 Ibidem, p. 673.

sūri (15th Century A.D.) had composed a *Kaṁsavadhanāṭaka*, but it is not now extant. His Prākrit poem *Haṁsasandeśa* also is lost to us.[29a] Among the Sanskrit poems dealing with this event we have *Kaṁsanidhana*,[30] a poem in seventeen cantos without labial, by Rāma ; and then there is *Kaṁsavadha*[31] by Rājacūḍamaṇi who flourished about the middle of the 17th century. Further there are two *Kaṁsavadha-campūs*[32] composed at the close of the last century : one by Keralavarman of Malbar and the other by Haridāsa of East Bengal. Whatever may be the literary merits of these compositions, especially on the back-ground of classical works, one thing is certain that the slaying of Kaṁsa has been an engrossing subject for writers throughout several centuries. Thus Rama Pāṇivāda has his predecessors and successors in handling this theme in the realm of Sanskrit literature.

In the field of Sanskrit classical poems we have already *Rāvaṇavadha*[33] of Bhaṭṭi and *Śiśupālavadha* of Māgha ; and, as shown below, Rāma Pāṇivāda shows an intimate acquaintance with the latter in composing his *Kaṁsavaho*. However in selecting this particular form of the title for his poem, it is more probable that Rama Pāṇivāda has in view the two earlier eminent poems, viz., *Dahamuhavaho* (or *Ravaṇavaho*, also called *Setubandha*) of Pravarasena and *Gaüḍavaho* of Vākpati.

iii) SUMMARY OF THE CONTENTS.

The author, being devoted to his Teachers and pressed by his ardent devotion for Viṣṇu-Kṛṣṇa, narrates the story of

29a *Proceedings and Transactions* of the 10th All India O. C. Trivandrum, 1940, pp. 502 etc.

30 *A Third Report of Mss.* etc. by P. PETERSON, p. 355.

31 *Classical Sanskrit Literature*, p. 235.

32 Ibidem, pp. 258 & 666

33 It is usually styled *Bhaṭṭikāvya*.

the slaying of Kaṁsa by Kṛṣṇa who is now adorning the settlement of cowherds as a son of Yasodā and attracting the attention of affectionate Gopīs (1-2).

One evening Akrūra comes to Gokula ; he has the rare opportunity of having an audience with Kṛṣṇa ; and he is plunged in joy at the vision of the divinity (i. 3-8). Kṛṣṇa received him affectionately, inquired about his welfare, treated him with dainty dishes, and expressed joy at his arrival. Akrūra draws the attention of Balarāma and Kṛṣṇa to the fact how, despite their potent valour, Kaṁsa is waxing strong ; and their parents are pining in the prison house. Kṛṣṇa offers an apologetic explanation that their attachment for their foster-parents is too deep, and then inquires of Akrūra about the special purpose of his arrival (i. 9-14). Akrūra adds in reply that Kaṁsa, as a rule, does not like anybody going to them ; but that he is lucky that Kaṁsa has sent him to invite Balarāma and Kṛṣṇa to Mathurā to attend the Bow-festival which, really speaking, is an open pretext to conceal his motive of killing them. Thus Akrūra delivers the royal invitation, indicates Kaṁsa's intention, and requests the brothers to see whether they would or would not attend the bow-festival at Mathurā (i. 16-26). Balarāma is in a mood of hesitation, but Kṛṣṇa fearlessly decides that he should start with his party with which his brother agrees ; and all of them start for Mathurā next morning (i. 27-34).

Kṛṣṇa was the very life of Gopīs ; his departure brings on them deep pangs of separation ; they curse Akrūra who took Kṛṣṇa to Mathurā ; and all of them begin to lament in various ways recollecting the image of Kṛṣṇa and their sports with him in Vṛndāvana (i. 35-55). On the instructions of Kṛṣṇa Akrūra consoled them requesting them to put up with this temporary separation because Kṛṣṇa was going out on an important mission (i. 56-60).

Akrūra drove the chariot ; they all halted on the banks of Yamunā ; and it is there that Akrūra had the wonderful experience of seeing Kṛṣṇa everywhere. Soon Kṛṣṇa and his party entered the town of Mathurā to the joy and satisfaction of all the young folk of the town (i. 61-64).

In that town of Mathurā Rāma and Kṛṣṇa met a washerman, carrying the clothes of Kaṁsa, from whom they demanded some clothes ; but they were warned by him that this audacity of theirs would cost them their heads, if the matter were to reach Kaṁsa's ears. Kṛṣṇa not only robbed him of the clothes but sent him also to the grave by plucking his head with his nails (ii. 1-10).

As they proceeded, they met a certain hunchbacked but beautiful lady who, on their inquiry, informed them that she was an artisan in the royal harem, that the adverse fate had made her physically crooked, that she was going to present the fragrant saffron to Kaṁsa, and that she would give a part of it to them as their bodies were quite worthy of it. They gladly accepted that saffron which added to their physical glow. By his divine touch Kṛṣṇa rendered her bent body straight. With a bit of audacity she made passionate advances to Kṛṣṇa who appreciated her love but told her that he was too busy with serious work on hand to dabble in love affairs at this stage. Kṛṣṇa bade good-bye to her who was pleased with a prospective assurance of his return, and proceeded towards the royal residence (ii. 11-30).

Rāma and Kṛṣṇa came to the gymnasium for archery which was duly decked for the function. There, despite the warning of the servant, Kṛṣṇa picked up the bow which was smashed to pieces as he tried to string it ; and there was such a great noise that Kaṁsa was thrilled to the core of his heart. The soldiers on guard who took the offensive received a good thrash. This success of the princes was a matter of joy to all (ii. 31-7).

Coming out of the gymnasium and strolling in the courtyard Kṛṣṇa described the various scenes which greeted his eyes in that town of Mathurā. Thus follows a picture of that town in the mouth of Kṛṣṇa who describes in poetical terms various scenes such as the lofty palaces, the extensive moat, the bright mansions, the amorous pleasures of loving couples, the dancing peacock, the singing and dancing parties, the disputes of grammarians etc. Kṛṣṇa is so much pleased by seeing that town that he waxed very eloquent and described Mathurā as the heaven itse f Then in the evening he retired to his place of residence (ii 38-60).

Early in the morning, at the appointed hour, the bards begin to sing eloquently just to wake up Kṛṣṇa and their songs inform Kṛṣṇa in an ornate style decked with various poetic embellishments how it is dawning, how the darkness is passing away, how the lotuses are blooming and the Cakravāka birds uniting again, how the rising sun is producing various scenes etc. (iii. 1-20).

Kṛṣṇa left his bed even before the bards pour out their verses, and offered his twilight worship. Putting on brilliant dress and attracting the attention of young ladies along the roads Rāma and Kṛṣṇa proceeded towards the city-gate (iii. 21-6). Ambaṣṭha, with the elephant Kuvalayāpīḍa, tried to stop them at the gate ; but Kṛṣṇa sent that elephant as well as its master to the grave after putting a vigorous and successful fight. With the tusks in their hands as trophies they were an object of pleasant sight for all the people. As desired by Kaṁsa there ensued an unfair duel in which Kṛṣṇa occupied himself with Cāṇūra and Rāma with Muṣṭika. People felt that it was an unequal duel, because Rāma and Kṛṣṇa were just boys while their partners were heavy wrestlers. There was a thrilling fight, and at last Rāma and Krsna killed their opponents and routed the wrestlers who tried to overpower them (iii. 27-51). When that wicked Kaṁsa expressed his intention to imprison them all, Krsna attacked him, felled him on the ground, and finished him to death with all vehemence. The naughty brothers of Kaṁsa too were killed. By way of congratulations gods showered from heaven flowers on their heads (iii. 52-60).

The slaying of Kaṁsa by Kṛṣṇa was a matter of relief to the whole world. Thereafter people became happy; ladies could move about freely; youths had no hindrance in their sports; and lastly even voluptuaries got a good deal of liberty (iv. 1-5). Kṛṣṇa appointed Ugrasena as the king and released his parents from the prison house. Both Balarāma and Kṛṣṇa paid respects to their parents who blessed them and embraced them with filial affection (iv. 6-9).

Then Akrūra comes, pays respects to Vasudeva and his wife, and then narrates the various events in the childhood of the princes: the transference of child Krsna to the bed of a cowherdess on a cloudy night when the river Yamunā became easily fordable; destruction of Pūtanā by Kṛṣṇa by sucking her blood; defeat and death of Tṛṇāvarta who had assumed the form of whirlwind; Yaśodā's binding of Kṛṣṇa to the mortar which he pulled through and uprooted a couple of Arjuna trees; destruction of Bakāsura and Aghasura; humiliation of Brahman by Kṛṣṇa; different sports of Kṛṣṇa in Vṛndāvana etc.; destruction of Dhenuka by Balarāma; Kṛṣṇa's dancing on the hood of Kāliya serpent and consequent banishment of it; his drinking of conflagration; smashing of Pralamba by Kṛṣṇa; Kṛṣṇa deprives Gopīs of their garments; refusal of the food by the sacrificial priests but the same respectfully offered by their pious wives; the worship of Gopas diverted from Indra to Govardhana; consequent rain-deluge was brought by Indra but all the people were protected by Kṛṣṇa who lifted up the Govardhana mountain on his little finger ; Kṛṣṇa coronated as Gopendra ; Kṛṣṇa's rescue of Nanda from Varuṇa's abode ; the graceful Rāsa sports of Kṛṣṇa ; disillusionment of proud maidens ; and the destruction of Śaṅkhacūḍa, Ariṣṭa, Keśi, Vyoma and lastly Kaṁsa who invited them with the pretence of the bow-festival (iv. 10-46). The parents were pleased to hear these events from Akrūra's mouth ; they embraced and blessed the princes who looked all the more graceful and glorious (iv. 47-8).

The author declares that this poem is like a ford for those who want to cross the ocean of Prākrit literature ; and in conclusion he solicits the protection of Viṣṇu.

iv) THE FORM, THE SOURCE AND THE MODEL.

It is clear from the perusal of the contents that our author has practically given the biography of Kṛṣṇa upto his slaying of Kaṁsa, though the title of the work is *Kaṁsavaho* which might tempt us to expect that the poem glorifies merely the slaying of Kaṁsa. The whole of the fourth canto is like an appendix narrating the various events from Kṛṣṇa's life including the slaying of Kaṁsa (iv. 45) artificially put in the mouth of Akrūra. Though they afford an opportunity for the author to exhibit his poetic skill, certain sections stand out a bit detached and come like intruders in that context, for instance, the elaborate description of Mathurā put in the mouth of Kṛṣṇa and that of the exploits of Kṛṣṇa in the mouth of Akrūra. There are other portions which are occupying more space than usual when we compare their length with the general scope of the poem : the lamentations of the Gopīs and the songs of bards. It is true that it is in these sections that Rāma Pāṇivāda is seen at his best as a poet.

Rāma Pāṇivāda appears to be an ardent devotee of Viṣṇu-

Kṛṣṇa and a close student of his biography. His *Bhāgavata-campū*, noted above, deals with the Tenth Skandha of *Bhāgavata* which is a fine biography of Kṛṣṇa. So far as the facts of the contents are concerned, *Kaṁsavaho* also is solely indebted to *Bhāgavata*. Every detail of Kṛṣṇa's life included in this work can be traced to *Bhāgavata*, as it is clear from the references given by me in the Notes. Though the handling of the topic and the poetic elaboration are quite independent and belong to our author, we find parallel ideas in similar contexts; and at times the wording also is alike (see my notes on i. 4; ii. 8, 15; iii. 38, 54; iv. 12, 21, 22, 37; etc.). Though the events are taken from *Bhāgavata*, our author shows originality and skill in narrating them with some dramatic effect, as we see in the case of his portrayal of the incidents of the washerman and the saffron girl (ii. 2-10, 11-30). The sentiment surrounding the meeting of Kṛṣṇa with the saffron girl (ii. 11-30) shows how our author is capable of creating artistic situations and weaving graceful conversations.

Apart from the fact that Rāma Pāṇivāda has composed some works in Sanskrit, the high-flowing style of *Kaṁsavaho* is sufficient to indicate the influence of classical Sanskrit writers like Kālidāsa, Māgha etc. on our author. Some of his poetic ornaments remind us of earlier Sanskrit works; and I have noted some such references in my Notes. *Kaṁsavaho* covers the same part of the life of Kṛṣṇa as depicted in the *Bālacarita* of Bhāsa, but I do not find any striking similarities between the two works. To me it appears that *Śiśupāla-vadha* was the model before our author when he composed *Kaṁsavaho*. There are close similarities between the two works, and they are far from being accidental. There are some parallel situations in both the texts: arrival of Nārada in *Ś*. i and that of Akrūra in *K*. i; Akrūra's address to Kṛṣṇa (*K*. i. 15-16) reminds us of Nārada's address (*Ś*. i. 31 etc.);

corresponding to the description of Dvārakā (S. iii. 33 etc.), we have here (*K*. ii. 39 etc.) the description of Mathurā put in the mouth of Kṛṣṇa; announcement of the morning by the bards (S. xi. 1 & *K*. iii. 2); and lastly just as Bhīṣma praises and narrates the various events from Kṛṣṇa's life in S. xiv, so also Akrūra is doing here in *K*. iv. Not only that there are common or parallel ideas, but some of them are expressed in similar words: Ś. ii. 13 & *K*. i. 14; Ś. i. 31 & *K*. i. 15; Ś. xvi. 35 & *K*. i. 29: S. xv. 17 & *K*. i. 40; Ś. xiv. 64, xx. 79 & *K*. ii. 9; Ś. iii. 79 & *K*. ii. 47; Ś. viii. 14 & *K*. ii. 5 *K*. ii. 50; Ś. xi. 24 & *K* iii. 5; Ś. xi. 49 & *K*. iii. 15; Ś. xi. 55 & *K*. iii. 17; Ś. xi. 43-5 & *K*. iii. 18; etc. In addition to these some other points of similarity might be noted as well. Ś. begins with the phrase *sriyah patim* and *K*. with *siria ṇāho*, and the titles of both works are of the same pattern. Though it is not a good criterion of parallelism, especially when the Sanskrit vocabulary is almost oceanic and the literature sufficiently extensive, still one must say that Rāma Pāṇivāda has much in common with the vocabulary and the turns of expression met with .. *Śiśupālavadha*. In the description of the town and the songs of the bards many ideas and words are common. Despite many points of agreement, it is really creditable that Rāma Pāṇivāda is not a slavish and mechanical imitator. One feels that Māgha is being followed, but Rāma Pāṇivāda has everywhere his touch of variety, if not speciality. I feel that it is not a case of a novice imitating and reproducing. Rāma Pāṇivāda has so thoroughly mastered *Śiśupālavadha* that ideas and expressions from Māgha are being echoed in this work without any special or intentional effort on the part of our author. This is not impossible when we remember that our old Paṇḍitas committed to memory not only *Amarakośa* but also *Raghuvaṁśa, Meghadūta, Śiśupālavadha* etc.

Any one who is acquainted with the classical poems like

Rāvaṇavaho and *Gaüḍavaho* would expect that *Kaṁsavaho* must be heavily indebted to these eminent predecessors in the field of Prākrit literature. I have carefully studied these texts, but I have not been able to detect their influence on our author to any appreciable extent. A few ideas, forms and turns of expression in *Kaṁsavaho* remind us of *Rāvaṇavaho*, and there is one verse in our text (i. 36) which closely agrees with that in *Rāvaṇavaho* (iv. 20). Between *Gaüḍavaho* and *Kaṁsavaho* there is hardly any similarity that could attract my attention. One idea is similar, but it is a common property of many authors as I have shown in the Notes. Though there is nothing particularly common, still the style of some verses reminds us of Rājaśekhara's verses in *Karpūramañjarī*.

v) ON THE PRĀKRIT DIALECT OF KAṀSAVAHO.

A) SPECIAL TRAITS OF THE AUTHOR'S DIALECT.

In studying the Prākrit dialect of this work we have to take into account many things : our author belongs to the last period of Prākrit literature ; with him the Prākrit language is a purely literary language in the sense that he studied Prākrit grammars and texts, and then wrote this poem ; he is writing in a place where the then spoken languages were not likely to influence his language ; and lastly he is a thorough master of Sanskrit in which too he could compose poems with equal if not greater fluency and elegance. Under these circumstances, a detailed grammatical analysis would not serve any great purpose ; so what is essential for us to know is how far Rāma Pāṇivāda conforms to the standards of Prākrit grammarians and in what details he has his specialities.

We have seen above that Rāma Pāṇivāda has written a commentary on the *Prākṛta-prakāśa* of Vararuci, and so we expect him to have followed this grammar in handling the Prākrit language. This expectation is fulfilled to a great extent, and we would not be wrong in saying that our author is mainly following Vararuci's grammar and its successors. In the vocabulary of *Kaṁsavaho* there are many conspicuous words and forms which are met with in the Sūtras of Vararuci and the commentaries thereon : *acchera, āmelo, gahira, ghola, ciṁdha, nolla, dualla, paṇolla, pariccemu, pāsutta, moha* (= *mayūkha*), *ruṁbha, ruva, vale, vijjulī, suṁdera, somāla* etc. So far as the substantial stock of vocabulary is concerned, our author is closely following the first nine chapters of Vararuci's grammar.

Secondly, we come across certain words and forms which, according to PISCHEL'S[34] analysis, are known to us from the Prākrit prose of the dramas : *adihi* (ii. 50), *assu* (i. 35), *tui* (i. 19), *païdi* (iii. 25), *paduma* (iii. 2), *pahudi* (iv. 34), *pidara* (i. 12), *bhavaṁ* (i. 14), *bhādara* (i. 27), *vivuda* (iii. 10), *radaṇa* (ii. 49), *sakkuṇa* (iii. 33), etc. Of course it is not claimed that these forms cannot be derived by a liberal and hypercritical application of the Sūtras of Vararuci.

Thirdly, we have in this work a large number of nominal and verbal forms which are direct corruptions of Sanskrit forms according to the well-known rules of phonetic change : *idaṁ vao* (i. 28), *joṇhāaṁ* (iii. 6), *thalīaṁ* (ii. 38), *puṇṇimāaṁ*[35]

---

34 PISCHEL : *Grammatik der Prākrit-Sprachen*, Strassburg 1900 ; and also its Index by Zilva WIKREMASINGHE, Bombay 1909.

35 It is interesting to note that Bhāsa's Prākrit shows such forms (PRINTZ : *Bhāsa's Prākṛta*, p. 27) in the Loc. sing. PISCHEL, as far as I remember, has not noted similar forms from any other source. If such forms are as old as Bhāsa, their absence in the subsequent literature is difficult to be explained. Or should we presume that they are the outcome of the Ms. tradition of Keraḷa country to which the Mss. of Bhāsa's dramas and of *Kaṁsavaho* belong ?

(ii. 19), *vihiāaṁ* (ii. 44), *dikkhu* (iv. 41) ; *caatthi* (i. 24), *musiṇā* (ii. 47), *vāharaï mha* (ii. 25), *daṁti* (ii. 52), *viiṇ-ṇaṁti* (i. 16), *suāṁti* (ii. 34), *ujjihāṇa* (iii. 20), etc. Such tendencies are bound to develop in the Prākrit stage especially when the Prākrits, as literary languages, were cultivated under the influence of classical Sanskrit and handled by authors who were themselves Sanskrit writers. Instances of this type are not altogether absent in earlier stages of Prākrit literature; but being rare they could be accepted as isolated cases of exception. Here, however, the tendency to introduce them is stronger and the number of instances is conspicuously large.

Fourthly, Rāma Pāṇivāda uses certain words and forms which, so far as I know, are his own and not of much frequency in earlier Prākrit literature : *kamaṇī* (ii. 19), *kāriä* (i. 48), *kūlaṁḍa* (i. 57, ii. 32, iii. 43), *kuvittha* or *kavittha* (i. 28, ii. 35), *koccaṇa* (ii. 52, 53, 55, 57), *kocci* (ii. 54), *ṇihela* (ii. 52), *talaüṁḍa* (i. 48), *paṇhi* (ii. 50), *rāsi* (= *raśmi*, iii. 17), *vuṁdara* (iii. 1, 57), *sāhaṁ* (i. 64), *siṁkharā* (iii. 31) ; *kaṇṇāü* (i. 62), *nisāü* (iii. 4), *tujjhaṇa* (i. 25) ; etc. Some of them can be explained analogically or by further changes in the known forms. I have discussed these in the Notes.

Fifthly, words like *ammaka* (i. 37), *ahake* (ii. 6) are not quite fitting in the dialect of our text. *Ahake* is justified according to Vararuci's Sūtras (xi. 9) but only in the Māgadhī dialect.

Sixthly, our author shows a confirmed habit of converting a string of Sanskrit words *en bloc* into Prākrit. Prākrit grammarians have to deal mainly with Tadbhava words ; they generalise certain tendencies according to which Prākrit Tadbhavas were derived from Sanskrit words ; and then these very generalisations served as rules for converting many other Sanskrit words into Prākrits when the latter became purely literary languages. It is an important rule that the intervocalic or, in grammarians' words, non-initial and non-conjunct *k*, *g*, *c*, *j*, *t*, *d*, *p*, *y* and *v* are generally dropped. The rule is a good one for all practical purposes. Even in the earlier stages of Prākrit literature we find that this rule has affected a few initial consonants also in some words : *iṁ* = *kiṁ*, *ira* = *kila*, *uṇa* = *punar*, *na yāṇāmi* = *na jānāmi*, *ya* = *ca* etc. It only means that these consonants were changed along with the previous words with which they went and thus became non-initial as it were. If at all, in the literary Prākrits, Sanskrit words were to be corrupted into Prākrit, the question may be asked whether a word is to be taken as an unit of corruption or a string of words say as in a compound phrase or in an elegant expression which is conceived by the author primarily in Sanskrit. Common sense demands that simple words should be taken as the units of corruption, and their non-initial and non-conjunct consonants may be dropped according to the above rule. The term 'simple words' included prepositions etc. ; so we have forms like *uvaïsaï*, *paäsaï*, *païṇṇa*. It also included some compound words of two members of frequent occurrence : *kara-ala*, *dharaṇī-yala*, *bhamara-ula* ; in these words the whole expression is treated as an unit of change. When the initial consonants of the various non-initial members of a compound expression are being elided, softened etc., on a large scale, it only means that the author first conceives an expression in Sanskrit, and then he converts it into Prākrit at a stretch. This difficulty faced the Prākrit grammarians, and Hemacandra (VIII. i. 177) allows an option admitting both forms like *jala-cara* and *jalayara*. *Aciram* and *svajana* would give *aïraṁ* and *saäṇa*, but on that account it would not be justified to use *iraṁ* for *ciram* and *aṇa* for *jana* when they are independent words. In our text we do come across some such cases, and both the Mss. agree to adopt the same reading : *iraṁ* = *ciram* (i. 12, 16, ii. 57, iv. 47), *ana* =

jana (i. 14, 29, iv. 28), *ulaṁ* = *kulam* (ii. 58). Some of these words occur more than once; so we cannot brush them aside by attributing them to scribes. These forms appear to be used by the author himself. In all probability the author was led to use such words from their occurrence in compound expressions like *aïraṁ, suïraṁ, kumiāṇa, muṇiāṇa, saāṇa, rāüla* etc. which are met with in standard texts like *Gaüḍavaho* and others. When these words (*ciram* etc.) stand as independent units and not as second members of a compound, the practice of eliding their initial consonants is not a healthy one, nor has it any stable foundation in the genuine Prākrit style of early authors. So I have emended these readings; and asterisks are put on them to indicate that they are subjected to editorial improvement. In the very interest of the language the elision of initial consonants in a compound expression, though optionally allowed by the grammarians, has to be practised with restraint. I have noted some striking cases of the elision of initial consonants in *Rāvaṇavaho*: *ṇa īṇam=na dīnam* (viii. 61), *aṇehim=janaiḥ* (viii. 65), *ūraṁ* = *pūram* (viii. 65); but in every case their presence is due to the necessity of rhyme. The treatment of aspirates like *kh* etc. is to be considered on the same lines as that of intervocalic *k* etc.

Seventhly, we may also note the treatment accorded to initial conjunct groups. In the light of Vararuci's Sūtras (iii. 50 & 57) there is no justification for forms like *kkhaäṁ* (i. 29), *kkhuḍiä* (iii. 19), *tthuo* (iv. 16), *ppaälaï* (iii. 35), *ppaïdi* (iii. 52), *ppaḍiṇava* (iii. 16), *ppamaüladaṁ* (iii. 37), *ppalavaï* (iii. 29, 49, 52), *ppavaḍiä* (iii. 55), *ppasahaṁ* (iii. 52), *ppaharisa* (iii. 37), *ppoṇṇidda* (iii. 41), *pphuḍa* or *pphuḍaṁ* (i. 29, ii. 5, 18, 38, iii. 18, 58). We get instances of this type in the various readings available for the Prākrit portions of the dramas. Here metre requires them, so they cannot be called scribal errors; even in the verses of *Karpūramañjarī*[36] there are some such cases: *ṇa ṭṭhāṇāhi* (ii. 1), *ṭṭhio* (ii. 46, iii. 4). This tendency can be explained on the supposition that the whole sentence or a string of words was first conceived in Sanskrit and then converted into Prākrit. This is manifest in some of the verses of Pravarasena, Vākpati and Rājaśekhara. This habit, so far as our author is concerned, is quite strong here as seen from the structure of various verses.

Lastly, our text shows the development of certain conjuncts in the following cases: *bhuvaṇa-ppanāidāe* (ii. 40), *pparusa* (iii. 47); and they are possibly due to the necessity of metre. PISCHEL has already collected many such cases from Prākrit literature.

To conclude, the above facts indicate that Rāma Pāṇivāda mainly follows Vararuci's Sūtras, especially the first nine chapters, with the commentaries thereon; his dialect is influenced by the Prākrit prose of the dramas; he shows a small number of words which are further deductions from the known forms; and, as he conceives the expressions first in Sanskrit, we find that many Sanskrit forms are directly corrupted into Prākrit, that some initial consonants are elided and that some initial duplicates are retained.

B) THE NAME OF THIS PRĀKRIT DIALECT.

The term Prākrit is used with various meanings. If we consider the views of the Prākrit grammarians, we find that it is used as a generic term to designate a number of Middle Indo-Aryan literary languages. In this sense Ardha-Māgadhī

---

36 I have noted these readings from Dr. KONOW'S text of *Karpūramañjarī* (Cambridge, Mass 1901). but I find that Dr. GHOSH has adopted some different readings in two places in his edition of *Karpūramañjarī* (Calcutta 1939) which has just reached my hands.

and Pāli, the canonical languages of the Jainas and Buddhists, can also be grouped under Prākrit. According to Daṇḍin the pre-eminent Prākrit is Māhārāṣṭrī (*mahārāṣṭrāśrayā bhāṣā*) and in *Mṛcchakaṭikam* the Sūtradhāra, remarking that he would then speak in Prākrit begins to speak in Śaurasenī. Māhārāṣṭrī and Śaurasenī being the popular dialects of the dramatic group of Prākrits, the term Prākrit often stood for them. Further, as PISCHEL[37] has remarked, the Māhārāṣṭrī is the language meant when one speaks of Prākrit in general; and it is also considered to be the best Prākrit in which we have classical poems like *Ravaṇavaho*, *Gaüḍavaho* etc. and compilations of lyrical songs like *Gāthāsaptaśatī* which has become a veritable treasure of quotations drawn by later rhetoricians. Now and then the term Prākrit is used even to indicate some of the Modern Indian languages like Marāṭhī and Kannaḍa[38] thereby distinguishing them from Sanskrit.

As we can imagine the territorial divisions and social groups in India in early days and as indicated by dialectal names like Māgadhī, Śaurasenī and Māhārāṣṭrī, it is clear that some of these dialects derived their names from territorial units. It appears that even by the time of Vararuci, if not earlier, they had become stereotyped literary languages in the sense that the writers of these dialects did not write so much from their personal touch with the spoken dialects as from the grammars and the works they studied. Such a procedure has its advantages as well as disadvantages: on the one hand the dialects gradually assume a standardised form and dignity and on the other they get isolated from the currents of spoken languages which evolve or degenerate in the popular mouths in their own way. Time, place and usage have created such barriers now and the evidence to the point is so meagre that to-day it

37 *Grammatik* etc. § 12.

38 S. B. JOSHI: *Kannadada Nele* (Dharwar 1939) p. 28.

is wellnigh impossible to get any idea of the original Māgadhī, the spoken language of Magadha. We may get a trace of it here and there, but these attempts are all guesses in the realm of probability. With us to-day, and especially with Rāma Pāṇivāda, names like Śaurasenī are conventional Prākrit dialects stereotyped and standardised by grammarians and play-wrights. Rāma Pāṇivāda composed this work after studying the language from grammars and literature.

Rāma Pāṇivāda is not explicit about the dialect in which he wrote *Kaṁsavaho.* As I understand, he simply hints that it is a Prākrit poem (iv. 48*1). To-day we are accustomed to the terminology of Prākrit dialects used by grammarians like Vararuci, Hemacandra and others and lately set on a scientific footing by PISCHEL who, for the first time, took an extensive linguistic survey of Prākrits with a marvellous critical acumen. So, in the light of the present terminology and material, we shall see whether our author is writing in Māgadhī, Śaurasenī or Māhārāṣṭrī ; and if he shows any dialectal admixture, to what extent can we ascertain it.

The material afforded by Prākrit literature and by the Prākrit grammars is such that it is always difficult to state individual exclusive characteristics of any dialect. When distinguishing one dialect from others what can be done at the best is to note essential characteristics not singly but along with other features of that dialect. By exclusive characteristics I mean those traits which exclusively belong to one dialect and are not found in any other dialects. For instance, use of the palatal sibilant alone is an exclusive characteristic of Māgadhī. In distinguishing one Prākrit dialect from the other, we may state a few essential characteristics of different dialects ; and all of them together characterise a particular dialect.

Our author uses *ahake* (ii. 6) which is noted as a speciality of Magadhī dialect by Vararuci, and there are about half a dozen words like *kālaṇa* (i. 14, 51), *kumāla* (iii. 29), *galula* (iv. 28), *calana* (iii. 34, 50), *muhala* (ii. 57) in which *r* is changed to *l*. It is true that *kālaṇa* and *kumāla* are not popular in dialects other than Māgadhī;[39] but words like *calaṇa* can occur in any other Prākrit dialect. In the absence of the Nom. Sing. of *a*-ending nouns in *e* and of the wholesale change of *r* to *l* and of *ṣ* and *s* to *ś*, we cannot say that the dialect of our text is Māgadhī. A word like *ahake* should be considered either as an intruder or a slip of the author.

A good deal has been written about Śaurasenī, its characteristics and its relation with Māhārāṣṭrī.[40] The use of Śaurasenī is prominent among the Prākrit dialects used in the prose of the dramas. But the Ms. material from which we have to generalise the nature of Śaurasenī is extremely unsatisfactory and the grammars are not quite exhaustive and they sometimes differ mutually. "In spite of all these difficulties" says PISCHEL, "it is however possible to get on the whole a fairly correct picture of Ś. In phonology the most characteristic feature is the change of *ta* into *da* and *tha* into *dha* (§ 203); in declension and conjugation the great variety of forms of

39 I am usually guided by the forms noted by PISCHEL.

40 PISCHEL: *Grammatik* etc. §§ 2, 12-15, 22 etc.; KONOW and LANMAN: *Karpūramañjarī*, the section of Rājaśekhara's Prakrit, pp. 199 etc.; R. SCHMIDT: *Elementarbuch der Śaurasenī*, Hannover 1924: M. GHOSH: Mahārāṣṭrī, a later phase of Śaurasenī in the Journal of the Department of Letters, Vol. XXIII, Calcutta 1933; A. M. GHATAGE: Śaurasenī Prākrit, the Journal of the University of Bombay, vol. III, part vi; S. K. CHATTERJI: The Study of New Indo-Aryan in the Journal of the Department of Letters, vol. XXIX, Calcutta 1936; A. M. GHATAGE: Māhārāṣṭrī Language and Literature, the Journal of the University of Bombay, vol. IV, part vi; etc.

M. AMg. JM. JS. has been greatly simplified. Thus in the case of *a*-stems only the abl. sing. in *-do* and the loc. sing. in *-e* are in use; in plural, in the case of all the stems, only the forms nasalised at the end are used in instr., gen. as well as in loc.; the *i*- and *u*-stems have in gen. sing. only *-ṇo,* not *-ssa* as well; in verbal flexion the Ātmanep. has almost completely disappeared; the opt. has only the endings *-eaṃ* (I. sing.), *-e*; many verbs have stem-forms different from M.; the fut. is formed only from stems in *-i,* and the passive only in *-īa,* the absol., in contrast to M., almost exclusively in *-ia* Skt. -ya, etc." By way of explanation and supplementation it may be added that in Śaurasenī *-di* in the Present and *-du* in the Imperative are the 3rd p. sing. terminations which being *-i* and *-u* respectively in Māhārāṣṭrī, that *d* and *dh* are retained, and sometimes *nt* is changed to *nd* and *ry* to *yy.*

With the above description of Śaurasenī in mind, if we look at our text, we find that there are many cases of *t* changing into *d* (*adi* ii. 20, *adihı* ii. 50, *cādaï* i. 60, *tado* i. 24, *dāva* iii. 49, *parāhada* i. 11, *vāmadā* i. 18 etc.) though this tendency is not uniformly carried out. In our text *th* is changed to *h* and not to *dh.* Some illustrations of abl. sing. in *-do* or *-ādo* are found (*laṁbhado* i. 12, *karādo* ii. 7, *sūrādo* iii. 8, also *matthaādu* iii. 15), besides we have those in *-ā* and *-hi* (*goravā* i. 19, *maāhi* i. 7 etc.). Loc. sing. in *-e* as well as in *-mmi* are found in our text (*samujjale* i. 30, *jaämmi* i. 13, *rahammi* i. 23, *vasuhammi* ii. 52, *vihummi* i. 10 etc). Nasalisation is unknown to our author, but whenever a long vowel is metrically needed *anusvāra* is added to the pl. terminations of the Instr., Gen. and Loc. The gen. sing. termination for the *i*- and *u*-stems is not only *-ṇo* but *-ssa* as well, though the latter is excluded by PISCHEL in Śaurasenī (*baṁdhuṇo* i. 10, *rassiṇo* i. 11, *bāhussa* i. 21, *Harissa* i. 41 etc.). We have many forms of the Atmanepada (*jaṁpaë, paäcchaë* i. 9). We come across Optative forms in

-jja (*bhaṇejja* i. 14). As against PISCHEL's expectation we come across Passive in *-ijj* (*kahijjaē* i. 15) and Absol. in *-ūṇa* and so also in *-ia* (*gamiūṇa* i. 34, *pariveḍhiūṇa* i. 53 *hakkāriā* i. 23, *samāaṇṇiā* i. 35 etc.). The 3rd p. sing. termination of the Present is *i* throughout and never *di*; there are only two cases of the softening of *t* in the 3rd p. sing. of the Imperative (ii. 6, 7). In this text *ry* is changed to *jj* and in one case *nt* is changed to *nd* (*sujjakaṁdā* iii. 14). The above scrutiny does not warrant us to conclude that the dialect of our text is Śaurasenī; but this much is to be admitted that it is sprinkled here and there with what are called Śaurasenī characteristics.[41]

It is already remarked above that our author closely follows Vararuci's grammar and his dialect fundamentally agrees with the one discussed in the first nine chapters of *Prākṛta-prakāśa*. Hemacandra and others who are indebted to Vararuci call the main dialect by the name Prākrit. The 12th chapter of *Prākṛta-prakāśa* mentions Māhārāstrī, but the text, as it is available, shows certain inconsistencies; so the genuineness of the 12th chapter can be called into question. Other grammarians like Mārkaṇḍeya start with Māhārāṣṭrī as the basic dialect, and according to their view Vararuci's Prākrit can be called Māhārāṣṭrī. Exception is taken to this view, and it is claimed that the Prākrit of Vararuci belongs to Indian Midland, and therefore it should be called Śaurasenī;[42] and this agrees well with the references to Śaurasenī in the 10th and 11th chapters. Admitting that it was once the dialect of the Indian Midland, we may still call it Māhārāṣṭrī following

41 Being a late work the text of *Kaṁsavaho* is not likely to be subjected to many changes at the hands of generations of copyists. The study of the dialect leaves the impression that our author did not discriminate one dialect from the other as rigorously as the modern scholars like WEBER, KONOW and others.

42 See the Papers of Drs. CHATTERJI and GHOSH noted above.

the lead of various grammarians. If it is once admitted that we are dealing with literary dialects, it is more safe to follow the terminology of the grammarians without always insisting on the territorial bias unless they show mutual contradictions and inconsistencies of an extraordinary character. Later grammarians have understood that the Prākrit of Vararuci is Māhārāṣṭrī ; and, as Rāma Pāṇivāda is following the nine chapters of *Prākṛta-prakāśa*, he is writing in Māhārāṣṭrī which is purely a literary language with no special territorial association at the time when he wrote this work.

Turning to the characteristics of Māhārāṣṭrī, as noted by grammarians and as gathered from the study of Māhārāṣṭrī literature, we find that intervocalic consonants ***k, g, c, j, t, d, p, y*** and ***v*** are usually dropped ; and aspirates like ***kh, gh, th, dh, ph*** and ***bh*** are changed to *h*. These are general rules ; Mss. do show irregularities ; and modern scholars want these rules to be applied rigorously as it is clear from the editions of *Sattasaï*, *Kappūramamjarī* etc. Grammarians allow even in Māhārāṣṭrī the change of *t* to *d* in a few words ;[43] and nowa-days it is held by some scholars[44] that the change of *t* to *d* is not prohibited in Māhārāṣṭrī. Rāma Pāṇivāda usually drops intervocalic consonants ***k, g, c, j, p, y*** and ***v***. His exceptions are either sanctioned by grammarians or very rare. His treatment of *t* is very uncertain : he may drop it or soften it as seen from the same words occurring in different places : (*aggao* i. 3 & *aggado* i. 5, *gao* i. 51 & *gada* ii. 11, *laā* iv. 25 & *ladā* i. 54, *haā* i. 36 & *hadā* iii. 51, etc.). As to *d*, it is sometimes dropped and sometimes retained (*vimaa* i. 30, *saā* i. 2, *savaï* i. 61 ; *jamādi* i. 16, ***pada*** i. 8, *paduma* iii. 2 ; *maa* iii. 60 & *mada* iv. 43 ; etc.). **The** most significant Māhārāṣṭrī trait of our author's dialect is the termination *i* or *e* in the 3rd p. sing.

43 PISCHEL : *Grammatik* § 204.

44 See the articles of Prof. A. M. GHATAGE noted above.

of the Present and *u* in that of the Imperative. There are only two cases of the termination *du* in the Imperative, and I should call them exceptional occurrences. It may be noted that even a rigorous editor like WEBER retains the termination *-du* once in his text of *Sattasaï* (verse 878) which is written in Māhārāṣṭrī. About the changes of *ṛ* there is no uniformity : it is changed to *a, i* or *u* ; and sometimes the same word shows two different forms (*maa* i. 50 & *mia* ii. 20). As to *kṣ* it is usually changed to *kkh,* but in a few words to *cch.* So far as the root *prekṣ* is concerned, both *pekkha* and *peccha* are available (ii. 11, iv. 11). The other Māhārāṣṭrī characteristics found in our author's dialect are the usual change of aspirates to *h* ; the change of *ry* to *jj* ; the Abl. sing. in *-ā,* the Loc. sing. in *-mmi* ; the Passive in *-ijj* ; the Future in *-hi-* ; and the Gerund in *-ūṇa.* In literary languages vocabulary is not a reliable criterion to distinguish one dialect from the other ; and therefore I have not scrutinised words like *laṭṭhī* which are restricted by certain grammarians for specific dialects.

Taking into account the essential characteristics of Śaurasenī and Māhārāṣṭrī, I might state, in conclusion, that the Prākrit dialect of *Kaṁsavaho* should be called Māhārāṣṭrī ; and as the author belongs to the decadent period of Prākrit literature and as he is thoroughly acquainted with the prose of the dramas, he shows some of the traits of Śaurasenī as well.

VI) METRES IN KAṀSAVAHO

In the Notes I have given the metrical analysis of every chapter at the close of it ; and I have also added there the mātrā-scheme and the author's definitions of different Vṛttas. Rāma Pāṇivāda has composed a treatise on classical metres, so I have mainly adopted his terminology ; and just in a few cases I have noted the variant names :

Avitatha, see Kaṭaka.
Indravajrā (1) : iv. 12.
Upajāti (12) : iv. 1, 2, 6, 8, 9, 11, 13-8.
Upendravajrā (7) : iv. 3-5, 7, 10, 19, 20.
Kaṭaka (1) : ii. 60.
Drutavilambita (1) : iv. 37.
Pṛthvī (3) : iii. 57, iv. 27, 40.
Praharṣiṇī (56) : iii. 1-56.
Mañjubhāṣiṇī (3): iv. 28, 43, 48*2 (Sanskrit).
Mandākrāntā (1) : iv. 33.
Mālabhāriṇī, see Vasantamālikā.
Mālinī (3) : i. 61-2, iv. 48.
Rathoddhatā (1) : iv. 29.
Vasantatilaka (7): iv. 21, 22, 34, 36, 42, 45, 48*1.
Vasantamālikā (60) : i. 63, ii. 1-57, iv. 24, 32.
Vaṁśastha (60) : i. 1-60.
Śālinī (2) : iv. 30-1.
Śikhariṇī (1) : i. 64.
Śārdūlavikrīḍita (6) : ii. 58, iii. 58, iv. 23, 26, 46, 47.
Sragdharā (5) : ii. 59, iv. 35, 39, 41, 44.
Svāgatā (3) : iii. 59, iv. 25, 38.
Hariṇī (1) : iii. 60.

If frequency is a good indication, Vaṁśastha, Vasantamālikā and Praharṣiṇī are the favourite metres of Rāma Pāṇivāda. Compared with the extent of the work, it has to be admitted that our author has used a greater variety of metres. On the whole the verses are metrically flawless; and there is only one case of Yati-bhaṅga (ii. 4, *cd*).

VII) STYLE OF KAṀSAVAHO.

Rāma Pāṇivāda has been brought up in the traditions of classical Sanskrit the tendencies of which are consequently deep-rooted in him. He shows a thorough mastery over the vocabulary which almost flows forth to serve his purpose. His language is simple in presenting the conversation and the narration, but it grows pretty difficult in descriptive portions especially due to the lengthy compounds. If the Prākrit language of the author becomes artificial now and then, the fault is due more to the age in which and the circumstances under which the work was composed than to any specific deficiency in the scholarship of our author. In many places we see his masterly grip over the language which vividly expresses the actions to be described. His style, though not very graceful, is full of vigour ; it inclines more towards elaboration than suggestion ; and sometimes the sound appears to dominate over the sense.

It is clear from the metrical analysis that our author has used a large number of metres in this work. The Gāthā, the Prākrit metre par excellence, is conspicuous by its absence. On the whole the verses flow with a vigour and dignity. Rāma Pāṇivāda's mastery over the language is seen also in some of his verbal devices. Identical syllables are repeated at the close of contiguous Pādas with the effect that we get a sonorous sound in reading these verses. In some verses the same syllable recurs so often that the reading of the verse adds to our pleasure. As in some of the Dravidian languages, our author shows the second syllable identical in all the Pādas ; and in some places we have the Yamaka of identical syllables with different meaning. Prākrit language affords a special facility in this regard since one and the same Prākrit word may stand for different Sanskrit words : in a few cases our author has availed himself of this advantage. Attention has been drawn to many of these cases in the Notes.

Some of the scenes sketched by Rāma Pāṇivāda in the section of the bards' songs or in the description of Mathurā are worthy of a genuine poet. These descriptions are spiced with poetic embellishments like Upamā, Utprekṣā, Rūpaka, Dṛṣṭānta etc. ; and we come across a few happy illustrations of Arthāntaranyāsa. Most of them are mentioned in the Notes on different verses.

Among the Sanskrit authors of note, Rāma Pāṇivāda can be favourably compared with Māgha whose influence he betrays in many places. We miss here the outstanding Utprekṣās and the natural scenes of the country-side seen in *Gaüḍavaho* ; nor do we get here the pedantic descriptions full of unwieldy compounds exhibited in *Rāvaṇavaho*. Antiquity may be an advantage but is not a virtue by itself ; nor is modernity a fault which should be allowed to obscure the genuine merits of a poet. Taking into consideration the able delineation of the subject, the successful handling of the language and the well-decorated presentation of poetry seen in *Kaṁsavaho,* it can be said that Rāma Pāṇivāda deserves a respectable seat in the gallery of his predecessors like Pravarasena, Vākpati Rājaśekhara and Guṇacandra.

5. THE CHĀYĀ AND ITS AUTHORSHIP

As already noted above, both the Mss. give the Sanskrit rendering or the Chāyā of the Prākrit text. It is practically identical in both the Mss. : there is a single case where the two Mss. differ with a corresponding difference in the Prākrit text (i. 38). There are a few variants on the common Prākrit text. So far as the tenses of the verbal forms are concerned, the Chāyā is not literal ; and in fact the forms of the Present are substituted by those of the Imperfect and Perfect. Who is the author of this Chāyā is a question for the solution of which no definite clue is available from the Mss. However some circumstantial evidence may be noted here : *Kaṁsavaho* belongs to an age and country in which Prākrit texts almost necessarily required a Chāyā ; the Sanskrit Chāyā in the Ms. is so closely associated with the text that it has not got independent colophons, those in the square brackets being added by the editor ; both the Mss. give the same Chāyā, and as yet no Ms. of *Kaṁsavaho* without the Chāyā has come to light; the Chāyā takes some liberty with the verbal forms of the text ; in some cases (i. 50) the metre is maintained even in the Sanskrit rendering ; and lastly Rāma Pāṇivāda himself has written a Chāyā for the Prākrit portions of his dramas like *Sītārāghavanāṭaka* etc.[45] Taking into account all these points, I am inclined to believe, of course tentatively, that Rāma Pāṇivāda himself might have added this Chāyā to make his work intelligible even to those who did not possess the first-hand knowledge of Prākrit.[46]

---

45 *A Triennial Catalogue of Mss.*, vol. VI-part 1. Sanskrit, Madras 1935, p. 7042, No. 5135 b.

46 A portion of this Introduction was read before the Prākrit Section of the Tenth All-India Oriental Conference, Tirupati, 1940.

राम-पाणिवाअ-कओ

कंसवहो

[पढमो सग्गो[1]]

सिरीअ णाहो सिहि-पिंछ-सेहरो[2]
सिणिद्ध-गोवी-णअणंचलंचिओ[3] ।
सअं जसोआ-तणअत्तणं[4] गओ
विहू विहूसावइँ गोव-वाडिअं ॥ १

कहं खु से कंसवहं सुहावहं
सुहं व गण्हेह वले सुहीअणा ।
सआ गुरूणं चलणे समल्लिओ[6]
भणामि जं भत्ति-गुणेण णोल्लिओ ॥ २

अहेक्कदा चंकमिरो वअंगणे
दिणंत-गो-दोहण-वावुडंगणे ।
सहग्गओ सो ऽहिसरंतमग्गओ
गदग्गओ दक्खइ गंदिणी-सुअं ॥ ३

रआइ रेहा-रहँ-संख-पंकअ-
द्धअंकिदाइं पुलऊण भूअले ।
तहिं णमंतं पुलआलि-पम्हल-
प्पमोअ-वाहोल्ल-विहुल्ल-विग्गहं ॥ ४

---

१ M begins thus: श्रीरस्तु ॥ कंसवधम् ॥, T begins thus: श्रीरामपाणिवादविरचितं कंसवधकाव्यम्. २ MT सेहरं. ३ MT लंचिअं. ४ M तणयत्तणं ५ M विगुसा° (विभूसा ?). ६ T समिल्लओ. ७ T रम. ८ T वोहोल.

खणे खणे झाण-णिमीलिएॅक्खणं[1]
णमंत-मोलि-प्पणिवेसिअंजलिं ।
असंभमं संभरमाणमग्गदो[2]
लसंतमप्पाणमणंत-कोङ्डअं ॥ ५

अदिङ्ग-पासट्ठिअ-वत्थु-सत्थअं
असुव्वमाणुच्चलिउच्च[3]-णिस्सणं ।
परं[4] परब्बम्ह-सुहाणुभाविणं[5]
ण बाहिरं बाहइ किं पि देहिणं ॥ ६

खणं रुवंतं विहसंतमंतरा
खणं च खंभं व णिरूसहं ठिअं ।
खणं चरंतं खणमुच्च-जंपिअं[6]
खणं पि तुण्हिक्क-मुहं मआहि व ॥ ७

पमोअ-तूरंत-पद-क्कमुच्चलं[7]-
क्खलंत-मोचा-गुण-फेण-मंडलो ।
सरि-प्पवाहं विअ संमुहागअं
स पच्चुवट्ठाइ णमच्चुअंबुही ॥ ८

करंबुएणं परिगण्हिऊण णं
घरं णिअं पावइ देवई-सुओ ।
अणामअं पुच्छइ मिट्ठ-भोअणं
पअच्छए किं पि अ जंपएं[8] पुणो ॥ ९

---

१ MT णिमीलिअक्खणं. २ M संभमरंतमग्गदो. ३ M -माणं चलिउच्च. ४ T वरं. ५ M सुखाणु°. ६ जंमिअं. ७ M क्कमुच्चलक्खिलंत, T क्कमुंचलंखीलं. ८ M जप्पए.

तुहावलोएण भुवीअ मे मणं
विसट्टमक्कूरं सिणिद्ध-बंधुणो ।
अहो किमच्छेरमिणं समुग्गए
वि[2]हुम्मि सज्जो विअसेइ केरवं ॥ १०

मुणामि तेएण खु भोअ-राइणो
दिण-प्पदीवा विव तिक्ख-रस्सि[3]णो ।
पलिज्जमाणेण पराहद-प्पहा
कहं पि तुम्हे बलिणो विजीवह ॥ ११

अवच्च-जुग्गे चिरं[4]मक्खंदे वि दे
सहंति जं णो पिदरा णिअंतणं ।
सरीरिणो ता दुरवच्च-लंभदो
वदंति सच्चं[5] णिरवच्चदा वरं ॥ १२

कहं परिच्चेमु सरीर-पोसए
इमे वि मादा-पिदरे व वच्छले ।
जअम्मि जे कोइल-रीइ-गामिणो
ण दे जुउ[6]च्छंति कहं महाअणा ॥ १३

कअं खु जं वा कहिदेण भूरिणा
किणो भणेज्जाअम[7]-कालणं भवं ।
इदं वदंतो विरमेइ माहवो
भणंति भव्वा हि जणा[8] मिदक्खरं ॥ १४

---

१ M विसट्ट-. २ M विहुव्वि, T विहुम्म. ३ T रंसिणो. ४ MT रमक्खदे.
५ T मच्चं ६ T जुगुच्छंति. ७ M -आयम. ८ MT जणा.

विसुद्ध-सीलेण विणम्म-मोलिणा
स कंस-दूएण कहिज्जए हरी ।
तुह व्व साहिट्ठ-जहिट्ठ-दंसणं
विसिट्ठमम्हाअमण-प्पओअणं ॥ १५

णिरत्थ-संगा णिअमंत-पंथओ[1]
जमादि-जोअब्भसणुब्भड-स्समा ।
चिरं[2] विइण्णंति तवोहणा वि जं
स दिट्ठिए[3] मज्झ सि दिट्ठि-गोअरो ॥ १६

जिअं जिअं मे णअणेहि जेहि दे
सुजाअ-सुंदेर-गुणेक्क-मंदिरं ।
पसण्ण-पुण्णामअ-मोह-सच्छहं
मुहं पहासुज्जलमज्ज पिज्जए ॥ १७

णिसिज्झए माहव माउलेण दे
विअंभमाणेण व पावरासिणा ।
इमस्स पच्चक्ख-णिरिक्खणूसवो
मुहस्स[4] जं वा विहि-वामदा खु सा ॥ १८

ममम्मि तुट्ठं विहिणा णु संपअं
महं मह च्चेअ[5] णु पुण्ण-संभवो ।
जमज्ज तेण च्चिअ भोअ-राइणा[6]
विसज्जिओ हं तुइ कज्ज-गोरवा ॥ १९

---

१ M पत्थआ. २ MT इरं. ३ M दिट्ठिं, T दिट्ठिअ. ४ T मुहुस्स. ५ M ममच्चेअ
६ M भोअराइणो.

सुणाहि तासेण सआ समाउलो
जमीहए माहव दे स माउलो[1] ।
स वंचिउं वंछइ तं पि संपअं
जअस्स जो देसि खु कं पि संपअं ॥ २०

पलंब-बाहुस्स वहस्स जस्स दे
पलंब-केसि-प्पमुहा ण पारिआ ।
तमप्पणा संपइ संपमद्दिउं
तम-प्पहाणो स हि सण्णहेइ हि[2] ॥ २१[3]

धराहिणाहो धणुहूसव-च्छला
खलो तिलोईवई[4] हिंसिउं तुमं ।
समं समारंभई[5] कुंभि-राइणा[6]
समं च मल्लेहि स मंचमाठिओ[7] ॥ २२

रहम्मि हक्कारिअ राअ-पंसणो[8]
भणीअ मं किं पि स तं पि सुव्वउ ।
अमंदमक्कूरअे[9] वच्च गोउलं
भणेहि बाले वि अ राम-केसवे ॥ २३

चअत्थि भोआहिव-बाहु-पालिए
सरास-जण्णो महुरा-महाघरे ।
तमिक्खिउं वो जइ किं पि कोदुअं
तदो समाअच्छह पेच्छहूसवं ॥ २४

---

१ M मादुलो. २ M ही. ३ T omits the 4th line. ४ T तिलोइपइ. ५ T समरंभइ. ६ T राएण. ७ Fourth line defective in T. ८ T वंस्सणो. ९ T अक्करम.

स णंदगोवो वि स-मित्त-बंधवो
जवा समावच्चउ मज्झ मंदिरं ।
अतुच्छओ तुज्झण विक्खणाअरो
मह त्ति तेण च्चिअ सव्वमीरिअं ॥ २५

इमस्स कज्जस्स सरीरमेरिसं
जहिं खु पाणाअइ विप्पलंभणं ।
ण वच्च वा णंदअ वच्च वा तुवं
विही-णिसेहो वि ण दूअ-कत्तओ ॥ २६

पवट्टए चावमहं ति कोदुअं
णिवट्टए वंचण-साहणं ति तं ।
दुहा वले भादर भाव-बंधणं
मह त्ति तं जंपइ रोहिणी-सुओ ॥ २७

इदं वओ भण्णइ वण्णमालिणा
अलं कवित्थेण[1] पलंब-सूअण ।
अकज्ज-सज्जाण हि सत्तु-संभवो
कुदो भअं कज्ज-पहुम्मुहाण णो ॥ २८

अह प्फुडं काहिइ साहसं जइ
क्खअं सअं जाहिइ पाअडो *जणो[2] ।
समिद्धमग्गि गासिउं समुट्ठिओ
ण डज्झए किं सलहाण संचओ ॥ २९

---

१ T कुवित्थेण. २ MT अणो.

विसुद्ध-सीले विमए[1]-च्छल-क्कमो
ण को वि अम्हे छिविउं पअब्भइ ।
णहम्मि तारा-णिअरे समुज्जले
णिसंधआरो मइलेइ किं भण ॥ ३०

भुअ-प्पआवो भुअ-दप्पसालिणो
रिवूण मज्झे च्चिअ संपआसइ ।
हिरण्ण-रेअस्स वि जाल-संचओ
सअं समिंधेइ[3] किमिंधणं विणा ॥ ३१

वअं वएसग्ग-सरा णिराउला
स-सिक्क-भंडा सअडाहिरोहिणो ।
समुच्चलामो सअला वि संपअं
सहाजिओ होज्ज स भोअ-भूवई ॥ ३२

इआलवंतो सह सीर-पाणिणा
रहं समारोहइ देवई-सुओ ।
करग्ग-संवग्गिअ-पग्गहो[5] जवा
स तस्स पढिम्मि अ गंदिणी-सुओ ॥ ३३

सुहं रहम्मि च्चिअ हम्मिओवमे ।
सअं सअंतो गमिऊण जामिणिं ।
पगे समं सम्मिलिदेहि माहवो
स णंद-गोव-प्पमुहेहि पढिओ ॥ ३४

---

१ M विणअ. २ M भुजप्पआवो. ३ M समिद्धेइ. ४ M वयं. ५ M पग्गवो.
६ T omits two lines.

अहो समाअण्णिअ कण्ण-दूसहं[1]
पवास-वत्तं पदएस-केउणो ।
गलुग्गलंतस्सु-जलुक्खदक्खरं
विओअ-भीआ विलवंति गोविआ ॥ ३५

असुद्धअंदम्मि व संभु-मत्थएं[2]
अकोत्थुहम्मि व्विव विण्हु-वच्छए ।
अणंदए णंद-घरम्मि का सिरी
हआ हआ हंत वअं वअंगणा ॥ ३६

अणण्ण-णाहा अविहा विहाअ णे[3]
घिणं विणा झत्ति गए विदालुणे ।
तहिं जणे लग्गइ संपअं पि जं
तमम्मकाणं खु मणं विणिंदिअं ॥ ३७

किमेत्थ अम्हे[4] कुणिमो *गुणुत्तरे[5]
जणे पिणद्धं जुवईण माणसं ।
ण तीरए चारु-पसूण-सोरहे
महीरुहे भिंगउलं च कड्ढिउं ॥ ३८

पहाण-पाणाणि खु णो जणद्दणो
स जेण दूरं गमिओ दुरप्पणा ।
कअंत-दूओ च्चिअ सो समागओ
ण कंस-दूओ त्ति मुणेह गोविआ ॥ ३९

---

१ T दुस्सअं (दुस्सहं ?).　२ T मत्थके.　३ T णो.　४ M किमम्मकाओ.
५ M गुणंतरे, T गुणत्तरे.

इमाहि कूरो ण परो त्ति से कआ
अवस्समक्कूरअ-सद्द-पक्किआ ।
अघोर-सद्दं जह घोर-मुत्तिणो
सिवस्स वक्खाइ तह त्ति मण्णिमो ॥ ४०

हरिस्स रूवं चिअ संभरेह हो
हरिम्मणी-सामल-कोमल-प्पहं ।
सिणिद्ध-केसंचिअ-मोर-पिंछिअं[1]
विसट्ट-कंदोट्ट-विसाल-लोअणं ॥ ४१

फुरंत[2]-दंतुज्जल-कंति-चंदिमा-
समग्ग-सुंदेर-मुहेंदु-मंडलं[3] ।
विसुद्ध-मोत्ता-गुणं[4]-कोत्थुह-प्पहा-
पलित्त-वच्छं फुड-वच्छ-लंछणं ॥ ४२

भुअंग-भोआकई[5]-चंग-भंगअ-
प्पआम-सोमाल-भुआ-लअंचिअं ।
मणि-प्पहाइण्ण-सुवण्ण-मेहला-
विलंबि-पीअंबर-सोणि-मंडलं ॥ ४३

णह-प्पहालिद्ध-णहप्पहामल-
प्पवाल[6]-तंबुज्जल-पाअ-पंकअं ।
मणोज्ज-हासोल्ल-कडक्ख-विक्खण-
क्खण-क्खुहिज्जंत[7]-वअंगणंगअं[8] ॥ ४४

१ M पंछिअं. २ T हुरंत. ३ T मंसलं. ४ M मोत्तागण, T मोत्ताउण. ५ T भोमा-कइ. ६ T प्पवाह. ७ M क्खुविज्जंत. ८ T वअंगणंगणं.

णिअंबिणीओ णिउलोल्ल-पल्लव-
प्पबद्ध-पल्लुंक-पमद्द-णिद्दअं ।
ण विम्हरिज्जेउ[1] णवं णवं कअं
जणद्दणेणं जउणाड-कीलणं ॥ ४५

जहिं[3] दु सा णिल्लुअ-फुल्ल-मंजरी
णमंत-चुंतग्ग-भमंत-छप्पआ ।
सुआणुवज्जंत-सुऊढ-जंपिआ
तडंत-वाणीर-लआ खु सक्खिणी ॥ ४६

मउंद-वेणूअर-णिंत-बंधुर-
स्सणामआसाअ-विरूढ-पल्लवा ।
दवुम्ह-सुक्का वि वणंत-पाअवा
जहिं खु गिम्हाअवमावुणंति[4] णो ॥ ४७

वणाणिला जत्थ कलिंद-णंदिणी-
तरंग-संपक्क-सिणिद्ध-सीअला ।
कुणंति णो[5] पंकअ-पंसु-मंसला
समाउराणं तलवुंड-कारिअं[6] ॥ ४८

सुवंति गोवद्धण-सेल-मेहला-
विलंबिउग्गज्जिअ-विज्जुला घणा ।
इमाण णो माण-विणोअणुम्मुहा
जहिं जइच्छागअ-पीढमद्दआ ॥ ४९

---

१ M विच्चुरिज्जेउ. २ T जउणाच. ३ M जहं. ४ M उणंति. ५ M णे. ६ M कारिणं. ७ T विज्जला.

जहिं च वुंदावणमेक्क-मंदिरं
मणि-प्पदीवो मअ-लंछणो सअं ।
णवा अ सेज्जा तरु-पल्लवावली
वसंत-पुप्फाइ अ भूसणाइ णो ॥ ५०

गओ स कालो गअ-गामिणी-अणा
मणोरहाणं कुणिमो तिलंजलिं ।
सुहस्स सव्वस्स वि मूल-कालणं
जणो गओ जं जण-लोअणंजणो ॥ ५१

कआ णु कण्हस्स कवोल-घोलिर-
प्फुड-प्पहा-मंडल-कुंडलुज्जलं[1] ।
सु-पिक्क-बिंबी-फल-पाडलाहरं
मुहुत्तअं[2] पेच्छिहिमो मुहंबुअं ॥ ५२

कआ णु पीण-त्थण-गाढ-पीडणा-
मलिज्जमाणुज्जल-वण्ण-मालिअं ।
इमेहिं दोहिं परिवेढिऊण से
विसालमालिंगिहिमो भुअंतरं ॥ ५३

असंक-संकेअ-लदा-घरोअर-
ट्ठिअस्स मग्ग-प्पहिएक्कवणस्स से ।
जवेण गंतूण जहिट्ठ-चेट्ठिअं
कआ णु वा पाइहिमो ऽहरामअं ॥ ५४

---

१ M कुंडलुज्जलं. २ M मुहुत्तअं.

इअ-प्पलावं पिअ-विप्पवासअ-
प्पआम-सोआउरमंगणा-अणं ।
मुउंद-वाआउ स गंदिणी-सुओ
समागओ जंपइ किं पि साअरं ॥ ५५

अहीरमाहीर-णिअंविणी-अणा
मुहा खु तुम्हे विलवेह वीहलं ।
कहं णु वो मुंचइ चंचलेक्खणा
खणं पि सो तुम्ह वसंवओ हरी ॥ ५६

विजिम्ह-तुम्ह-ब्भुमआ-कुअंडअ-
प्पमुत्त-णेत्तंचल-बाण-कीलिओ ।
कहं खु सो कंपइ संपइ क्खणं
सहेज्ज कज्जाहिमुहस्स साहसं ॥ ५७

उसंम्मि संमज्जइ साअरम्मि जो
स साअमुम्मज्जइ किं ण चंदमो ।
अलं विसाएण विलासिणीण वो
गअस्स पच्चाअमणं ण दुल्लहं ॥ ५८

समत्थ-लोअस्स पआस-हेदुणो
तमप्पवंचस्स णिरासआरिणो ।

---

१ M मुहा तु.

पडिप्पआणं पडिवालएह से
सरोइणीओ व सहस्स-रस्सिणो ॥ ५९

विओअ-सोउम्हल-गिम्ह-ताविअं
वइ[1]त्थिओ-सत्थअ-चादई-उलं ।
वअंबु-धाराहि सु-सीअलाहि सो
सुहावए माहव-दूअ-वारिओ ॥ ६०

अह दिअह-विआस-प्पक्कमे पारुहंतो
सवइ हरि-सणाहं संदणं गंदिणेओ ।
णयणं[2]-पदुम-राई-रोअणिज्जं जणाणं
लहइ सुहमहिक्खं कं पि सो कस्सवी व ॥ ६१

जव-जिअ-पवणेणं वच्चमाणो रहेणं
सह पसुव-वरेहिं गाहए माहवो सो ।
कसण-गिरि-सिहाली-तुल्ल-कल्लोल-माला-
फिडिअं[3]-तड-तमालं सूर-कण्णाउ वेलं ॥ ६२

जउणा[4]-सलिलम्मि बुड्डमाणो
पडिबिंबं व तहिं पि वासुदेवं ।
पुलऊण भुवीअ विम्हअंतो
पुलउब्भिण्ण-तणू स गंदिणेओ ॥ ६३

---

१ MT वळत्थिआ. २ T णअण. ३ M विडिम. ४ M जुउणा.

तरंतो तं तो सो तरुण-मण-संतोस-महुरो
स-वुंदेहिं साहं विसई महुरं णाम णअरं ।
तहिं वीहीगाही कुणइ वणिआणं समहिअं
समाणंदं चंदो विव कुमुइणीणं महुमहो ॥ ६४

इअ राम-पाणिवाअ-कए कंसवहे
पढमो सग्गो ।

[बीओ सग्गो]

अह मालिअे-दिण्ण-माल-भारी
वणमाली मुसली अ वच्चमाणं ।
परिधोअ-वरिल्ल-भंडवौहं
रअअं कं पि णिअंति राअमग्गे ॥ १

मउ-हास-मणोहराणणेहिं
कुमरेहिं वसणाइ जाइदो सो ।
कुमणो घण-गव्व-दुव्विणीओ
कुविदो भासइ भोअराअ-भिच्चो ॥ २

---

१ M विसअ. २ T माल्मि. ३ M भंणवाहं.

ण हु संभरिउं पि सक्कए जं
तमिणं जंपह डिंभआ किमेव्वं ।
णणु खादइ तज्जिओ वि जो सो
छिविओ किं ण कुणेइ कण्हभोई ॥ ३

णवरं ण लहिस्सइ त्ति णेअं
वसणं भोअवइस्स जच्चमाणं ।
णमिणं चिअ तुम्ह सीस-छेअ-
स्स वि हो होस्सइ कालणं मुणेह ॥४

अभणिज्ज-वउग्गमेण जम्मा
अणुहोंति प्फुडमप्पणो विणासं ।
चवलं लहिऊण पक्खवालिं[1]
सलहा किं ण मरंति हव्ववाहे ॥ ५

अह होदु सहेमि एक्कवारं
अहके[2] तुज्झण बाल-चावलाइं ।
ण सहेज्ज णराहिवो इमाइं
जइ सो सोच्छिइ वच्छलिज्ज-वंझो ॥ ६

इअ सो कडु भासिऊण जाहे
पहसंतो च्चिअ वोलिउं पवुत्तो ।
सहसा महु-मूअणेण ताहे
वसणाइं हरिआइ से करादो ॥ ७

---

१ T पक्खवाली, M पक्खवाहिं. २ T अहहे.

अहिहोदु-मणस्स कोह-भारा
रहसुट्ठाविअ-लट्ठि-पाणिणो से[1] ।
अह तक्खण-णक्ख-कोडि-रुग्गं
परिपाडेइ सिरं सिरीअ णाहो ॥ ८

णिअ-पंक-विसोहणावदाओ
रअअस्सब्भहिअं लहू-भवंतो ।
पविसेइ[2] सइप्पआसमप्पा
वसणाणं णिअरो अ वासुदेवं ॥ ९

सिअएहि सिएहि से सरीरं
वसिएहिं लसए तमाल-णीलं ।
कणउज्जल-मेहलाहिरामं
ससि-मोहेहि व णील-सेल-सिंगं ॥ १०

अह पेक्खइ वंकदं गदाए
तणु-लट्ठीअ वि दिट्ठि[3]-रम्म-रूवं ।
मअणस्स व सो कुअंड-लट्ठिं
वणिअं कं पि समुण्णमंत-पिट्ठं[4] ॥ ११

अणुसप्पिर-छप्पअं वहंतिं
मणि-पत्तं भिद-कुंकुमं करग्गे ।
सणिअं सणिअं समावडंतिं[5]
समुवागच्छिअ पुच्छए हरी णं ॥ १२

---

१ T सो. २ M परिसेइ. ३ M दट्ठि. ४ M पीठं, T वट्ठी. ५ M समावसंतिं.

कुडिलच्छि वले कुदो सि बाले
कुडिली-होइ कहं तुहं सरीरं ।
मसिणं घुसिणं च कस्स दाउं[1]
सणिअं गच्छसि पेच्छणिज्ज-रूवे ॥ १३

अह जंपइ सा विहिस्स सच्ची
वलिअं जिंभइ वामिआ ममस्सिं ।
हिअअम्मि पसिद्धमित्थिआणं
मह गत्ते वि कुणीअ वंकदं जा ॥ १४

सुण सुंदर सिप्पआरिआ हं
णिवरंतेउर-वासिणी विणीआ ।
घुसिणं पुण कंस-राइणो से
पणिदाउं पअलामि तण्णिएदं ॥ १५

सुउमारमिणं च दे सरीरं
सुरही[2] कुंकुम-पंकओ अ एसो ।
परिगण्हउ ता भवं चिएअं
सरिसाणं हि[3] समाअमो सुहस्स ॥ १६

इअ तप्पाविइण्ण-कुंकुमाहि-
प्फुसिअंगा विलसंति कण्ह-रामा ।
स-पसूण-कला अ सिंदुवारा
विव संझाअव-संछिविज्जमाणा ॥ १७

---

१ T दाइं. २ M सरई. ३ स समाअमो.

चिबुए कर-पल्लवेण कण्हो
सणिअं गण्हिअ सारसेक्खणं तं ।
अह खुज्जिअमुज्जुइं कुणीअ
प्फुड-लज्जावलिआणणेंदु-बिंबं ॥ १८

पढमं[1] कुडिला वि चंद्लेहा
जह संपुण्णदमेइ पुण्णिमाअं ।
तह सा सहसा भुवीअ पुण्णा
कमणी-कोमल-कंति-कोमुईहिं ॥ १९

अदिभूमिमुवागअं मिअच्छी
मअणाअल्लुअ-सल्लमुव्वहंती ।
णमिऊण भणाइ णंदसूणुं
धुअ-लज्जा-णिअलेहि अक्खरेहिं ॥ २०

इमिणम्हि[2] जिओ सरीर-सोहा-
विहवेण त्ति तुमंसि रूढ-वेरो ।
तुमए अणुकंपिद त्ति दाणिं
किमु मं वाहइ वम्महो महप्पं ॥ २१

विस-रुक्ख-पसूणएहि मण्णे
विसमेसू विसिहे ऽहुणा कुणाइ ।
मउएहि किमण्णहा मणं मे
इमिणा डज्झइ णिज्जए अ मुच्छं ॥ २२

१ MT पढमं. २ M इमिणम्मि.

अवसं सवसं पि मार-घोर-
ज्जर-दूमंत-मणं मणोज्ज-मुत्ति ।
अणुगण्ह मि कण्हसार-सार-
च्छवि-सारेहि कडक्ख-विक्खणेहिं ॥ २३

हरि-णील-सिणिद्ध-मुद्ध-सोहे
तुह संकंतमुरम्मि रम्म-रूवं ।
कसणाअल-धाउ-राअ-कप्पं[1]
थण-उंभेहि[2] लुहामि[3] कुंकुमं णं ॥ २४

अह वाहरई म्ह वासुदेवो
सुमहंतं तुह सुब्भु साहसिक्कं ।
इह जाइ मए विवक्खिदाइं
हरिदाइं तइ ताइ अक्खराइं ॥ २५

विअसंत-मुहारविंद-णिंतं-*
ब्भमरालाव-छलाहिलास-वाअं ।
पडिवालइ किं णु मल्लिअक्खो
णलिणिं किं दु सरेइ दिट्ठमत्तं ॥ २६

मह माणिणि कज्ज-गोरवेण
परवंतस्स ण तुब्भ कुंभ-थोरे ।
परिरंभिउमोसरो उरोए
सवसो च्चेअ खमो हि काम-तंते ॥ २७

---

१ Defective line in T. २ M उंफेहिं. ३ T ल्हामि. ४ M वासरइ.
५ MT णिंत.

अहमेहिमि दाव भूव-सेवा-
णिअलादो मह जाव होज्ज मोक्खो ।
ण हि केरविणिं छिवेउमीसो
घण-रुद्ध-प्पसरो स चंदमो वि ॥ २८

अह णो हिअएच्छिआइ पच्छा
ससि-जोण्हुप्फुसिआसु जामिणीसुं ।
सुअणाण सहासु सक्कवीणं
वअणाइं व पहंतु कीलिआइं[1] ॥ २९

इअ तं पिअ-दंसणं भणंतो
मुदिअं चेअ विसज्जिऊण कण्हो ।
सअणेहि सहग्गओ गओ सो
साणिअं तो विसए अ राअहाणिं ॥ ३०

महणिज्ज-महुज्जलंग-लच्छी-
विहवालोअ-विहुल्ल-कोउहल्ला[2] ।
पदिसंति पिहज्जणा चि मग्गं
तहि से कं ण हरंति पुण्णभाआ ॥ ३१

मणि-दीव-सिहा-पलिज्जमाणं
कणअ-क्खंभ-विलग्ग-हार-गुंफं ।
महिसक्खअ-धूव-गंध-गब्भं
महु-वेरी विसए कुअंड-सालं[3] ॥ ३२

---

१ M कीलआइं, T कीलिआहिं. २ M कोउहल्लो. ३ M कुअंडवालं.

महिअं बहु-गंध-मल्लएहिं
धणुहं गण्हिअ पाणि-पल्लवेहिं ।
सहस[1] च्चिअ सज्जिअं कुणंतो
स समाकड्ढइ मुट्ठि-पीडिअं णं ॥ ३३

अइ[2] बालअ राअ-पूइदं णं
धणुहं मा छिव मा छिवेत्ति[3] जाहे ।
वअणाइ सुअंति[4] किंकराणं
खुडिअं तं महु-सूअणेण[5] ताहे ॥ ३४

थणिअं किमिणं कुदो पओओ
णर-सिंघ[6]-द्धणिअं णु तं णिवुत्तं ।
इअ[8]वित्थ[7]-सएण दुत्थ-चित्तो
धणु-भंग-द्धणिणा सुवीअ कंसो ॥ ३५

अह रक्खि-भडे परक्कमंते
परुसेहिं वअणेहि अक्खिवंते ।
पमलंति परोस-विड्डिरिल्ला
धणु-खंडेहि रणम्मि राम-कण्हो[9] ॥ ३६

मिहिरम्मि विअ प्पआसमाणे
वणमालिम्मि मणाइ सज्जणाणं ।
कमलाइ व होंति फुल्लआइं
कुमुआइं व कुअंति दुज्जणाणं ॥ ३७

---

१ M सहसु. २ T अयि. ३ T मा च्छिव मा च्छिवेत्ति. ४ T सुवंति. ५ M सूह-णेण. ६ M णरणीह (-सीह ?). ७ M अयवित्थ, T अअपित्थ. ८ M Defective reading. ९ M रामकण्हो.

अह चाव-घराहि णिक्कमंतो
सह रामेण स देवई-तणूओ ।
जुवई-णयणेहि[1] पिज्जमाणो
विअरेइ प्फुडमंकण[2]-त्थलीअं ॥ ३८

समुवट्ठिअ भोअ-राअहाणिं
सरसं तं पुलऊण राअहाणिं ।
भणए सणिअं मणोहिरामं
स हि वाआहि स-वित्थराहि[3] रामं ॥ ३९

उव णो भुवण-प्पणाइदाए
महुराए महुरत्तणं पुरीए ।
मणि-हम्मिअ-पालि-मोलि-कुंभ-
क्खलणोवाहिअ-सूर-संदणाए ॥ ४०

इअमुण्णमिउच्चे[4]-केउ-हत्थ-
प्पअलिज्जंत-पडाइअंगुलीहिं ।
स-विहूइ-लहूइदं स-गव्वा
णअरिं तज्जइ किं णु णिज्जराणं ॥ ४१

कणआअल-सोह-सोह[5]-सिंग-
त्थल-कीलंत-पुरंगणच्छरोहा[6] ।
परिहण्णव-मज्झ-वट्टिणीअं[7]
सअमोलंबइ जंबुदीव-लच्छि ॥ ४२

---

१ T णअणेहिं. २ M प्फुड. ३ T वित्थदाहि. ४ T इयमु-. ५ M omits सोह.
६ M च्छलोहा. ७ T वट्टणीअं.

फलिहोवल-कुट्टिम-प्पएसो
हरिणीलालअ-रस्सि-मिस्सिदो ऽअं ।
इह संपइ संभरावए णो
जउणुग्गणिहअ-जण्हवी-पवाहं ॥ ४३

कसणोवल-केलि-पव्वआणं
तम-सामाहि रुईहि णिण्हुआअं[1] ।
दिअहे वि सरंति वीहिआअं[2]
विहुआसंकमिहाहिसारिआओ ॥ ४४

इह कंचण-गेह-कंति-लित्ते
गअणे बाल-दिणेस-मोह-मोहा ।
विहडेइ ण दिग्घिआसु दिग्घं
रअणीअं पि रहंगणाम-जुग्गं ॥ ४५

इह वप्प-मणि-प्पहा-कडप्पा
गअणं मंडल-सोहिणो लिहंता ।
रइणो ससिणो अ कंचि कालं
परिवेस-प्पहमुज्जलं कुणंति ॥ ४६

वलही[3]-वलएसु गोउराणं
विहरंताण विलासिणीअणाणं ।
मुसिणाइ मुहेंदु-सेअ-बिंदु-
च्छल-मोत्ताफलआइ सग्ग-वाओ[4] ॥ ४७

---

१ M णिण्हुआसं. २ M वीहिआइं. ३ T वलहिं. ४ T वावो.

इह चंद-मणी-घरोअरेसुं
समअं चंद-मुहीहि संविसंता ।
ण लहंति रइ-स्ससं जुवाणा
तव-रत्तीसु वि णाम तामसीसुं ॥ ४८

इअमुण्णमिउच्च-सोह-सीसा
पविसंट्टेहि[1] गवक्ख-लोअणेहिं ।
रदणाअर-मेहला-कलावं
कुदुउल्ली पुलइ व्व भूअ-धात्तिं ॥ ४९

अदिहीण कुणंति पज्ज-कज्जं
पअलंतं[2]-प्पसवासवोदएहिं ।
इह णिक्खुड-वाड-बाल-रुक्खा
सुह-पण्हि च रवेहि कोइलाणं ॥ ५०

सर-सीअर-वाहिणो समीरा
सरसामोअं[3]-हरा सरोरुहाणं ।
मिहुणाण रइ-स्समं समेउं
सइ सज्जंति णमेत्थ वित्थरंतं ॥ ५१

इह कोञ्चण पिच्छिलम्मि णिञ्चु-
ब्भड-दोग्घट्ट-कडावडोज्झरेहिं ।
लगिआ वसुहम्मि दंति भिंगा
ण णिहेलोवल-कुट्टिम-ब्भमं किं ॥ ५२

---

१ M पविसंदेहि. २ M वलअंत. ३ T सरसामोद. ४ T Defective reading.

आणिअंतण-जंत-मग्ग-णित-
द्धणिउग्घोसिर-वारि-धोरणीहिं ।
इह कोच्चण णिच्च-सिच्चमाणे
णिलए णच्चइ पच्चहं[1] मऊरो[2] ॥ ५३

इह सुव्वइ णिव्वहंत-ताल-
प्फुड-संगीअ-णडंगहार-इंधं ।
गहिरो घण-गज्जिआणुरूवो
महुरो कोच्चि मइंग-तुंग-णाओ ॥ ५४

सुणँ[3] पुव्वअ-सुंदरीअणाणं
महु-गोट्ठीसु मआणुसंग-संदं ।
ललिअं कलअंठ-कंठ-णाअ-
प्पडिमं कोच्चण णच्चणम्मि गीअं ॥ ५५

परदो सुर्णं[4] थाणिइल्ल-भावा[5]
विहलं पच्चअ-लक्खणस्स सुत्तं ।
सहलं तमलल्लुअम्मि कज्जे
इअ वय्याँअरणार्णं[6] वाअ-घोसं ॥ ५६

स-सलाह-सिलोअ-पाढँएहिं[7]
मुहलं कोच्चण बंदि-वुंदरेहिं ।
इणमम्मउरं चिँरं[8] पि दिट्ठं
ण हु दिट्ठिं परदो णिवट्टएइ ॥ ५७

---

१ M पंचमं. २ M मयूरो. ३ T सुणु. ४ T सुणु. ५ M भावा. ६ M वय्आअर-णाण, T वआअ ७ MT पाठएहिं. ८ MT इरं.

गंधव्वा ण किमेत्थ संति ण हु किं विज्जंति विज्जाहरा
किं वा चारु ण चारणाण अ कुँलं[1] जिण्णंति णो किंणरा।
किं णेअं सुमणाण धाम किमहो णाहो महिंदो ण से
सग्गो च्चेअ वसूण ठाणमिणमो रम्मं सुधम्मुज्जलं ॥ ५८

कीला[3]-सेलग्ग-लग्ग-त्थणिअ-घण-घणुस्सिट्ठ-विट्ठि-प्पणाली-
झंकारुक्कंठ-मोर-प्फुड-णडण-हलब्बोल-दिप्पंत-कामा ।
वामा वामा वि पीण-त्थण-कणअ-घडे संघडेऊण गाढं
कंठे गण्हंति कुंठेअरमिहँ[4] पिहु-राओल्लिरा वल्लहा णं ॥ ५९

इअ बहु-वित्थआइ विसआण बहुत्तणदो
सअमह गो-सआइमुवसंहरिऊण सुहं ।
वसहिमुवासरेइ वसुदेव-सुओ स जआ
तइ खु दिवाअरो वि चरमाअलँ[5]-मोलि-मुवं ॥ ६०

इअ कंसवहे बीओ सग्गो ।

[तीओ सग्गो]

पच्चूसे पर-मण-सल्ल-मल्ल-जुज्झ-
प्पत्थाव-प्पढम-पवुत्त-सुत्तहारो ।
पाढत्तो पडह-रवो पबोह-वेलं
वोलंतिं भणइ व बंदि-वुंदराणं ॥ १

---

१ MT उलं. २ M चेअ. ३ M किला. ४ M कुंठेम्मरमिव, T कंठेम्मरमिहं.
५ T वरमाम्मल.

बुज्झंती[1] बुह-पडिहा व कव्व-बंधे
बज्झंती बहल-रसेहि अक्खरेहिं ।
पासुत्तं पदुम-विलोअणं पबोहं
पावेउं कमइ कमेण बंदि-पाली ॥ २

कल्लाणं कमल-सिरी-कडक्ख-विक्खा-
विक्खेव-प्पअडुल-चंचलीअ-मालं ।
कल्लाणं कुणउ[2] पुरस्सरस्स तुज्झं
कल्लं णं[3] सुहअँ[4] सुह-प्पबोह-हेदु ॥ ३

होस्संति तुह मुह-लच्छिमच्छि-सोहा-
विच्छाई-कअ-णिअ-चिण्ह-कण्हिमाणं ।
पेच्छंतो[5] पढममिमो तुह प्पबोहा
णिक्खंतो णिहुअ-गई णिसाउँ[6] णाहो ॥ ४

जाओ दे जउ-सुअ णेत्त-तारआओ
णिस्सेसं जणमणुगण्हिहिंति बोहे ।
ताहिंतो लहु इदराउ तारआओ
वीलाए धुवमुव होंति णिप्पहाओ ॥ ५

जोण्हाअं तुहिणअरस्स रुक्ख-छाआ-
पच्छण्णा कह वि ठिआ खु अंधआरा ।
उल्लासे तुह मुहअंद-चंदिमाएँ[7]
संकंता णिअ-खअमेण्हिमोसरंते ॥ ६

---

१ T बुज्झंति. २ M कुणइ. ३ M कल्लाणं. ४ M सुहअं. ५ M पेच्छंते. ६ T णिसाइ. ७ M चंदमाए.

तूरंतो विरह-विसूरणा-विसोहं
राहाए सुहअ तुवं व भाणुमंतो ।
मीलंतं मुह-कमलं सरोइणीए
संपत्तो परिफुसिउं[2] करंचलेहिं ॥ ७

बीभंता विमअ-भडा जहा तुइत्तो
सूरादो मुइरमुदेउमुम्मुहादो ।
अण्णाअ-प्फिडिअँ[3]-पसण्णआ-दुअल्ला
णिल्लीणा कुहइ मुउंद चंद-मोहा ॥८

झीणाअं विहडण-कालणे णिसाअं
चक्काआ णिअ-वणिआहि संघडंति ।
संताअं विअ णिअ-पाव-संतदीअं
संता दे स-अलुण-विक्खण-च्छडाहिं ॥ ९

भिंगालिं[4] पुलइअ पंकआण गब्भे
संभंतं दर-विवुदाण संभरामो ।
उब्बोह-क्कम-विअसंत-दीहरच्छी-
दच्छंत-प्पसरमए कणीणिअं दे ॥ १०

संभिण्ण-प्पहमिणमीसि चंदिमाए
बंधूआरुणमरुणस्स रस्सि-जालं ।
मोत्तालीं[5] सु-विसअ-दंत-कंति-सिट्ठं
दिट्ठिं[6] णो हरइ तुव व्विवाहरोट्ठं ॥ ११

---

१ M संपत्ते. २ M परिपुसिउं. ३ M अण्णाहिंच्छिअडिम. ४ T भिंगाली.
५ T मोत्तालिं, ६ M दिट्ठी.

आलिद्धो दिअहवइस्स पाडलेहिं
मोहेहिं मरगअ-कुट्टिमो विहाइ ।
गोवीणं. घण-कुअ-कुंभ-कुंकुमेहिं
संकंतो तुहमिव कण्ह वच्छ-भाओ ॥ १२

उम्मिल्लावइ कमलाअरो ण जाहे
सच्छंदं मुउलमआइ लोअणाइं ।
उण्णिद्दो णिअ-णअणुप्पलाइ ताहे
फुल्लाइं कुणसु तुवं पि वासुदेव ॥ १३

आविज्झा रवि[1]-किरणेहि सुज्ज-कंदा
उम्हाणं[2] वमिउममी उवक्कमंति ।
णो खुद्दा[3] अवि हि सहंति अण्ण-तेओ-
विच्छड्डं किमुअ तुमारिसा महंता ॥ १४

तिक्खंसु-प्फुड-हरि-णक्ख-विक्खदादो*[4]
विक्खोह-प्पवडिअ-रिक्ख-मोत्तिआदो ।
अंधार-त्थिर-करि-मत्थआदु संझा-
राओ ऽअं विअलइ सोणिअ-प्पवाहो ॥ १५

णिद्दाणं कुमुइणिमुज्झिऊण सज्जो
बुज्झंतिं कमलिणिमल्लिएइ भिंगो ।
पच्चूहो ण हि बहु-वल्लहस्स कोच्चिं
तुज्झ व्व प्पडिणव-कीलणूसवेसुं[5] ॥ १६

---

१ M रइ. २ T उम्माणं. ३ M णो वखुद्दा. ४ M विक्खणादो, T विक्खदोदो.
५ M किल्लणूसवेसु.

आअंबो कुणइ दिणेस-रासि-रासी
णिंतीणं पिअ-वसहीउ बंधईणं ।
थोरेसुं थण-अलसेसु वल्लहोर-
प्पम्मट्ठं घुसिण-रसं पुणो व लित्तं ॥ १७

किंचेमो जलहि-जलम्मि संमिलंतो
संदाइ प्फुड-वलआमुहग्गि-संकं ।
अम्मेलावइ[1] पुण हत्थि-मत्थएसुं
सिंदूर-प्पअर-पिसंगिमाणमेसो ॥ १८

सच्छंदं छुरउ णिहेल-सामले दे
वच्छम्मि क्खुडिअ-पवाल-खंड-सोहो ।
सोहग्गं लहिउमिमो ग्वु सुज्ज-मोही
तल्लच्छी-घण-थण-कुंकुमंकणस्स ॥ १९

पुव्वासा-जुवइ-सव-प्पवाल-भूसा-
ताडंकं गअण-सरो-सहस्स-पत्तं ।
पाईणाअल-मणि-सोह-मोलि-कुंभं
पेच्छेणं दिणअर-बिंबमुज्जिहाणं ॥ २०

एव्वं सिं थुइ-वअणुग्गमाहि पुव्वं
पल्लंकं मुअइ जणद्दणो विणिद्दो ।
उम्मेसं[2] लहइ पुरो सरोअ-वाडो
पच्छा णं पसरइ राअहंस-णाओ ॥ २१

---

१ M अंमोलावइ. २ T उम्मेसुं.

पच्चूसे[1] च्चिअ णिअ-सच्छ-गत्त-लच्छी-
विच्छड्ड-च्छिविअ-विअप्पहावआसो ।
पच्चक्खो भुवइ रईव पाअ-सेवा-[2]
तप्पज्ज-प्पवण-मणाण सो जणाणं ॥ २२

संझं तो विअअ-जवा-पसूण-तंबं
तंबुल्लारुण-वणिआहरोट्ठ-सोहं ।
राहाए[3] मुह-विहु-संभरावअं सो
वंदंतो चलइ पुरी-दुवार-हुत्तो ॥ २३

पालेअ-च्छइ-तणुणो बलस्स पच्छा
वच्चंतो पअडुल-हार-चारु-वच्छो ।
कण्हो सो बहु विलसेइ विज्जुलिल्लो
चंदस्स व्विव णव-णील-वारिवाहो ॥ २४

सोएणं[4] बहु-दिअहे समाउराए
वामच्छी फुरइ तआ स-माउराए ।
कंसादीण अ कुहणा-समल्लआणं
सत्तूणं पइदि-हदास-मल्लआणं ॥ २५[5]

सोहग्ग-ट्ठिअ-णअरंगणा-कडक्ख-
च्छाआली-मसिण-मसार-मंडिआए ।
वीहीए विविह-विलास-वेस-लच्छी-
भासंतां[6] सणिअमअंति राम-कण्हाँ[7] ॥ २६

१ M पच्चूस. २ M पावसेवा. ३ M राहाहे, T राजाए. ४ M सेएणं. ५ Wanting in T. ६ T भासंतो. ७ T रामकण्हो.

अंवट्ठो णरवइ-सासणा दुवारे
दुव्वार-प्पसर-पआवमीसरं तं ।
रुंभेउं पअदइ कुंभिणा स-पाणि-
च्छत्तेणं विअ भअवंतमुण्ह-मोहं ॥ २७

आमेलं कुवलअ-पुव्वमुव्वराअं
कीलंतं विअ सअमब्भमग्गअ णाहं ।
कुज्झंतं कुलिस-कढोर-दंत-डंडं
कुंभिंदं कुडिल-मणो पणोल्लए सो ॥ २८

मत्तुं किं जम-घर-म त वारणस्स
पच्चक्खं णिवडह मत्त-वारणस्स ।
अण्णत्तो ऽवसरह कुदमा कुमाला
झत्ति त्ति प्पल्लवइ हत्थिवो स-गव्वं ॥ २९

अण्णत्तो जइ ण णिअत्तएसि णाअं
सज्जीवो वसिहिइ ता खणं पि णाअं ।
इत्थं तो भणिअ हरी सहग्गअम्मो
पाढत्तो परिभुविउं णमुग्गअम्मो ॥ ३०

उव्वंत-क्खुडिअ-कडंबु-णिज्झरोल्लं
मज्झम्मि प्पवडिअ-सिखरो-भुअंगं ।
दोग्घट्टं णिअ-भुअं-कड्ढिअं मुउंदो
भामेंतो विहरइ मंदरं व पुव्वं ॥ ३१

---

१ MT कठोर. २ M पघडअ-सिंघरा. ३ T भुज.

कुज्झंतं गअमह कुंडली·कआए
सुंडाए कअ-पग्गिंढ-मूढ-हेलं ।
भंसंतो भमर-करंबिअम्मि गंडे
चंडाहिं पहरइ सो चवेडिआहिं ॥ ३२

कीलाए लगइ हरी महिम्मि जाला
नाला सो डसण-जुएण वारणिंदो ।
विज्झंतो महिअलमेत्थ बुड्डमाणं
कड्ढेउं तमिणमहो ण सक्कुणेइ ॥ ३३

कुंभं तो कुविअ-मणो खणद्ध-आलं
वोलंतो[1] चलण-अलेण वामएणं ।
उक्खाइ क्खुडिअ-पढिल्ल-मूल-बंधं
कण्हो से कर-जुअलेण दंत-जुग्गं ॥ ३४

जाहे सो णिवडइ वज्ज-रुग्ग-पक्ख-
प्पक्खित्तो कसण-गिरीव णाअ-राओ ।
ताहे खु प्पअलइ सेस-सीस-अक्क-
प्पब्भट्ठं विअ वलअं वसुंधराए ॥ ३५

अंबट्ठ-प्पहद-पहेण केच्चिरं[3] सो
हत्थिंदो सरइ सअं ति चिंतअंतो ।
अंबट्ठं गमइ धुवं तआणि दुट्ठं
हत्थिंद-प्पहद-पहेण वासुदेवो ॥ ३६

---

१ M बोलंतो. २ T णावराओ. ३ M कच्चिरं.

गेहं ता गहिरअरुम्ह-सोम्म-सीला
गाहंता गअण-अलं व पुप्फवंता ।
केसिं चि प्पहरिस-फुल्लदं कुणंते
केसिं चि प्पमॅउलदं[1] च राम-कण्हा ॥ ३७

घोलंतुज्जल-वण-माल-हारि-वच्छे
कीलंते करिवर-दंत-पाणिणो[2] दे ।
पेच्छंता[3] जह-सुहमच्छि-जम्म-कज्जं
सच्छंदं सवइ लहंति सव्व-लोआ ॥ ३८

वेरं जे हिअअ-ठिअं वहंति ताणं
वत्ताइं मइलदमाइ होंति ताहे ।
रुक्खाणं सइ णिअ-कोडर-प्पडिट्ठो
पुप्फाइं[4] दव-दहणो हि वाअएइं[5] ॥ ३९

आदिट्ठा णवरि अ दुण्णएण रण्णा
रण्णेहा विअ रहसेण सिंघ-पोदे ।
जेउं[6] दे जउ-कुमरे कअ-प्पडिण्णा
सण्णद्धा समहिसरंति मल्ल-जोहा ॥ ४०

मंचग्ग-ट्ठिअ-णिअ-भत्तु-दिट्ठि-विट्ठी-
सिंचंता विअ मअ-पल्लवुल्लसंता ।
चाणूरो सअमहँ[7] मुट्ठिओ अ बेण्णि
प्पोण्मिद्दा णिहिलमवंति मल्ल-सेणं[8] ॥ ४१

---

१ MT प्पमइल्दं. २ M पाणिणे. ३ M पच्छंता. ४ M पुप्फाणं. ५ M एवाअएइ, T हि पाअएइ. ६ T जेडुं. ७ M सअमअ. ८ T सेण्णं.

चाणूरो कइढवं-सूअणं सरंतो
साडोवं भणइ वले वएस-सूणू ।
इच्छंतो णिवसइ तुज्झ जुज्झ-कीला-
पंडिच्चं पुलइउमेस भोअ-राओ[2] ॥ ४२

भूवालो च्चिअ कुसलो[3] कुअंड-सत्थे
गोवालो च्चिअ णिउणो णिउज्झ-तंते ।
जो जस्सिं कुणइ परिस्समं पआमं
सो तस्सिं च्चिअ विणिउंजिओ विहाइ ॥ ४३

मल्लेहिं सह मह-विक्कमेहि पाडि-
प्फद्धीअं कह किर होज्ज दुक्खरा दे ।
बालेण च्चिअ तुमए पलंब-केसि-
प्पाआ किं ण हु णिहआ दइच्च-वीरा ॥ ४४

ता जुज्झं कुणह दुवे वि णाम तुम्हे
धम्मेण च्चिअ खु दुवेहि मल्लएहिं ।
अम्हाणं[4] मुणउ सअं कुऊहलिल्लो
भोएसो भुअ-विहवम्मि तारतम्मं ॥ ४५

एवं से सुणिअ वआइ सुप्पसण्णो
सण्णद्धो समहिघडेइ णेण कण्हो ।
कुप्पंतो कुलिस-विघट्ट-णिट्ठुराहिं
मुट्ठीहिं मुसलहरो वि मुट्ठिएण ॥ ४६

---

१ M कइढव. २ T भोअरावो. ३ M कुसले. ४ T अम्माणं.

थिव्वोल[1]-प्परुस-परप्फर-प्पलावं
घेप्पंत-प्फिडिअ-पडंत-बाहु-जंतं ।
अप्फाल-प्फुड-कडु-सद्द-विड्डिरिल्लं
खुब्भंत-त्तिहुवणमासि ताण जुज्झं ॥ ४७

कड्ढंता कर-जुअलेण जाणु-जंघा
संघट्ट-क्खुडिअ-विलित्त-रत्त-गत्ता ।
उद्दाम-ब्भमण-धुणंत-भूमि-अक्का
विकंतिं विविहमिमा समार[*]हंति[2] ॥ ४८

कट्ठं हो कढि[*]ण-मणो[3] पणाल्लए को
सद्दूले सस-सिसुएहि संपहंतुं[4] ।
गच्छामो विसममिणं[5] ण पंच्छणिज्जं
जुज्झं ति प्पलवइ दाव साहु-लोओ ॥ ४९

चाणूरं चलण-जुअम्मि गण्हमाणो
कण्हो णं खिवइ ताडित्ति धत्ति-वट्ठे ।
जंट्ठो से तह किर मुट्ठिअं च दुट्ठं
दिट्ठंतं समुवगआ दुवे वि मल्ला ॥ ५०

जुज्झंता कदि वि हदा गदग्गएणं
विब्भंता[6] कदि वि पलाइदा खु मल्ला ।
मत्तंडे फुडअरमुग्गए गहा वि
प्पम्मट्ठा[7] कहि उण जोइरिंगिणोहा ॥ ५१

---

१ M घिप्पोल., T चिप्पोल. २ M समाहरंति, T समारणंति. ३ M कठिन, T कठिण. ४ संपहत्तुं. ५ M विस[म]मिमं. ६ M वीभंता. ७ T प्पमुट्ठा.

वज्झंतु प्पइदि-कइ बइ बलादो
वज्झंतु प्पसहमिमा वि गोव-संघा ।
मुच्चंता मुणह विणासिहिंति[1] जिम्हा
तुम्मे त्ति प्पलवइ दाव भोअ-राओ[2] ॥ ५२

बिब्भाणं विसमाहिअं सहाव-वंकं[3]
कंसं तं कसण-भुअंगमं व घोरं ।
पक्खिदो विअ विणअत्ति-भंजणो सो
मंचग्ग-ट्ठिअमहिसंपडेइ कण्हो ॥ ५३

उट्ठंतो कर-जुअ-लग्ग-खग्ग-चम्मो
जाहे णं पहरिउमारहेइ कंसो ।
मंचादो महु-महणो हढेण[4] ताहे
भू-वट्ठे पडिअममुं खणा कुणाइ ॥ ५४

वच्छम्मि प्पवडिअ खिप्पमत्थिवत्थिं
वित्थिण्ण-त्थण-अड-चंदणोल्लिए से ।
कण्हो सो कुणइ तहा गहीद-खग्गो
भूवो सो भुवइ[5] जहा कहावसेसो ॥ ५५

कड्ढंतो गल-पह-णित-रत्त-सित्तं
गत्तं से गलुल-धओ गआणुकंपं ।
सेरं सो लहइ तहिं खु वेर-संतिं
धीराणं पि हि हिअअं धुणाइ[6] कोहो ॥ ५६

---

१ T विणस्सिर्विति. २ T भोअरात्रो. ३ M वकं. ४ MT हठेण. ५ T भुवउ
६ M धुणाहि, T सुणाइ.

सिणिद्ध-घण-कुंतल-प्फुरिअ-मोर-पिंछंचिए
सिरीअ पइणो सिरे सुर-करंचलुम्मुंचिअं[1] ।
भमंत-भमरावली-कलअलेहि वाआलिआ
सुर-दु-कुसुम-च्छडा पडइ दाव देवालआ ॥ ५७

णच्चंति प्फुडमच्छरा णह-पहे सेच्छं[2] मिहो मच्छरा
दिव्वा दुंदुहिणो धणंति गहिरं सग्गाणिलुग्गूरिओ[3] ।
पुण्णा भिण्ण-कडावडोज्झर-दिसा-दोग्घट्ट-थट्टुब्भड-
प्पप्फुज्जंत-पमोअ-बंहिअ-महा-घोसेहि वीसंभरा ॥ ५८

अट्ठ दाव णिवरस्स कणिट्ठा
णिट्ठुरट्टहसिआदि-गरिट्ठा ।
दुट्ठ-रुट्ठ-मणसो वि पविट्ठा
विट्ठरस्सव-हआ सुर-गोट्ठिं ॥ ५९

इअ सब्भुअ[4]-संभार-प्फार-प्पआवमआअ[5]व-
क्खविअ-विमअंधारो वीरो विसुद्ध-गुणुत्तरो ।
बुह-अण-मणंभोअव्वाअं णिआम-विअस्सरं[6]
कुणइ कुसलालोओ लोए मुउंद-दिवाअरो ॥ ६०

इअ[7] कंसवहे तीओ सग्गो ।

---

१ T °मुंचिअं. २ T सेच्छा. ३ T °लुल्लूरिआ. ४ T सुभुअ. ५ M मआअम T विकस्सरं. ७ T इअ राम-पाणिवाअकए.

[चउत्थो सग्गो]

तदो अ भोएस-भुअ-प्पआव-
गिम्होम्ह-भारेण पडज्झ*माणं[1] ।
कण्हंबुवाहो खु कडक्ख-लच्छी-
धाराहि सिंचावइ जीवलोअं ॥ १

धंसं गए[2] कंस-णिवे जणाणं
मणाइ गे*हेइं[3] पसाअ-लच्छी ।
परिच्चुए पाउस-वारिवाहे
सरोअ-वुंदाइ व हंस-राई ॥ २

पवित्त-चारित्त-विलोव-संका-
विवज्जिआओ कुल-वालिआओ[4] ।
तआ पआसं पसरंति सेरं
ससि-प्पहाओ व तमुज्झिआओ ॥ ३

जुवाण रामाहिमणंतराअं
विहत्तु-कामाणमणंत-राअं ।
करेइ तावं सरसा वि साअं
विरामइल्लि त्ति णिसा विसाअं ॥ ४

विढत्त-रत्त-प्पणआ विवंका
विसट्ट-कंदोट्ट-पहा विडेसुं ।
विअड्ढ-णारीण विलास-दिट्ठी
पडेइ णो पत्थिव-खग्ग-लट्ठी ॥ ५

---

१ MT पढज्जमार्ण. २ M गहे. ३ MT वाहेइ. ४ M पालिआओ. ५ M णे.

काऊण भोअंधअ-चक्कवट्टिं
पआण रक्खित्तरमुग्गसेणं ।
मोएइ माआ-पिदरे तदो सो
काराघरादो[1] कमला-सहाओ[2] ॥ ६

सहग्गओ णे समुव्वासरंतो
सिणेह-वाहोच्छइअच्छि-पम्हे ।
कुणीअ दीहं कुमरो पणामं
स-णाम संगाण्हिअ[3] विण्हि-वीरो ॥ ७

दिग्घाउणो[4] होह चिरस्स वच्छा
तुम्हे त्ति बाह-क्खलिअक्खराहिं[5] ।
आसीहि वड्ढावइ[6] देवईए
समं खु सो आणअदुंदुही णे[7] ॥ ८

एक्कस्स[8] सच्छ-प्फालिअ[9]-प्पआसं
अण्णस्स भिण्णंजण-मंजुलाहं ।
मलिज्जमाणुज्जलं[10]-वण्ण-मालं
वच्छं समालिंगइ ताण तादो ॥ ९

तदो समागच्छिअ गंदिणेओ
कअ-प्पणामो कम-सोहिदाइं[11] ।
कहाणुबद्धाइ कुमारआणं
वआइ संजंपई[12] मंजुलाइ ॥ १०

---

१ M कराघरादो. २ T यमला. ३ T संगच्छिअ. ४ M दिग्घायुणो. ५ M अक्खरोहिं, T अक्खराही. ६ M वज्झावइ. ७ M णो. ८ MT एकस्स. ९ M सच्चप्पडिअ, T सच्छहलिअ. १० MT मणिज्ज°. ११ M कमसोहिदालं, T कमणोइदाइं. १२ M संजप्पइ.

अअं खु गो जस्स णिहेल-णीलं
वच्छत्थलुग्घोलिर-वण्णमालं ।
चउब्भुअं विग्गहमग्गभाए
जाअस्स णं पेच्छह पेच्छणिज्जं[1] ॥ ११

घेत्तूण[2] जं सम्हर[3]-रत्ति-मज्झे
तुज्झं तरंतस्स तरंगइल्ली ।
कूलंत-वोलंत[4]-जला वि ताहे
जंघाण लंघीअ कलिंद-अण्णा ॥ १२

तप्पम्मि जं ठाविअ गोविआए
पच्चाणिआ सोरि तुए सुआ से ।
कज्जाणुरोहा गरुअत्तणं णो
मुणंति मुद्धस्स हि विक्कएसुं ॥ १३

इमो खु सो च्चेअ थण-प्पदाए
थणेण[5] पीदेण वि पूदणाए ।
तण्हा-पडीघाअमलंभमाणो
पाणे वि जो दुल्ललिओ पिबीअ ॥ १४

एसो खु सो णंद-घरेसएण
जिणा तिणावत्त[6]-दइच्च-वीरो ।
कओ ऽब्भुवंतो वि स चक्कवाओ
कअंत-भूमी-सर-चक्कवाओ ॥ १५

---

१ M पेच्छसपेच्छणिज्जं. २ M घोत्तूण, T घेरूण. ३ T सम्मर. ४ T खोलंत.
५ T थणोण. ६ M तणावत्त.

सत्तूण सव्वं मुसिणाउं[1] गव्वं
कुदो खु बंधूण वि वल्लवाणं ।
इअ त्थुओ[2] जो किर गव्व-चोरो
पहास-सीलेहि सुरेहि सो ऽअं[3] ॥ १६

जो च्चेअ[4] माआ-पणिबज्झमाणं
जणं विमुंचावइ बंधणादो ।
सो च्चेअ माआउ महाणुभावो
उलूहले बज्झइ सो खु एसो ॥ १७

भग्गो णमेक्को च्चिअ भग्गवेण
पुरज्जुणो[5] सोरि सहस्स-बाहू ।
णेणं सहस्साहिअ-दीह-साहा-
बाहूण भग्गं जुअमज्जुणाणं ॥ १८

पआरअंतं णिअ-गो-सआइं
पराम्मुवेउं किर संपवुत्तो ।
बआसुरो णं खु सअं पणट्ठो
तमिस्स-संघो व सहस्स-मोहं ॥ १९

सउस्स रूवेण सअं सअंतो
पवड्ढिएणं जढर[6]-ट्ठिएणं ।
अहासुरो णेण हदो हदासो
स गुम्म-रोएण व कम्म-दोसो ॥ २०

---

१ T मुसिणाइ. २ T इअत्थुवो. ३ T सो णं. ४ T चिअ. ५ M पुरज्जुणे, T पुरज्जणो. ६ जठर, T जठरा.

माआ[1]-बलेणमिममब्भअमुब्भमेउं
जो पक्कमेइ स सअं चिअ वंचिओ से ।
माअंबुहिम्मि गहिरे पडिओ विरिंचो
पत्तो णमेव सरणं[2] कवलद्धपाणिं ॥ २१

वुंदावणम्मि जउणा-पुलिणम्मि रम्मे
गोवद्धणद्दि-सिहरम्मि अ हम्मिआहे[3] ।
गोवाल-बाल-कुल-लालिअ-कीलिआइं
णेणं बहूइ दिअहाइ खु वोलिआइं ॥ २२

णेणं धेणुअ-गद्दह-प्पहुदिणो वग्गस्स दुग्गव्विरं
चेअं चेअ बलेण ताल-विविण-व्वाएण धूअं बला ।
पीओ णिब्भर-तप्फलंबु-छलदो लोआण सोआअमो
सत्तु-प्पाण-मिसा खुं साहु पुहवी-भारो समुद्धारिओ ॥२३

परिरक्खिवउमंग धेणुअं[5] तं[6]
पअरंतो विहणासि धेणुअं किं ।
कह वीससिमो तुमं ति रामं
पहसंतो किर वाहरेइ कण्हो ॥ २४

कालिआहि-विस-धूम-लआहिं
कालिआहि गअणं व करालं ।
जाउणंबु विरएइ विसुद्धं
जाउ णंद-त्तणओ सरओ व ॥ २५

---

१ M माआ. २ M सरणिं. ३ M हम्मिआए. ४ M इ. ५ M मग्गधेणुअं ६ T तुं.

पाढंतो[1] फणिराअ-पव्वअ-फणा-सिंगेसु पाए समं
सिग्घं णिक्खिविऊण णच्चिउमिमो पच्चूस-सुज्जोव्वमो ।
आअंबाअव-सोह-पीअ-वसणो साणंद-वुंदारअ-
स्सेणी-णेत्त-सरोअ-रोअण-गुणुद्दामो खु दामोअरो ॥ २६

झणज्झणिअ-णेउरं चलण-पल्लवाणोल्लणा-
णमंत-फणि-मत्थअं कम-पढिल्ल-कंची-लअं ।
चलंत-सिहि-पिंछिआ-वलअ-रम्म-धम्मिल्लअं[2]-
ब्भमंत-भमर-च्छडं णडइ बाल-गोवालओ ॥ २७

गल्लुलाहि से गलिअ-गव्व-सालिणो
अभअं पुणो दिसइ एस भाइणो ।
रूसिआ विसं जइ वि साहुणो जणो[3]
अमअं खु दे तह वि णाम तोसिआ ॥ २८

णाअ-जोव्वअ-समप्पिएहि तो
णाअ-हार-णिअरेहि[4] भूसिओ ।
एस भाइ हरि-णील-सामलो
तारएहि व सुहो णहोवहो ॥ २९

सुप्पंतेसुं गोव-गो-वुंदरेसुं
दिप्पंतो तो णिप्पडंतो दवग्गी ।
सज्जो णेणं पिज्जए विज्जुलाहो
सव्वावाओ होइ लोउत्तराणं ॥ ३०

---

१ M पडंतो, T पाढतो. २ MT धम्मल्लअ. ३ MT जणा. ४ T णिहरेहि.

गोवाअंतो गोउलं कामवालो
गोवाअंतं कंस-भिच्चं दइच्चं ।
आकंखंतं विप्पलंभं पलंबं
रुट्ठो दुट्ठं मुट्ठिणा पिट्ठवंतो ॥ ३१

जउणा-सलिले कआ वि जाओ
जुवईओ किल कीलणं कुणंति ।
हिअआइ व णिम्मलाइ ताणं
वसणाइं मुसिणाइ वासुदेवो[1] ॥ ३२

रण्णे जण्णे कुहइ महिए भोअणं जाइदेहिं
भूदेवेहिं किर पडिणिराचक्खिआं दिक्खिएहिं ।
भत्ताहिंतो सरस-महुरं साअरं चावि ताणं
भज्जाहिंतो लहइ तमिमो मुत्तिमोसिं च देइ ॥ ३३

एसो खु णंद-पहुदिस्स पुरंदरादो[2]
भत्तिं णिवत्तिअ करेइ गिरिंद-हुत्तं ।
आअड्ढिऊण दिअहा कुमुआअरादो
भिंगस्स दिट्ठिमिव पंकअ-वाड-हुत्तं ॥ ३४

सज्जो गज्जंत-विज्जुज्जल-जलअ-घडा-गब्भ-पब्भार-थोर-
प्पब्भट्ठं पट्ठविट्ठंभिअं[3]-भुवण-अलं विट्ठिमब्भावडंतिं ।
गोवालो एस गोवड्ढणमअलवरं तक्खणं उक्खणंतो
छत्तं काऊण घेत्तूण अ कर-अमले डिंभओ रुंभए णं ॥३५

---

1 T वासुदेओ. 2 M पुरंदराओ. 3 T फट्ठविट्ठंभिअ.

णिव्वाणं[1]-गव्व-सिहि-पव्वअं[2]-वेरि-जुट्ठं
तुट्ठं सअं ण्हुअ-पओहर-णिस्सिदेहिं ।
एअं पओहि सुरही अहिसिंचमाणी
गोविंद-णाम सु-सिलिट्ठअरं करेइ ॥ ३६

अह खु णं चिअ कंचण-कुंभिआ-
विअलिएहि किलब्भमु-वल्लहो ।
सुरणई-सलिलेहिं[3] णिसिंचए
पमुदिरो मुदिरो विअ सारओ ॥ ३७

जाउ दाव जउणा[4]-जल-मग्गं
वारुणेण हरिअं पुरिसेणं ।
अच्चुओ बअ पएद-णिएदा
पच्चुवाहरइ णंदममंदं ॥ ३८

जोण्हा-विच्छड्ड-पच्चुप्फुसिअ-ससिमणी-संद-णीसंद-सीए
वुंदारण्णे कलिंद-प्पिअ-दुहिउ-महा-तूँहे[5]-रोहत्थलीसुं ।
वेला-सेलाणिलालोलिअ-सरस-रसालग्ग-लग्गालिवग्गे
काले संते वसंते कुणइ घणमिमो केसवो रास-कीलं[6] ॥ ३९

उवट्ठिअ-तरट्टिआवलि[7]-सिलिट्ठ-गोट्ठी-गओ
पवंचिअ-विवंचिआ-मुरलि-सिंग-सिंगारिअं ।
विडंबिअ-विडक्कमं विमल-मंजु-संजंपिअं
तरंगिअ-सुरंगणं कुणइ बालओ खेलणं ॥ ४०

---

१ M णिव्वार. २ M पव्वर. ३ M सलिले. ४ T ताव जवुणा. ५ MT महारूह
६ M रासलीलं. ७ M उवट्ठिदविरट्ठिआ.

रास-कीलासु वीला-विअल-वअ-वहू-णेत्त-कंदोट्ट-माला-
पालंबालंकिदंगो मउ-हसिअ-सुहा-सित्त-वत्तेंदु-बिंबो ।
संगाअंतो णडंतो सरसअरमिमो संचरंतो सअंतो
सव्वासुं दिक्खु दक्खिज्जइ सअल-अणाणंदणो णंदणो दे ॥४१

सोहग्गं-गव्विर-मणाण णिअंबिणीणं
पत्तो तहा बहु-तणू वि परोक्ख-भावं ।
एसो तम-प्पइदिआण ण दक्खणिज्जो
सुज्जो व वित्थअ-पहो वि विहावरीणं ॥ ४२

विरदे मदे विरहिणीण ताण तो
पअडेइ विग्गहमिमो कुमारओ ।
पसमं गअम्मि सिसिरम्मि तक्खणं
कुसुमं पआसइ हि चूद-पादवो ॥ ४३

संखोही संखऊडो वि स वुसह-तणू किं चरिट्ठो गरिट्ठो
विट्ठो रुट्ठूण केसी विअ तुरअ-वऊ धंसिओ केसवेणं[2] ।
वामारंभी स वोमो वि खु परिखुडिओ सोरि वेरि-द्दुमाणं
दावग्गी णंदणो दे किमिह हि बहुणा संपअं जंपिएणं ॥४४

आणाइओ धणुह-जण्ण-छलेण एसो
कंसेण तेण धुवमत्त-णिबंहणत्थं ।
साहग्ग-संघरिस-संघडिआ हि वण्ही
सुण्णी-करेइ तरस च्चिअ किं ण रुक्खं[3] ॥ ४५

---

१ T सोफ [भ ?] ग्ग. २ M केसवो णं. ३ T रुष्वा [क्खा ?].

अक्कूराणण-सिप्पि-गब्भ-गलिअं तं सुत्ति-मुत्तावलिं
गण्हेऊण कुणंति हंत पिदरा कण्णाण दे मंडणं ।
अच्चारूढ-हिरी-दरोणअ-सिरो-णंचंत-पिंछंचलं
गाढं किं च परिस्सजंति बहुसो माअग्गअं सग्गअं ॥ ४६

पालेआअल-मोलि-घोलिर-महा-कल्लोल-हल्लोहल-
प्फारुड्डामर-चारु-चारण-धुणी-सच्छाहि वच्छा चिरं[1] ।
तुम्हे[2] जीवह पुण्णिमामअ-मऊहुण्णिद्द-जोण्हा-झरी-
पंडिच्च-च्छिउर-च्छईहि महिआ कित्तीहि धत्तीअले ॥ ४७

इअ मुदिअ-मणाणं ताणमासीहि ताहे
सर-समअ-सिरीहिं चंद-सूरा व सूरा ।
समहिअमहिरामं राम-कण्हा पसण्णा
सअल-जण-मणोज्जं लंभिआ कं पि लच्छि ॥ ४८

इअ राम-पाणिवाअ-कए[3] कंसवहे
चउत्थो सग्गो ।[4]

दुव्वाह[5]-पाअड-पओ-णिलए गहीरे
बालाणं[6] वाहिउमिणं खु मुणेह रूहं ।
णव्वं हि कव्वमिह कंसवहाभिहाणं
सव्वे वि भव्व-मंदिणो[7] परिसीलएह[8] ॥ ४८*१

---

१ M हिरं, T झरं. २ T तुम्मे. ३ T omits कए. ४ M ends here and has the phrase सम्मत्तमिणं कव्वं which is put later. ५ T alone gives this verse and the subsequent portion. ६ T बालण्ण. ७ T भावमभिणो. ८ T परिसील्सेह.

सिरि-गुरु-पाआणं णमो । सुहमत्थु ।
समत्तमिणं कव्वं ॥[1]

[3]कमलासहाय कमलासनादिभिः
शमलापनोदमभिलाषकैः सुरैः ।
समुपास्यमानचरणाम्बुज प्रभो
कमलालयेश परिपालयाशु माम् ॥ ४८*[2]

---

१ T omits this phrase which is given by M above.
२ T alone gives this verse. ३ T कमलासादिभिः.

कंसवधकाव्यस्याज्ञातप्रणेतृका

संस्कृतच्छाया

[प्रथमः सर्गः]

[१ **सिरीअ णाहो**]—श्रियो नाथः शिखिपिञ्छशेखरैः[1] स्निग्ध-गोपीनयनाञ्चलाञ्चितैः[2], स्वयं यशोदातनयत्वं गतो विभुर्व्यभूषयद्[3]गोप-वाटिकाम् ॥ १ ॥

[२ **कहं खु**]—कथां[4] खल्वस्य कंसवधं[5] सुखावहां[6] सुधामिव गृह्णीत वले सुधीजनाः, सदा गुरूणां चरणौ समाश्रितो भणामि यां भक्तिगुणेन नुन्नः ॥ २ ॥

[३ **अहेक्कदा**]—अथैकदा चङ्क्रमणशीलो व्रजाङ्गणे[7] दिनान्त-गोदोहनव्यापृताङ्गने, सहाग्रजः सोऽभिसरन्तमग्रतो गदाग्रजोऽद्राक्षीद्गा-न्दिनीसुतम्[8] ॥ ३ ॥

[४ **रआइ**]—रजांसि रेखारथशङ्खपङ्कजध्वजाङ्कितानि प्रविलोक्य[9] भूतले, तस्मिन्ननमन्तं[10] पुलकालिपक्ष्मलप्रमोदबाष्पार्द्रविफुल्लविग्रहम्[11] ॥४॥

[५ **खणे खणे**]—क्षणे क्षणे ध्याननिमीलितेक्षणं नम्यमान-मौलिप्रणिवेशिताञ्जलिम्, असंभ्रमं संस्मरन्तमग्रतो लसन्तमात्मानमनन्त-कौतुकम् ॥ ५ ॥

---

१ M शेखरं. २ M °ञ्चितम्. ३ [विभुविभूषयति गोप°] ४ T कथं. ५ T कंसवधः. ६ T सुधावहा. ७ T व्रजाङ्कणे. ८ [पश्यति (द्रक्ष्यति) गान्दिनी°]. ९ T प्रलोक्य. १० T नमन्तः. ११ T विग्रहः.

[६ **अदिट्ठ-पासट्ठिअ**]—अदृष्टपार्श्वस्थितवस्तुसार्थमश्रूयमाणोच्चलितोच्चनिस्वनम्, वरं परब्रह्मसुखानुभाविनं न बाह्यं बाधते किमपि देहिनम् ॥ ६ ॥

[७ **खणं रुवंतं**]—क्षणं रुवन्तं[1] विहसन्तमन्तरा क्षणं च स्तम्भमिव निरुच्छ्वसंस्थितम्, क्षणं चरन्तं क्षणमुच्चजल्पितं क्षणमपि च तूष्णीकमुखं मदादिव ॥ ७ ॥

[८ **पमोअ-तूरंत**]—प्रमोदत्वर्यमाणपदक्रमोच्चलस्खलन्मुक्तागुणफेनमण्डलः, सरित्प्रवाहमिव सम्मुखागतं स प्रत्युपातिष्ठद्[2] एनमच्युताम्बुधिः ॥ ८ ॥

[९ **करंबुएणं**]—कराम्बुजेन परिगृह्यैनं गृहं निजं प्रापयद्[3] देवकीसुतः, अनामयम् अपृच्छन्मृष्टभोजनं[4] प्रायच्छत्[5] किमपि चाजल्पत्[6] पुनः ॥ ९ ॥

[१० **तुहावलोएण**]—तवावलोकेन बभूव मे मनो विकसितमक्रूर स्निग्धबन्धोः, अथो किमाश्चर्यमिदं समुद्गते विधौ सद्यो विकसति कैरवम् ॥ १० ॥

[११ **मुणामि तेएण**]—जानामि तेजसा खलु भोजराजस्य दिनप्रदीपा इव तीक्ष्णरश्मेः, प्रदीप्यमानेन पराहतप्रभाः कथमपि यूयं बलिनो[7] विजीवथ ॥ ११ ॥

---

१ T रुदन्तं. २ [प्रत्युपतिष्ठते]. ३ [प्रापयति]. ४ [पृच्छति मृष्ट°]
५ [प्रयच्छति]. ६ [च जल्पति]. ७ T बलिनोपि.

[१२ अवच्च-जुग्गे]—अपत्ययुग्मे चिरमक्षतेऽपि तौ सहेते यन्त्रः पितरौ नियन्त्रणाम्[1], शरीरिणस्तस्माद्दुरपत्यलाभतो[2] वदन्ति सत्यं निरपत्यता वरम् ॥ १२ ॥

[१३ कहं परिच्चेमु]—कथं परित्यजानि[3] शरीरपोषकाविमावपि मातापितरौ वा[4] वत्सलौ, जगति ये कोकिलरीतिगामिनो न तान् जुगुप्सन्ते कथं महाजनाः ॥ १३ ॥

[१४ कअं खु जं]—कृतं खलु यद्वा कथितेन भूरिणा किणो[5] भणेदागमकारणं भवान्, इदं वदन् विररामै[6] माधवो भणन्ति भव्या हि जना मिताक्षरम् ॥ १४ ॥

[१५ विसुद्ध-सीलेण]—विशुद्धशीलेन विनम्रमौलिना स कंस-दूतेन अकथ्यत[7] हरिः, तवैव साधिष्ठयथेष्टदर्शनं विशिष्टमस्मदागमन-प्रयोजनम् ॥ १५ ॥

[१६ णिरत्थ-संगा]—निरस्तसङ्गा निगमान्तपान्था यमादि-योगाभ्यसनोद्भटश्रमाः, चिरं विचिन्वन्ति तपोधना अपि यं स दिष्ट्या ममासि दृष्टिगोचरः ॥ १६ ॥

[१७ जिअं जिअं]—जितं जितं मे नयनाभ्यां याभ्यां [तव] सुजातसौन्दर्यगुणैकमन्दिरम्, प्रसन्नपूर्णामृतमयूखसदृशं[8] मुखं प्रहासो-ज्ज्वलमद्य पीयते ॥ १७ ॥

---

१ T नियन्त्रणा (णं ?). २ [°लम्भतो]. ३ [परित्यजावः]. ४ [इव].
५ T तिणो, M (किंनु ?). ६ [विरमति]. ७ [कथ्यते]. ८ [सच्छायं].

[१८ **णिसिज्झए**]—निषिध्यते माधव मातुलेन ते विजृम्भमाणेनेव पापराशिना, अमुष्य[1] प्रत्यक्षनिरीक्षणोत्सवो मुखस्य यद्वा विधिवामता खलु सा ॥ १८ ॥

[१९ **ममंमि तुहं**]—मयि तुष्टं विधिना नु सांप्रतं महान्ममैव नु पुण्यसंभवः, यदद्य तेनैव भोजराजेन विसृष्टोऽहं त्वयि कार्यगौरवात् ॥ १९ ॥

[२० **सुणाहि तासेण**]—शृणु त्रासेन सदा समाकुलो यदीहते माधव ते स मातुलः, स वञ्चयितुं वाञ्छति त्वामिह[2] सांप्रतं जगते यो ददासि खलु कामपि संपदम् ॥ २० ॥

[२१ **पलंब-बाहुस्स**]—प्रलम्बबाहोर्वधाय यस्य ते प्रलम्बकेशिप्रमुखा न पारिताः, तमात्मना संप्रति संप्रमर्दितुं तमःप्रधानः स हि सन्नह्यति[3] हि ॥ २१ ॥

[२२ **धराहिणाहो**]—धराधिनाथो धनुरुत्सवच्छलात् खलत्रिलोकीपते हिंसितुं त्वाम्, समं समारभते कुम्भिराजेन समं च मल्लैः स मञ्चमास्थितः ॥ २२ ॥

[२३ **रहम्मि**]—रहस्याहूय राजपांसनो बभाण[4] मां किमपि स तदपि श्रूयताम्, अमन्दमक्रूर व्रज गोकुलं भण बालावपि च रामकेशवौ ॥ २३ ॥

[२४ **चअत्थि भोआहिव**]—चकास्ति भोजाधिपबाहुपालिते शरासयज्ञो मधुरा[5]महागृहे, तदीक्षितुं वां यदि किमपि कौतुकं ततः समागच्छतं पश्यतमुत्सवम् ॥ २४ ॥

---

१ [अस्य]. २ [त्वामपि]. ३ T omits some portion. ४ [अभणत्]. ५ [मथुरा].

[२५ स णंदगोवो]—स नन्दगोपोऽपि समित्रबान्धवो जवात् समाव्रजतु मम मन्दिरम्, अतुच्छो युष्माकं वीक्षणादरो ममेति तेनैव सर्वमीरितम् ॥ २५ ॥

[२६ इमस्स कज्जस्स]—अमुष्य[1] कार्यस्य शरीरमीदृशं यस्मिन् खलु प्राणायते विप्रलम्भनम्, न व्रज वा नन्दजे[2] व्रज वा त्वं विधिर्निषेधोऽपि[3] न दूतकर्तृकः ॥ २६ ॥

[२७ पवट्टए चाव-]—प्रवर्तते चापमख इति कौतुकं निवर्तते वञ्चनसाधनमिति तद्, द्विधा वले भ्रातर्भावबन्धनं ममेति तमजल्पत्[4] रोहिणीसुतः ॥ २७ ॥

[२८ इदं वओ]—इदं वचो अभण्यत[5] वन्यमालिना अलं कुतर्केण प्रलम्बसूदन, अकार्यसज्जानां हि शत्रुसंभवः कुतो भयं कार्यपथोन्मुखानां नः ॥ २८ ॥

[२९ अह प्फुडं]—अथ स्फुटं करिष्यति साहसं यदि क्षयं स्वयं यास्यति प्राकृतो जनः, समिद्धमग्निं ग्रसितुं समुत्थितो न दह्यते किं शलभानां संचयः ॥ २९ ॥

[३० विसुद्ध-सीले]—विशुद्धशीलान्[6] विमदच्छलक्रमो[7] न कोऽप्यस्मान् स्प्रष्टुं प्रगल्भते, नभसि तारानिकरान्समुज्ज्वलान् निशान्धकारो मलिनयति किं भण ॥ ३० ॥

---

१ [अस्य]. २ M नन्द. ३ M निषेधो हि. ४ [तं जल्पति]. ५ [भण्यते]. ६ M विशुद्धशीलो, T °शीला. ७ T विमत°, M विमच्छल°.

[**३१ भुअ-प्पआवो**]—भुजप्रतापो भुजदर्पशालिनो रिपूणां मध्य एव संप्रकाशते, हिरण्यरेतसोऽपि जालसंचयः[1] स्वयं समिन्धे किमिन्धनं विना ॥ ३१ ॥

[**३२ वअं वएसग्ग**]—वयं व्रजेशाग्रसरा[2] निराकुलाः सशिक्य-भाण्डाः शकटाधिरोहिणः, समुच्चलामः सकला अपि सांप्रतं सभाजितो[3] भवतु स भोजभूपतिः ॥ ३२ ॥

[**३३ इआलवंतो**]—इत्यालपन् सह सीरपाणिना रथं समारोहति[4] देवकीसुतः, कराग्रसंवल्गितप्रग्रहो जवात्स तस्य पृष्ठे च गान्दिनीसुतः ॥ ३३ ॥

[**३४ सुहं रहम्मि**]—सुखं रथ एव हर्म्योपमे स्वयं शयानो गमयित्वा यामिनीम्, प्रगे समं संमिलितैर्माधवः स नन्दगोपप्रभुखैः[6] प्रस्थितः ॥ ३४ ॥

[**३५ अहो समाअण्णिअ**]—अथो समाकर्ण्य कर्णदुस्सहां प्रवासवार्तां पतगेशकेतोः, गलोद्गलदश्रुजलोक्षताक्षरं[7] वियोगभीता[8] व्यलपन्[9] गोपिकाः ॥ ३५ ॥

[**३६ अमुद्धअंदम्मि**]—अमुग्धचन्द्र इव शम्भुमस्तके अकौस्तुभ इव विष्णुवक्षसि, अनन्दजे नन्दगृहे का श्रीः हता हता वयं व्रजाङ्गनाः ॥ ३६ ॥

---

१ [ज्वालासंचयः]. २ M व्रजेशाग्रेसरा. ३ T सभाजिको. ४ T समारोहद्देवकी. ५ M संवाहित. ६ T omits some portion. ७ [जलोक्षिताक्षरं]. ८ M भीत्या. ९ [विलपन्ति].

[३७ **अणण्ण-णाहा**]—अनन्यनाथा अपि हा विहाय नो घृणां विना झटिति गते विदारुणे, तस्मिन् जने लगति सांप्रतमपि यत्तद-स्मादृशीनां खलु मनो विनिन्दितम् ॥ ३७ ॥

[३८ **किमेत्थ अम्हे**]—किमत्र वयं[1] कुर्मो गुणोत्तरे जने पिनद्धं युवतीनां मानसम्, न तीर्यते चारुप्रसूनसौरभे महीरुहे भृङ्ग-कुलं च क्रष्टुम् ॥ ३८ ॥

[३९ **पहाण-पाणाणि**]—प्रधानप्राणाः खलु नो जनार्दनः स येन दूरं गमितो दुरात्मना, कृतान्तदूत एव स समागतो न कंसदूत इति जानीत गोपिकाः ॥ ३९ ॥

[४० **इमाहि कूरो**]—अस्मात् क्रूरो न परं[2] इति अस्य कृता अवश्यमक्रूरशब्दप्रक्रिया, अघोरशब्दं यथा घोरमूर्तेः शिवस्य व्याचष्टे तथेति मन्यामहे ॥ ४० ॥

[४१ **हरिस्स रूवं**]—हरेः रूपमेव संस्मरत भो हरिन्मणिश्यामल-कोमलप्रभम्, स्निग्धकेशाञ्चितमयूरपिञ्छिकं विकसितेन्दीवरविशाल-लोचनम् ॥ ४१ ॥

[४२ **फुरंत-दंतुज्जल**]—स्फुरद्दन्तोज्ज्वलकान्तिचन्द्रिकासमग्र-सौन्दर्यमुखेन्दुमण्डलम्, विशुद्धमुक्तागुणकौस्तुभप्रभाप्रदीप्तवक्षःस्फुटवत्स-लाञ्छनम् ॥ ४२ ॥

[४३ **भुअंग-भोआकइ**]—भुजङ्गभोगाकृतिसौन्दर्यभङ्गदप्रकाम-सौकुमार्यभुजालताञ्चितम्[3], मणिप्रभाकीर्णसुवर्णमेखलाविलम्बिपीताम्बर-श्रोणिमण्डलम् ॥ ४३ ॥

---

१ M किमस्मादृश्यः. २ M क्रूरो वर इति. ३ [°प्रकामसुकुमार°]

[४४ **णह-प्पहालिद्ध**]—[1]नखप्रभास्पृष्टनभःपथामलप्रवालताम्रो-ज्ज्वलपादपङ्कजम्, मनोज्ञहासार्द्रकटाक्षवीक्षणक्षणक्षोभ्यमानव्रजाङ्गनाङ्ग-जम् ॥ ४४ ॥

[४५ **णिअंबिणीओ**]—नितम्बिन्यो निचुलार्द्रपल्लवप्रबद्धपर्यङ्क-प्रमर्दनिर्दयम्, न विस्मर्यतां नवं नवं कृतं जनार्दनेन यमुनातटक्रीड-नम् ॥ ४५ ॥

[४६ **जहिं दु सा**]—यस्मिंस्तु सा निर्लूनफुल्लमञ्जरी नमद्-वृन्ताग्रभ्रमत्षट्पदा, शुकानूद्यमानसुगूढजल्पितौ[3] तटान्तवानीरलता खलु साक्षिणी ॥ ४६ ॥

[४७ **मउंद-वेणूअर**]—मुकुन्दवेणूदरनिर्यद्बन्धुरस्वरामृतास्वार्द[4]-विरूढपल्लवाः, दवोष्मशुष्का अपि वनान्तपादपा यस्मिन्खलु ग्रीष्मातपम् आवृण्वन्[5] नः ॥ ४७ ॥

[४८ **वणाणिला जत्थ**]—वनानिला यत्र कलिन्दनन्दिनी-तरङ्गसंपर्कस्निग्धशीतलाः, अकुर्वन्[6] नः पङ्कजपांसुमांसलाः श्रमातुराणां तालवृन्तकार्यम् ॥ ४८ ॥

[४९ **भुवंति गोवद्धण**]—अभवन्[7] गोवर्धनशैलमेखलात्रि-लम्बितोद्गर्जितविद्युतो घनाः, आसां नो मानविनोदनोन्मुखा यस्मिन् यदृच्छागतपीठमर्दाः[8] ॥ ४९ ॥

---

१ M नवप्रभा. २ M Defective reading. ३ T सुरूढ. ४ [स्वनामृतास्वाद] ५ [आवृण्वन्ति]. ६ [कुर्वन्ति]. ७ [भवन्ति]. ८ M °गतिपीठमर्दनाः, [पीठमर्दकाः].

[**५० जहिं च**]—यस्मिंश्च वृन्दावनमेकमन्दिरं मणिप्रदीपो मृगलाञ्छनः स्वयम्, नवा च शय्या तरुपल्लवावली वसन्तपुष्पाणि च भूषणानि नः ॥ ५० ॥

[**५१ गओ स कालो**]—गतः स कालो गजगामिनीजना मनोरथेभ्यः कुर्मः तिलाञ्जलिम्[1], सुखस्य सर्वस्यापि मूलकारणं जनो गतो यज्जनलोचनाञ्जनम् ॥ ५१ ॥

[**५२ कआ णु कण्हस्स**]—कदा नु कृष्णस्य कपोलघूर्णनशील-स्फुटप्रभामण्डलकुण्डलोज्ज्वलम्, सुपक्वबिम्बीफलपाटलाधरं मुहूर्तं प्रेक्षिष्यामहे मुखाम्बुजम् ॥ ५२ ॥

[**५३ कआ णु पीण**]—कदा नु पीनस्तनगाढपीडनामृद्यमानोज्ज्वलवन्यमालिकम्, आभ्यां दोर्भ्यां परिवेष्ट्यास्य विशालमालिङ्गिष्यामो भुजान्तरम् ॥ ५३ ॥

[**५४ असंक-संकेअ**]—अशङ्कसङ्केतलतागृहोदरस्थितस्य मार्ग-प्रहितेक्षणस्यास्य, जवेन गत्वा यथेष्टचेष्टितं कदा नु वा पास्यामोऽधरामृतम् ॥ ५४ ॥

[**५५ इअ-प्पलावं**]—इतिप्रलापं[2] प्रियविप्रवासजप्रकामशोकातुरमङ्गनाजनम्, मुकुन्दवाचा स गान्दिनीसुतः समागतो अजल्पत्[3] किमपि सादरम् ॥ ५५ ॥

[**५६ अहीरमाहीर**]—अधीरमाभीरनितम्बिनीजना मुग्धा[4] खलु यूयं विलपथ विह्वलम्, कथं नु वो मुञ्चति चञ्चलेक्षणाः क्षणमपि स युष्मद्वशंवदो हरिः ॥ ५६ ॥

---

१ M तिलकाञ्जलिं. २ M इति प्रकामं, T इति प्रलापः. ३ [जल्पति]. ४ T मुग्धा.

[५७ **विजिम्ह-तुम्ह**]—विजिह्मयुष्मद्भ्रूकोदण्डप्रमुक्तनेत्राञ्चलबाणकीलितः, कथं खलु स कम्पते संप्रति क्षणं सह्यतां कार्याभिमुखस्य साहसम् ॥ ५७ ॥

[५८ **उसम्मि संमज्जइ**]—उषासि संमज्जति सागरे यः स सायमुन्मज्जति किं न चन्द्रमाः, अलं विषादेन विलासिनीनां वो गतस्य प्रत्यागमनं न दुर्लभम् ॥ ५८ ॥

[५९ **समत्थ-लोअस्स**]—समस्तलोकस्य प्रकाशहेतोः तमःप्रपञ्चस्य निरासकारिणः, प्रतिप्रयाणं प्रतिपालयतास्य सरोजिन्य इव सहस्ररश्मेः ॥ ५९ ॥

[६० **विओअ-सोउम्हल**]—वियोगशोकोष्मलग्रीष्मतापितं व्रजस्त्रीसार्थचातकीकुलम्, वचोऽम्बुधाराभिः सुशीतलाभिः स सुखयामास[1] माधवदूतवारिदः ॥ ६० ॥

[६१ **अह दिअह**]—अथ दिवसविकासप्रक्रमे प्रारोहत्सपदि हरिसनाथं स्यन्दनं गान्दिनेयः, नयनपद्मराजिरोचनीयां जनानाम् अलभत[2] शुभामभिख्यां[3] कामपि स काश्यपिरिव ॥ ६१ ॥

[६२ **जव-जिअ-पवणेणं**]—जवजितपवनेन व्रजन् रथेन सह पशुपवरैः अगाहत[4] माधवः स, कृष्णगिरिशिखालीतुल्यकल्लोलमालाभ्रंशिततटतमालां सूर्यकन्याया वेलाम् ॥ ६२ ॥

[६३ **जउणा-सलिलम्मि**]—यमुनासलिले मज्जन्[5] प्रतिबिम्बमिव

---

१ [सुखयति]. २ [लभते]. ३ M शुभाभिख्यां. ४ [गाहते]. ५ M मज्जत्.

तस्मिन्नपि वासुदेवम्, प्रलोक्य बभूव विस्मयमानः पुलकोद्भिन्नतनुः[१] स गान्दिनेयः ॥ ६३ ॥

[६४ **तरंतो तं**]—तरंस्तां ततः स[२] तरुणमनस्सन्तोषमधुरः स्ववृन्दैः सार्धम् अविशत्[३] मधुरां[४] नाम नगरम्, तस्मिन् वीथीगाही चकार[५] वनितानां समधिकं समानन्दं चन्द्र इव कुमुदिनीनां मधुमथनः[६] ॥ ६४ ॥

[इति रामपाणिवादकृते कंसवधे प्रथमः सर्गः]

[द्वितीयः सर्गः]

[१ **अह मालिअ**]—अथ मालिकदत्तमालभारी वनमाली मुसली च व्रजन्तम्, परिधौतवस्त्रभाण्डवाहं रजकं कमपि अपश्यतां[७] राजमार्गे ॥ १ ॥

[२ **मउ-हास**]—मृदुहासमनोहराननाभ्यां कुमाराभ्यां वसनानि याचितः सः, कुमना घनगर्वदुर्विनीतः कुपितो अभाषत[८] भोजराजभृत्यः ॥ २ ॥

[३ **ण हु संभरिउं**]—न खलु संस्मर्तुमपि शक्यते यत्तदिदं जल्पथो डिम्भकौ किमेवम्, ननु खादति तर्जितोऽपि यः स स्पृष्टः किं न करोति कृष्णभोगी ॥ ३ ॥

---

१ M °वपुः २ T omits स, M Defective reading. ३ [विशति]. ४ M मधुरा. ५ [करोति]. ६ T मदनः ७ [पश्यतः]. ८ [भाषते].

[**४ णवरं ण लहिस्सइ**]—केवलं न लप्स्यत इति नेदं वसनं भोजपतेर्याच्यमानम्, नन्विदमेव युष्मच्छीर्षच्छेदस्यापि भो भविष्यति कारणं जानीतम् ॥ ४ ॥

[**५ अभणिज्जवउ-**]—अभणितव्यवचउद्गमेन जाल्मा अनुभवन्ति स्फुटमात्मनो विनाशम्, चपलां लब्ध्वा पक्ष्मपालीं[१] शलभाः किं न म्रियन्ते हव्यवाहे ॥ ५ ॥

[**६ अह होदु**]—अथ भवतु सह एकवारमहं युवयोर्बालचापलानि, न सहेत नराधिप इमानि यदि स श्रोष्यति वात्सल्यवन्ध्यः ॥ ६ ॥

[**७ इअ सो कडु**]—इति स कटु भाषित्वा यावत्प्रहसन्नेवापक्रमितुं प्रवृत्तः, सहसा मधुसूदनेन तावद्वसनानि हृतान्यस्य करात् ॥७॥

[**८ अहिहोदु-मणस्स**]—परिभवितुमनसः[२] क्रोधभाराद्रभसोत्थापितयष्टिपाणेरस्य, अथ तत्क्षणनखकोटिरुग्णं पर्यपाटयत्[३] शिरः श्रियो नाथः ॥ ८ ॥

[**९ णिअ-पंक**]—निजपङ्कविशोधनावदातो रजकस्याभ्यधिकं लघूभवन, प्राविशत्[४] सदाप्रकाशमात्मा वसनानां निकरश्च वासुदेवम् ॥९॥

[**१० सिअएहि**]—सिचयैः सितैरस्य[५] शरीरं वसितैः अलसत्[६] तमालनीलम्, कनकोज्ज्वलमेखलाभिरामं शशिमयूखैरिव नीलशैलशृङ्गम् ॥ १० ॥

---

१ [पक्ष्मपालीं]. २ [अभिभावितु]. ३ [परिपाटयति]. ४ [प्रविशति]. ५ M सितैरस्य. ६ [लसति].

[११ अह पेक्खइ]—अथ अपश्यत्[1] वक्रतां गतया तनुयष्ट्यापि दृष्टिरम्यरूपाम्, मदनस्येव स[2] कोदण्डयष्टिं[3] वनितां कामपि समुन्नमत्पृष्ठाम् ॥ ११ ॥

[१२ अणुसप्पिर]—अनुसर्पणशीलषट्पदं वहन्तीं मणिपात्रं भृतकुङ्कुमं कराग्रे, शनैः शनैः समापतन्तीं समुपागम्य अपृच्छत्[4] हरिरेनाम् ॥ १२ ॥

[१३ कुडिलच्छि]—कुटिलाक्षि वले कुतोऽसि बाले कुटिलीभवति कथं तव शरीरम्, मसृणं घुसृणं च कस्मै दातुं शनैर्गच्छसि प्रेक्षणीयरूपे ॥ १३ ॥

[१४ अह जम्पइ]—अथ अजल्पत्[5] सा विधेः शक्तिर्बलवज्जृम्भते त्वामा मयि, हृदये प्रसिद्धां स्त्रीणां मम गात्रेऽप्यकरोत्[6] वक्रतां या ॥ १४ ॥

[१५ सुण सुंदर]—शृणु सुन्दर शिल्पकारिकाहं नृवरान्तःपुरवासिनी विनीता, घुसृणं पुनः कंसराजायास्मै प्रणिदातुं प्रचलामि तन्निकेतम् ॥ १५ ॥

[१६ सुउमारमिणं]—सुकुमारमिदं च ते शरीरं सुरभिः कुङ्कुमपङ्कजश्चैषः[7], परिगृह्णातु तस्माद्भवानेवेदं सदृशयोर्हि समागमः सुखाय ॥ १६ ॥

[१७ इअ तप्पविइण्ण]—इति तत्प्रवितीर्णकुङ्कुमाभिमृष्टाङ्गो[8]

———

१ [प्रेक्षते]. २ T च. ३ M कोपदण्ड. ४ [पृच्छति]. ५ [जल्पति]. ६ M गात्रे न्यकरोत्. ७ [पङ्कश्चैषः]. ८ M तत्प्रविकीर्ण.

व्यलसतां[1] कृष्णरामौ, सप्रसूनकलायौ[2] सिन्दुवाराविव सन्ध्यातपसंस्पृश्य-माणौ ॥ १७ ॥

[१८ **चिबुए कर**]—चिबुके करपल्लवेन कृष्णः शनैर्गृहीत्वा सारसेक्षणां ताम्, अथ कुब्जामृज्वीमकरोत् स्फुटलज्जावलिताननेन्दु-बिम्बाम ॥ १८ ॥

[१९ **पढमं कुडिला**]—प्रथमं कुटिलापि चन्द्रलेखा यथा संपूर्णतामेति पूर्णिमायाम्, तथा सा सहसा बभूव[3] पूर्णा कमनीकोमल-कान्तिकौमुदीभिः ॥ १९ ॥

[२० **अदिभूमि**]—अतिभूमिमुपागतं मृगाक्षी मदनायल्लक-शल्यमुद्वहन्ती, नत्वा अभणत्[4] नन्दसूनुं धुतलज्जानिगलैरक्षरैः ॥ २० ॥

[२१ **इमिणम्हि**]—अनेनास्मि शरीरशोभाविभवेनेति त्वयि रूढवैरः, त्वयानुकम्पितेतीदानीं किमु मां बाधते मन्मथो महा-त्मन् ॥ २१ ॥

[२२ **विस-रुक्ख**]—विषवृक्षप्रसूनैर्मन्ये विषमेषुर्विशिखानधुना करोति, मृदुभिः किमन्यथा मनो मे अनेन दह्यते नीयते च मूर्छाम् ॥ २२ ॥

[२३ **अवसं सवसं**]—अवशां स्ववशामपि मारघोरज्वरदूय-मानमनसं मनोज्ञमूर्ते[5], अनुगृहाण मां कृष्णसारशारच्छाविसारैः कटाक्ष-वीक्षणैः ॥ २३ ॥

---

१ [विलसतः]. २ [सप्रसूनकलौ च]. ३ [अभवत्]. ४ [भणति]. ५ T मनःसमोहनमूर्ते

[२४ हरिणील-सिणिद्ध]—हरिनीलस्निग्धमुग्धशोभे तव संक्रान्तमुरसि रम्यरूपम्, कृष्णाचलधातुरागकल्पं स्तनकुम्भाभ्यां मार्ष्टि कुङ्कुममेनत् ॥ २४ ॥

[२५ अह वाहरइ]—अथ व्याहरति स्म वासुदेवः सुमहत्तव सुभ्रु साहसिक्यम्, इह यानि मया विवक्षितानि हृतानि त्वया तान्यक्षराणि ॥ २५ ॥

[२६ विअसंत]—विकसन्मुखारविन्दनिर्यद्भ्रमरालापच्छलाभिलाषवाचम्, प्रतिपालयति किं नु मल्लिकाक्षो नलिनीं किंतु सरति दृष्टिमात्राम्[1] ॥ २६ ॥

[२७ मह माणिणि]—मम मानिनि कार्यगौरवेण परवतो न तत्र कुम्भस्थूलौ, परिरब्धुमवसर उरोजौ स्ववश एव क्षमो हि कामतन्त्रे[2] ॥ २७ ॥

[२८ अहमेहिमि]—अहमेष्यामि तावद्भूपसेवानिगलान्मम यावद्भवेन्मोक्षः, न हि कैरविणीं स्प्रष्टुमीशो घनरुद्धप्रसरः स चन्द्रमा अपि ॥ २८ ॥

[२९ अह णो]—अथ नौ हृदयेप्सितानि पश्चात् शशिज्योत्स्नोन्मृष्टासु यामिनीषु, सुजनानां सभासु सत्कवीनां वचनानीव प्रथन्तां क्रीडितानि ॥ २९ ॥

[३० इअ तं पिअ]—इति तां प्रियदर्शनां भणन मुदितामेव

---

१ [दृष्टमात्रम्]. २ T कामतन्त्रः.

विसृज्य कृष्णः, स्वजनैः सहाग्रजो गतः स शनैस्ततो अविशत्[1] च राजधानीम् ॥ ३० ॥

[३१ **महणिज्ज**]—महनीयमहोज्ज्वलाङ्गलक्ष्मीविभवालोकविफुल्ल-कौतूहलाः, प्रादिशन्[2] पृथग्जना अपि मार्गं तस्यामस्मै कं न हरन्ति पूर्णभागाः[3] ॥ ३१ ॥

[३२ **मणि-दीव**]—मणिदीपशिखाप्रदीप्यमानां कनकस्तम्भ-विलग्नहारगुम्फाम्, महिषाक्षधूपगन्धगर्भां मधुवैरी[4] विवेश[5] कोदण्ड-शालाम् ॥ ३२ ॥

[३३ **महिअं बहु**]—महितं बहुगन्धमाल्यैर्धनुर्गृहीत्वा पाणि-पल्लवाभ्याम्, सहसैव सज्यं कुर्वन् स समाकर्षत्[6] मुष्टिपीडितमेनत् ॥३३॥

[३४ **अइ बालअ**]—अयि बालक राजपूजितमेतद्धनुर्मा[7] स्पृश मा स्पृशेति यावत्, वचनानि अश्रूयन्त[8] किंकराणां त्रुटितं मधुसूदनेन तावत् ॥ ३४ ॥

[३५ **थणिअं किमिणं**]—स्तनितं किमिदं कुतः पयोदो नर-सिंहध्वानितं नु तन्निवृत्तम्, इति वितर्कशतेन दुःस्थाचित्तो धनुर्भङ्ग-ध्वनिना बभूव[9] कंसः ॥ ३५ ॥

[३६ **अह रक्खिभडे**]—अथ रक्षिभटान् पराक्रमतः परुषै-र्वचनैराक्षिपतः, प्रामृद्नीतां[10] प्ररोषभयङ्करौ धनुःखण्डाभ्यां रणे राम-कृष्णौ ॥ ३६ ॥

---

१ [विशति]. २ [प्रदिशन्ति]. ३ [पुण्यभाजः]. ४ M वैरिर्विवेस. ५ [विशति]
६ [समाकर्षति] ७ T पूजितमेनं.धनुर्मा, ८ [श्रूयन्ते]. ९ [अभवत्]. १० [प्रमृद्नीतः].

[३७ मिहिरम्मि]—मिहिर इव प्रकाशमाने वनमालिनि मनांसि सज्जनानाम्, कमलानीव अभवन्[1] फुल्लानि कुमुदानीव अकुचन्[2] दुर्जनानाम् ॥ ३७ ॥

[३८ अह चावघराहि]—अथ चापगृहान्निष्क्रामन् सह रामेण स देवकीतनूजः, युवतिनयनैः पीयमानो व्यचरत्[3] स्फुटमक्कणस्थल्याम् ॥ ३८ ॥

[३९ समुवट्ठिअ]—समुपस्थितैर्भोजराजधानीं सरसं तां प्रलोक्य राजधानीम्, अभणत्[4] शनैर्मनोभिरामं स हि वाग्भिः सविस्तराभिराम[5][6] ॥ ३९ ॥

[४० उव णो भुवण]—पश्य नो[7] भुवनपणायिताया मधुराया मधुरत्वं पुर्याः, मणिहर्म्यपालिमौलिकुम्भस्खलनापवाहितसूर्यस्यन्दनायाः ॥ ४० ॥

[४१ इअमुण्णमि]—इयमुन्नमितोच्चकेतुहस्तप्रचाल्यमानपताकिकाङ्गुलीभिः, स्वविभूतिलघूकृतां सगर्वा[8] नगरीं तर्जयति किं नु निर्जराणाम् ॥ ४१ ॥

[४२ कणआअल]—कनकाचलशोभसौध[9]शृङ्गस्थलक्रीडत्पुराङ्गनाप्सरौघोः, परिखार्णवमध्यवर्तिनीयं स्वयमालम्बते जम्बूद्वीपलक्ष्मीम् ॥ ४२ ॥

[४३ फलिहोवल]—स्फटिकोपलकुट्टिमप्रदेशो हरिनीलाक्य-

---

१ [भवन्ति]. २ [कुचन्ति]. ३ [विचरति]. ४ [समुपस्थाय]. ५ [न्ति]. ६ [सविस्तराभी रामम्]. ७ M पश्यन्तौ. ८ M सगर्वा. ९ M omits सौध.

रश्मिमिश्रितोऽयम, इह संप्रति संस्मारयति नो यमुनोद्गृहीतजाह्नवी-प्रवाहम् ॥ ४३ ॥

[४४ **कसणोवल**]—कृष्णोपलकेलिपर्वतानां तमःश्यामाभी रुचिभिर्निह्नुतायाम्, दिवसेऽपि सरन्ति वीथ्यां[1] विधुताशङ्कमिहाभि-सारिकाः ॥ ४४ ॥

[४५ **इह कंचण**]—इह काञ्चनगेहकान्तिलिप्ते गगने बाल-दिनेशमयूखमोहात्, विघटते न दीर्घिकासु दीर्घं रजन्यामपि रथाङ्ग-नामयुग्मम् ॥ ४५ ॥

[४६ **इह वप्प-मणि**]—इह वप्रमणिप्रभासमूहा गगनं मण्डल-शोभिनो लिहन्तः[2], रवेः शशिनश्च कांचत्कालं परिवेषप्रभामुज्ज्वलां कुर्वन्ति ॥ ४६ ॥

[४७ **वलही-वलएसु**]—वलभीवलयेषु गोपुराणां विहरतां विलासिनीजनानाम्, मुष्णाति मुखेन्दुस्वेदबिन्दुच्छलमुक्ताफलानि स्वर्गवातः ॥ ४७ ॥

[४८ **इह चंद-मणी**]—इह चन्द्रमणिगृहोदरेषु समं चन्द्रमुखीभिः संविशन्तः, न लभन्ते रतिश्रमं युवानः तपरात्रिष्वपि नाम तामसीषु ॥४८॥

[४९ **इअमुन्नमिउच्च**]—इयमुन्नमितोच्चसौधशीर्षा प्रविकसितैर्ग-वाक्षलोचनैः, रत्नाकरमेखलाकलापां कुतुकवती प्रलोकत इव भूत-धात्रीम् ॥ ४९ ॥

---

१ [वीथिकायां]. २ [लिखन्तः].

[५० अदिहीण]—अतिथीनां कुर्वन्ति पाद्यकार्यं प्रचलत्प्रसवासवोदकैः, इह निष्कुटवाटबालवृक्षाः सुखप्रश्नं च रवैः कोकिलानाम् ॥ ५० ॥

[५१ सर-सीअर]—सरश्शीकरवाहिनः समीराः सरसामोदहराः सरोरुहाणाम्, मिथुनानां रतिश्रमं शमयितुं सदा सज्जन्ति नन्वत्र विस्तृणन्तम् ॥ ५१ ॥

[५२ इह कोच्चण]—इह क्वचन पिच्छिलायां नित्योद्भटगजकटावटनिर्झरैः, लग्ना वसुधायां ददति[1] भृङ्गा नेन्द्रनीलोपलकुट्टिमभ्रमं किम् ॥ ५२ ॥

[५३ आणिअंतण]—अनियन्त्रणयन्त्रमार्गनिर्यद्ध्वनितोद्घोषणशीलवारिधोरणीभिः, इह क्वचन नित्यसिच्यमाने[2] निलये नृत्यति प्रत्यहं मयूरः ॥ ५३ ॥

[५४ इह सुव्वइ]—इह श्रूयते निर्वहत्तालस्फुटसंगीतनटाङ्गहारचिह्नम्, गभीरो घनगर्जितानुरूपो मधुरः क्वचिन्मृदङ्गतुङ्गनादः ॥ ५४ ॥

[५५ सुण पुव्वअ]—शृणु पूर्वजसुन्दरीजनानां[3] मधुगोष्ठीषु मदानुषङ्गसान्द्रम्, ललितं कलकण्ठकण्ठनादप्रतिमं क्वचन नर्तने गीतम् ॥ ५५ ॥

[५६ परदो सुण]—परतः शृणु स्थानिवद्भावाद्विफलं प्रत्ययलक्षणस्य सूत्रम्, सफलं तदलाश्रये कार्ये इति वैयाकरणानां वादघोषम् ॥ ५६ ॥

---

१ M दधति. २ T नित्यदीप्यमानो. ३ M पूर्वसुन्दरी.

[५७ स-सलाह]—सश्लाघश्लोकपाठकैर्मुखरं क्वचन बन्दिवृन्दैः, इदमस्मत्पुरं चिरमपि दृष्टं न खलु दृष्टिं परतो[2] निवर्तयति ॥ ५७ ॥

[५८ गंधव्वा ण]—गन्धर्वा न किमत्र सन्ति न खलु किं विद्यन्ते विद्याधराः किं वा चारु न चारणानां च कुलं जयन्ति नो किन्नराः, कि नेदं सुमनसां धाम किमहो नाथो महेन्द्रो[3] नास्य स्वर्ग एव वसूनां स्थानमिदं रम्यं सुधर्मोज्ज्वलम् ॥ ५८ ॥

[५९ कीलासेलग्ग]—क्रीडाशैलाग्रलग्नस्तानितघनघनोत्सृष्टवृष्टि-प्रणाली झंकारोत्कण्ठमयूरस्फुटनटनकोलाहलदीप्यमानकामाः, वामा वामा अपि पीनस्तनकनकघटौ संघटय्य गाढं कण्ठे गृह्णन्ति कुण्ठेतरमिह पृथुरागार्द्रशीला वल्लभानाम् ॥ ५९ ॥

[६० इअ बहु-वित्थआइ]—इति बहुविस्तृतानि विषयाणां बहुत्वतः स्वयमथ गोशतानि उपसहृत्य सुखम्, वसतिम् उपासरत्[4] वसुदेवसुतः स यदा तदा खलु दिवाकरोऽपि चरमाचलमौलिभुवम् ॥ ६० ॥

[इति कंसवधे द्वितीयः सर्गः]

[तृतीयः सर्गः]

[१ पच्चूसे पर]—प्रत्यूषे[5] परमङ्गल्य ल्लियुद्धप्रस्तावप्रथम-प्रवृत्तसूत्रधारः, प्रारब्धः पटहरवः प्रबोधवेलामप न्ताम् अभणत्[6] इव बन्दिवृन्देभ्यः ॥ १ ॥

---

१ M सुश्लाघ. २ M परितो. ३ M महीन्द्रो. [उपसरति]. ५ M प्रत्यूहे.
६ [भणति].

[२ बुज्झंती बुह]—बुध्यमाना बुधप्रतिभेव काव्यबन्धान् बध्नती[1] बहलरसैरक्षरैः, प्रसुतं पद्मविलोचनं प्रबोधं प्रापयितुम् अक्रमते[2] क्रमेण बन्दिपाली ॥ २ ॥

[३ कल्लाणं कमल]—कल्याणं कमलश्रीकटाक्षवीक्षाविक्षेपप्रचटुलचञ्चरीकमालम्[3], कल्याणं करोतु पुरस्सरस्य तव कल्यं ननु सुभग सुखप्रबोधहेतुः ॥ ३ ॥

[४ होस्संतिं तुह]—भविष्यन्तीं तव मुखलक्ष्मीमक्षिशोभाविच्छायीकृतनिजचिह्नकृष्णिमानम्, पश्यन् प्रथममयं तव प्रबोधान्निष्क्रान्तो निभृतगतिर्निशाया नाथः ॥ ४ ॥

[५ जाओ दे जउ]—यास्ते यदुसुत नेत्रतारका निश्शेषं जनमनुग्रहीष्यन्ति बोधे, ताभ्यो लघ्वितरास्तारका व्रीडया ध्रुवं पश्य भवन्ति निष्प्रभाः ॥ ५ ॥

[६ जोण्हाअं तुहिण]—ज्योत्स्नायां तुहिनकरस्य वृक्षच्छायाप्रच्छन्नाः कथमपि स्थिताः खल्वन्धकाराः, उल्लासे तवमुखचन्द्रचन्द्रिकायाः शङ्कमाना निजक्षयमिदानीमपसरन्ति ॥ ६ ॥

[७ तूरंतो विरह]—त्वरमाणो विरहवेदनाविशोभं राधायाः सुभग त्वमिव भानुमान्, मीलन्मुखकमलं सरोजिन्याः संप्राप्तः परिमार्ष्टुं कराञ्चलैः ॥ ७ ॥

[८ बीभंता विमअ]—बिभ्यतो विमतभटा यथा त्वत्सूर्यात्

---

१ M बध्नन्ती. २ M अक्रमत, [क्रमते]. ३ T चञ्चरीक.

सुचिरमुदेतुमुन्मुखात्, अज्ञातभ्रष्टप्रसन्नतादुकूला निर्लीना कुहचिन्मुकुन्दचन्द्रमयूखाः ॥ ८ ॥

[९ **झीणाअं विहडण**]—क्षीणायां विघटनकारणे निशायां चक्रवाका निजवनिताभिः संघटन्ते, शान्तायामिव निजपापसंततौ सन्तस्ते सकरुणवीक्षणच्छटाभिः ॥ ९ ॥

[१० **भिंगालिं पुलइअ**]—भृङ्गालिं[1] प्रलोक्य पङ्कजानां गर्भे संभ्रान्तां[2] दरविवृतानां संस्मरामः, उद्बोधक्रमविकसद्दीर्घतराक्षिद्रक्ष्यमाणप्रसरामये कनीनिकां ते ॥ १० ॥

[११ **संभिण्ण-प्पह**]—संभिन्नप्रभामिदमीषच्चन्द्रिकया बन्धूकारुणमरुणस्य रश्मिजालम्, मुक्ताली[3] सुविशददन्तकान्तिश्लिष्टं दृष्टिं नो हरति तवेवाधरोष्ठम् ॥ ११ ॥

[१२ **आलिद्धो दिअह**]—आस्पृष्टो[4] दिवसपतेः पाटलैर्मयूखैर्मरकतकुट्टिमो विभाति, गोपीनां घनकुचकुम्भकुङ्कुमैः संक्रान्तस्तवेव कृष्ण वक्षोभागः ॥ १२ ॥

[१३ **उम्मिल्लावइ**]—उन्मीलयति कमलाकरो न यावत् स्वच्छन्दं मुकुलमयानि लोचनानि, उन्निद्रो निजनयनोत्पले तावत् फुल्ले कुरु त्वमपि वासुदेव ॥ १३ ॥

[१४ **आविज्झा रवि**]—आविद्धा रविकिरणैः सूर्यकान्ता ऊष्माणं वमितुममी उपक्रमन्ते, नो क्षुद्रा अपि सहन्तेऽन्यतेजोविच्छर्दं किमुत त्वादृशा महान्तः ॥ १४ ॥

---

१ T भृंगालीः. २ M गर्भं° ३ T मुक्तालिं. ४ M अस्पृष्टो, [आश्लिष्टो].

[१५ **तिक्खंसु-प्फुड**]—तीक्ष्णांशुस्फुटहरिनखविक्षताद्दिक्षोभप्रपतितर्क्षमौक्तिकात्, अन्धकारस्थिरकरिमस्तकात् सन्ध्यारागोऽयं विगलति शोणितप्रवाहः ॥ १५ ॥

[१६ **णिद्दाणं कुमुइणि**]—निद्राणां कुमुदिनीमुज्झित्वा सद्यो बुध्यमानां कमलिनीमाश्रयति भृङ्गः, प्रत्यूहो न हि बहुवल्लभस्य कचित्तवेव प्रतिनवक्रीडनोत्सवेषु ॥ १६ ॥

[१७ **आअंबो कुणइ**]—आताम्रः करोति दिनेशरश्मिराशिर्नीयन्तीनां[1] प्रियवसतेर्बन्धकीनाम्, स्थूलयोः स्तनकलशयोर्वल्लभोरःप्रमृष्टघुसृणरसं पुनरिव लिप्तम्[2] ॥ १७ ॥

[१८ **किंचेमो जलहि**]—किं चायं जलविजले संमिलन्संददाति[3] स्फुटवडवाग्निशङ्काम्, आम्रेडयति पुनर्हस्तिमस्तकेषु सिन्दूरप्रकरपिशङ्गिमानमेषः ॥ १८ ॥

[१९ **सच्छंदं छुरउ**]—स्वच्छन्दं छुरतु[4] इन्द्रनीलश्यामले ते वक्षसि त्रुटितैप्रवालखण्डशोभः, सौभाग्यं लब्धुमयं खलु सूर्यमयूखस्तलक्ष्मीघनस्तनकुङ्कुमाङ्कनस्य ॥ १९ ॥

[२० **पुव्वासा-जुवइ**]—पूर्वाशायुवतिश्रवः प्रवालभूषाताटङ्कं गगनसरस्सहस्रपत्रम्, प्राचीनाचलमाणिसौधमौलिकुम्भं पश्येदं दिनकरबिम्बमुज्जिहानम् ॥ २० ॥

[२१ **एवं सिं**]—एवमेषां स्तुतिवचनोद्गमात् पूर्वं पर्यङ्कम्

---

१ M राशिं नीतानां. २ M पुनरिवालिप्तम्. ३ M संमिलत् संदधाति, T स ददाति. ४ [स्फुरतु]. ५ M छुरित.

अमुचर्त्[1] जनार्दनो विनिद्रः, उन्मेषं लभते पुरस्सरोजवाटः पश्चान्नु प्रसरति राजहंसनादः ॥ २१ ॥

[२२ पच्चूसे च्चिअ]—प्रत्यूष एव निजस्वच्छगात्रलक्ष्मीविच्छर्द-स्पृष्टवियत्पथावकाशः, प्रत्यक्षो अत्रभर्त्[2] रविरिव पादसेवातात्पर्यप्रवण-मनसां स जनानाम् ॥ २२ ॥

[२३ संझं तो]—सन्ध्यां ततो विकचजपाप्रसूनताम्रां ताम्बूला-रुणवनिताधरोष्ठशोभाम्, राधाया मुखविधुसंस्मारकं[3] स वन्दमानो अच-लर्त्[4] पुरीद्वाराभिमुखः ॥ २३ ॥

[२४ पालेअ-च्छइ]—प्रालेयच्छवितनोर्बलस्य पश्चाद् व्रजन् प्रचटुलहारचारुवक्षाः, कृष्णोऽसौ बहु व्यलसर्त्[5] विद्युत्वांश्चन्द्रस्येव नव-नीलवारिवाहः ॥ २४ ॥

[२५ सोएणं बहु]—शोकेन बहुदिवसात् समातुराया वामाक्षि अस्फुरर्त्[6] तदा स्वमातुः, कंसादीनां च कुहनासमाश्रयाणां शत्रूणां प्रकृतिहतप्रशमल्लकानाम् ॥ २५ ॥[7]

[२६ सोहग्ग-ट्ठिअ]—सौवाप्रस्थितनगराङ्गनाकटाक्षच्छायाली-मसृणमसारमण्डितया, वीथ्या विविधविलासवेषलक्ष्मीभासमानौ शनैः आयेतां[8] रामकृष्णौ ॥ २६ ॥

[२७ अंबट्ठो णरवइ]—अम्बष्ठो नरपतिशासनाद्द्वारे दुर्वार-

---

१ [मुञ्चति]. २ [भवति]. ३ [संस्मारकां]. ४ [चलति]. ५ [विल-सति]. ६ [स्फुरति]. ७ T omits this. ८ [भवतः]

प्रसरत्प्रतापमीश्वरं[1] तम्, रोद्धुं प्रायतत[2] कुम्भिना स्वपाणिच्छत्रेणेव भगवन्तमुष्णमयूखम् ॥ २७ ॥

[२८ आमेलं कुवलअ]—आपीडं कुवलयपूर्वमुर्वरायां क्रीडन्तमिव स्वयमभ्रम्वा नाथम्[3], क्रुध्यन्तं कुलिशकठोरदन्तदण्डं कुम्भीन्द्रं कुटिलमनाः प्राणुदत्[4] सः ॥ २८ ॥

[२९ मत्तुं किं जम]—मर्तुं किं यमगृहमत्तवारणस्य प्रत्यक्षं निपततो मत्तवारणस्य, अन्यतो अपसरतं दुर्दमौ कुमारौ झटितीति प्रालपत्[5] हस्तिपः सगर्वम् ॥ २९ ॥

[३० अण्णत्तो जइ]—अन्यतो यदि न निवर्तयासि नागं सजीवो वत्स्यति क्षणमपि नायम्, इत्थं ततो भणित्वा हरिः सहाग्रजन्मा प्रारब्ध परिभवितुमेनमुग्रकर्मा ॥ ३० ॥

[३१ उव्वंत-क्खुडिअ]—उद्वान्तत्रुटितकटाम्बुनिर्झरार्द्रं मध्ये प्रघटित[6]शृङ्खलाभुजङ्गम्, गजं निजभुजकृष्टं मुकुन्दो भ्रामयन् व्यहरत्[7] मन्दरमिव पूर्वम्[8] ॥ ३१ ॥

[३२ कुज्झंतं गअमह]—क्रुध्यन्तं गजमथ कुण्डलीकृतया शुण्डया कृतपरिवेषमूढहेलम्, मृश्यन् भ्रमरकरम्बिते गण्डे चण्डाभिः प्राहरत्[9] स चपेटिकाभिः ॥ ३२ ॥

[३३ कीलाए लगइ]—क्रीडया अलगत्[10] हरिर्महीं यावत्तावत्स

१ M प्रसरत्स्फुरत्प्र. २ [प्रयतते]. ३ M °मभ्रमूसनाथं, T Blank. ४ [प्रणुदति सः], T प्राणदत्स्कम्. ५ [प्रलपति]. ६ M प्रकटित. ७ [विहरति]. ८ M प्रहरन्मन्दराद्रिमिव. ९ [प्रहरति]. १० [लगति].

दशनयुगेन वारणेन्द्रः, विघ्यन्महीतलमत्र मज्जत्कृष्टुं तदिदमथो न अशक्नोत्[1] ॥ ३३ ॥

[**३४ कुंभं तो कुविअ**]—कुम्भं ततः कुपितमनाः क्षणार्ध-कालमाक्रामंश्चरणतलेन वामेन, उदखनत्[2] त्रुटितप्रशिथिलमूलबन्धं कृष्णोऽस्य करयुगलेन दन्तयुग्मम् ॥ ३४ ॥

[**३५ जाहे सो**]—यावत् स न्यपतत्[3] वज्ररुग्णपक्षप्रक्षिप्तैः[4] कृष्णगिरिरिव नागराजः, तावत् खलु प्राचलत्[5] शेषशीर्षचक्रप्रभ्रष्टमिव वलयं वसुन्धरायाः ॥ ३५ ॥

[**३६ अंबट्ठ-प्पहद**]—अम्बष्ठप्रहतपथेन कियच्चिरं स हस्तीन्द्रः सरति स्वयमिति चिन्तयन्, अम्बष्ठम् अगमयत्[6] ध्रुवं तदानीं दुष्टं हस्तीन्द्रप्रहतपथेन वासुदेवः ॥ ३६ ॥

[**३७ गेहं ता गहिर**]—गेहं तावद्गभीरतरोष्मसौम्यशीलौ गाह-मानौ गगनतलमिव पुष्पवन्तौ, केषांचित्प्रहर्षफुल्लताम् अकुरुतां[7] केषां-चित् प्रमुकुलतां[8] च रामकृष्णौ ॥ ३७ ॥

[**३८ घोलंतुज्जल**]—घूर्णमानोज्ज्वलवनमालभारिवक्षसौ क्रीडन्तौ करिवरदन्तपाणी तौ, पश्यन्तो यथासुखमक्षिजन्मकार्यं स्वच्छन्दं सपदि अलभन्त[9] सर्वलोकाः ॥ ३८ ॥

[**३९ वेरं जे हिअअ**]—वैरं ये हृदयस्थितम् अवहन्[10] तेषां

---

१ [शक्नोति]. २ [उत्खनति]. ३ [निपतति]. ४ M पक्षः. ५ [प्रचलति]. ६ [गमयति]. ७ [कुरुतः]. ८ मुकुलतां. ९ [लभन्ते]. १० [वहन्ति].

वक्त्राणि मुकुलतमानि अभवन्[1] तावत्, वृक्षाणां सदा निजकोटरप्रतिष्ठः पुष्पाणि दवदहनो हि[2] म्लापयति ॥ ३९ ॥

[४० आदिट्ठा णवरि]—आदिष्टा अनन्तरं दुर्नयेन राज्ञा अरण्येभा इव रभसेन सिंहपोतौ, जेतुं तौ यदुकुमारौ कृतप्रतिज्ञाः सन्नद्धाः समभ्यसरन्[3] मल्लयोधाः ॥ ४० ॥

[४१ मंचग्ग-ठ्ठिअ]—मञ्चाग्रस्थितानिजभर्तृदृष्टिवृष्टिसिच्यमानाविव मदपल्लवोल्लसन्तौ, चाणूरः स्वयमथ मुष्टिकश्च द्वौ प्रोन्निद्रौ निखिलम् आवर्तां[4] मल्लसैन्यम् ॥ ४१ ॥

[४२ चाणूरो कइढव]—चाणूरः कैटभसूदनं सरन् साटोपम् अभणत्[5] वले[6] व्रजेशसूनो, इच्छन्निवसति तव युद्धक्रीडापाण्डित्यं प्रलोकितुमेष भोजराजः ॥ ४२ ॥

[४३ भूवालो च्चिअ]—भूपाल एव कुशलः कोदण्डशास्त्रे गोपाल एव निपुणो नियुद्धतन्त्रे, यो यस्मिन्करोति परिश्रमं प्रकामं स तस्मिन्नेव विनियोजितो विभाति ॥ ४३ ॥

[४४ मल्लेहिं सह]—मल्लैः सह महाविक्रमैः प्रतिस्पर्धिरियं कथं किल भवेद्दुष्करा त्वया[7], बालेनैव त्वया प्रलम्बकेशिप्रायाः किं न खलु निहता दैत्यवीराः ॥ ४४ ॥

[४५ ता जुज्झं कुणह]—तस्माद्युद्धं कुरुतं द्वावपि नाम युवां

---

१ [भवन्ति]. २ M omits. हि. ३ [समभिसरन्ति]. ४ [अवतः]. ५ M अवदत्, [भणति]. ६ T बटो. ७ T °दुष्कराख्या, [तव].

धर्मेणैव खलु द्वाभ्यां मल्लाभ्याम्, अस्माकं जानातु स्वयं कुतूहलवान् भोजेशो भुजविभवे तारतम्यम् ॥ ४५ ॥

[४६ एवं से सुणिअ]—एवमस्य श्रुत्वा वचांसि सुप्रसन्नः सन्नद्धः समभ्यघटत[1] अनेन कृष्णः; कुप्यन् कुलिशविघट्टनिष्ठुराभिः मुष्टिभिः मुसलधरोऽपि मुष्टिकेन ॥ ४६ ॥

[४७ धिब्बोल-प्परुस]—धिक्कारपरुषपरस्परप्रलापं गृह्यमाण-भ्रष्टपतद्बाहुयन्त्रम्, आस्फालस्फुटकटु[2]शब्दभयंकरं क्षुभ्यत्त्रिभुवनमासीत्[3] तेषां युद्धम् ॥ ४७ ॥

[४८ कड्ढंता कर]—कर्षन्तः करयुगलेन जानुजङ्घासंघट्टत्रुटित विलिप्तरक्तगात्राः, उद्दामभ्रमणधूयमानभूमिचक्रा विक्रान्तिं विविधामिमे समारभन्ते[4] ॥ ४८ ॥

[४९ कट्ठं हो]—कष्टं भोः कठिनमनाः प्रणुदाति कः शार्दूलौ शशशिशुभ्यां संप्रहन्तुम्[5], गच्छामो विषममिदं न प्रेक्षणीयं युद्धमिति प्रालपत्[6] तावत्साधुलोकैः[7] ॥ ४९ ॥

[५० चाणूरं चलण]—चाणूरं चरणयुगे गृह्णन् कृष्ण एनम् आक्षिपत्[8] तडिति धात्रीपृष्ठे, ज्येष्ठोऽस्य तथा किल मुष्टिकं च दुष्टं दिष्टान्तं समुपगतौ द्वावपि मल्लौ ॥ ५० ॥

[५१ जुज्झंता कदि]—युध्यन्तः कत्यपि हता गदाग्रजेन

---

१ [समभिवट्टते]. २ M पट्ठ. ३ M आस. ४ [समारभन्ते]. ५ M संमहर्तुं. ६ [प्रलपति]. ७ M तावत्से वनः. ८ [क्षिपति].

बिभ्यन्तः कत्यपि पलायिताः खलु मल्लाः, मार्ताण्डे स्फुटतरमुद्गते ग्रहाः अपि प्रमृष्टाः क्व पुनर् ज्योतिरिङ्गणौघाः ॥ ५१ ॥

[५२ बज्झंतु प्पइदि]—बध्येतां प्रकृतिकटू बटू बलाद्दृप्यन्तां प्रसभमिमेऽपि गोपसंघाः, मुच्यमाना जानीत विनाशयिष्यन्ति जिह्माः युष्मानिति प्रालपत्[1] तावद्भोजराजः ॥ ५२ ॥

[५३ बिब्भाणं विसम]—बिभ्राणं विषमधियं स्वभाववक्रं[2] कंसं तं कृष्णभुजङ्गमिव घोरम्, पक्षीन्द्र इव विनतार्तिभञ्जनः स मञ्चाग्रस्थितम् अभिसमपतत्[3] कृष्णः ॥ ५३ ॥

[५४ उट्ठंतो कर]—उत्तिष्ठन् करयुगलात्तखड्गचर्मा यावदेनं प्रहर्तुमारभते[4] कंसः, मञ्चान्मधुमथनो हठेन तावद्भूपृष्ठे पतितममुं क्षणात् अकरोत्[5] ॥ ५४ ॥

[५५ वच्छम्मि प्पवडिअ]—वक्षसि प्रपत्य क्षिप्रमस्तिप्रास्र्ति[6] विस्तीर्णस्तनतटचन्दनार्द्रेऽस्य, कृष्णः सो अकरोत्[7] तथा गृहीतखड्गो भूपः सो अभवत्[8] यथा कथावशेषः ॥ ५५ ॥

[५६ कड्ढंतो गल]—कर्षन् गलपथनिर्यद्रक्तसिक्तं गात्रमस्य गरुडध्वजो गतानुकम्पम्, स्वैरं सोऽलभत[9] तस्मिन्खलु वैरशान्तिं धीराणामपि हि हृदयं धुनाति क्रोधः ॥ ५६ ॥

[५७ सिणिद्ध]—स्निग्धघनकुन्तलस्फुरितमयूरपिञ्छाञ्चिते श्रियः

---

१ [प्रलपति]. २ T °धियान्धभाववक्रं. ३ [अभिसंपतति]. ४ T °मारभत. ५ [करोति]. ६ [क्षिप्रमस्थिवर्त्ति]. ७ [स करोति]. ८ [स भवति]. ९ [स लभते]

पत्युः शिरसि सुरकराञ्चलोन्मुक्ता, भ्रमद्भ्रमरावलीकलकलैर्वाचालिता सुरद्रुकुसुमच्छटा अपतत् तावद्देवालयात्[2] ॥ ५७ ॥

[५८ णच्चंति फ्फुड]—अनृत्यत्[3] स्फुटमप्सरसो नभःपथे स्वैच्छं[4][5] मिथो मत्सरा दिव्या दुन्दुभयो अध्वनन्[6] गभीरं स्वर्गानिलोद्गूर्णाः, पूर्णा भिन्नकटावटनिर्झरदिग्गजसार्थोद्भटप्रस्फूर्जत्प्रमोदबृंहितमहाघोषैर्विश्वंभरा ॥ ५८ ॥

[५९ अह दाव]—अष्ट तावन्नृवरस्य कनिष्ठा निष्ठुरा[7]ट्टहसितातिगरिष्ठाः, दुष्टरुष्टमनसोऽपि प्रविष्टा विष्टरश्रवहता सुरगोष्ठीम् ॥५९॥

[६० इअ सभुअ]—इति स्वभुज[8]संभारस्फारप्रतापमयातपक्षपितविमतान्धकारो वीरो विशुद्धगुणोत्तरः, बुधजनमनोऽम्भोजव्रातं निकामविकस्वरम् अकरोत्[9] कुशलालोको लोके मुकुन्ददिवाकरः ॥६०॥

[इति कंसवधे तृतीयः सर्गः]

[चतुर्थः सर्गः]

[१ तदो अ भोएस]—ततश्च भोजेशभुजप्रतापग्रीष्मोष्मभारेण प्रदह्यमानम्, कृष्णाम्बुवाहः खलु कटाक्षलक्ष्मीधाराभिः असेचयत्[10] जीवलोकम् ॥ १ ॥

[२ धंसं गए]—ध्वंसं गते कंसनृपे जनानां मनांसि अगाहत[11]

---

१ [पतति]. २ M तावदेव देवालयात्. ३ [नृत्यन्ति]. ४ T omits some portion. ५ M स्वेच्छा. ६ [ध्वनन्ति]. ७ M निष्ठुराट्ट. ८ [स्वभुज]. ९ [करोति]. १० [सेचयति]. ११ [गाहते.]

प्रसादलक्ष्मीः, परिच्युते प्रावृड्वारिवाहे सरोजवृन्दानीव हंसराजिः ॥२॥

[३ पवित्त-चारित्त]—पवित्रचारित्रविलोपशङ्काविवर्जिताः कुल-पालिकाः, तदा प्रकाशं प्रासरन्[1] स्वैरं शशिप्रभा इव तमउज्झिताः ॥३॥

[४ जुवाण रामाहि]—यूनां रामाभिरनन्तरायं विहर्तुकामाना-मनन्तरागम्[2], अकरोत्[3] तावत् सरसापि सायं विरामवतीति निशा विषादम् ॥ ४ ॥

[५ विढत्त-रत्त]—विधृतरक्तप्रणया विवक्रा विकसितेन्दीवरप्रभा विटेषु[4], विदग्धनारीणां विलासदृष्टिः अपतत्[5] नो पार्थिवखड्गयष्टिः ॥ ५ ॥

[६ काऊण भोअंधअ]—कृत्वा भोजान्धकचक्रवर्तिनं प्रजानां रक्षितारमुग्रसेनम्, अमोचयत्[6] मातापितरौ ततः स[7] कारागृहात्कमला-सहायः ॥ ६ ॥

[७ सहग्गओ णे]—सहाग्रज एनौ समुपासरन् स्नेहबाष्पाव-च्छादिताक्षिपक्ष्माणौ, चकार दीर्घं कुमारः प्रणामं स्वनाम संगृह्य वृष्णिवीरः ॥ ७ ॥

[८ दिग्घाउणो होह]—दीर्घायुषौ भूयास्तं चिरस्य वत्सौ युवामिति बाष्पस्खलिताक्षराभिः, आशीर्भिः अवर्धयत्[8] देवक्या समं खलु स आनकदुन्दुभिरेनौ[9] ॥ ८ ॥

[९ एक्कस्स सच्छ]—एकस्य स्वच्छ[10]स्फटिकप्रकाशमन्यस्य

---

१ [प्रसरन्ति]. २ T °रायम्. ३ [करोति]. ४ M वितेषु. ५ [पतति]. ६ [मोचयति]. ७ M ततोसौ. ८ [वर्धापयति]. ९ T दुन्दुभिः. १० M स्वच्छं.

भिन्नाञ्जनमञ्जुलाभम्, मर्द्यमानोज्ज्वलवन्यमालं वक्षः समालिङ्गते[1] तयोस्तातः ॥ ९ ॥

[१० **तदो समागच्छिअ**]—ततः समागत्य गान्दिनेयः कृतप्रणामः क्रमशोभितानि, कथानुबद्धानि कुमारयोर्वचांसि समजल्पत्[2] मञ्जुलानि ॥ १० ॥

[११ **अअं खु**]—अयं खलु स यस्य इन्द्रनीलनीलं वक्षःस्थलोद्घूर्णनशीलवन्यमालम्, चतुर्भुजं विग्रहमग्रभागे जातस्य ननु अपश्यतं[3] प्रेक्षणीयम् ॥ ११ ॥

[१२ **घेत्तूणं जं**]—गृहीत्वा यं संस्मररात्रिमध्ये तव तरतस्तरङ्गवती, कूलान्तातिक्रान्तजलापि तावज्जङ्घानां[4] लंघयतु[5] कलिन्दकन्या ॥ १२ ॥

[१३ **तप्पम्मि जं**]—तल्पे यं स्थापयित्वा गोपिकायाः प्रत्यानीता शौरे त्वया सुतास्याः, [6]कार्यानुरोधाद्गुरुत्वं नो जानन्ति मूल्यस्य हि विक्रयेषु ॥ १३ ॥

[१४ **इमो खु सो**]—अयं खलु स एव स्तनप्रदायाः स्तन्येन पीतेनापि पूतनायाः, तृष्णाप्रतीघातमलभमानः प्राणानपि यो दुर्ललितोऽपिबत् ॥ १४ ॥

[१५ **एसो खु सो**]—एष खलु स नन्दगृहेशयेन येन तृणावर्तदैत्यवीरः, कृतोऽभवन्नापि स चक्रवातैः[7] कृतान्तभूमीसरश्चक्रवाकः ॥ १५ ॥

---

१ [समालिङ्गति]. २ [संजल्पति]. ३ [पश्यतं]. ४ T जङ्घेनालङ्घ्यत. ५ [लङ्घया]. ६ M कर्मानु°. ७ T चक्रवाकः

[१६ सत्तूण सव्वं]—शत्रूणां सर्वं मुष्णातु गर्वं कुतः खलु बन्धूनामपि बल्लवानाम्, इति स्तुतोऽयं किल गव्यचोरः प्रहासशीलैः सुरैः सोऽयम् ॥ १६ ॥

[१७ जो च्चेअ माआ]—य एव मायाप्रणिबध्यमानं जनं विमोचयति बन्धनात्, स एव मात्रा[1] महानुभावः उलूखले अबध्यते[2] स खलु एषः ॥ १७ ॥

[१८ भग्गो]—भग्नो नन्वेक एव भार्गवेण पुरार्जुनः शौरे सहस्रबाहुः, अनेन सहस्राधिकदीर्घशाखाबाह्वोर्भग्नं युगमर्जुनयोः ॥१८॥

[१९ पआरअंतं निअ]—प्रचारयन्तं निजगोशतानि पराभवितुं किल संप्रवृत्तः, बकासुर एनं खलु स्वयं प्रणष्टस्तमिस्रासंघ इव सहस्रमयूखम् ॥ १९ ॥

[२० सउस्स रूवेण]—शयो रूपेण स्वयं शयानः प्रवृद्धेन जठरस्थितेन, अघासुरोऽनेन हतो हताशः स गुल्मरोगेणेव कर्मदोषात्[3] ॥ २० ॥

[२१ माआ-बलेण]—मायाबलेनेममर्भकमुद्धमथितुं यः प्राक्रमते[4] स स्वयमेव वञ्चितोऽस्य, मायाम्बुधौ गभीरे पतितो विरिञ्चः प्राप्तः एनमेव शरणं कबलार्धपाणिम् ॥ २१ ॥

[२२ वुंदावणम्मि]—वृन्दावने यमुनापुलिने रम्ये गोवर्धनाद्रिशिखरे च हर्म्याभे, गोपालबालकुललालितक्रीडितानि अनेन बहूनि दिवसानि खल्वतिक्रान्तानि ॥ २२ ॥

---

१ M मात्रा. २ [बध्यते]. ३ [दोषः]. ४ [प्रक्रमते]

[**२३ णेणं धेणुअ**]—अनेन धेनुकगर्दभप्रभृतेर्वर्गस्य दुर्गर्वशीलं चेत एव बलेन तालविपिनव्याजेन धूतं बलात्, पीतो निर्भरतत्फलाम्बुच्छलतो लोकानां शोकागमः शत्रुप्राणमिषात्खलु साधु पृथिवीभारः समुद्धृतः ॥ २३ ॥

[**२४ परिरक्खिउमंग**]—परिरक्षितुमङ्ग धेनुकं त्वं प्रचरन् विहंसि धेनुकं किम्, कथं विश्वसिमस्त्वामिति रामं प्रहसन् किल व्याहरत्[1] कृष्णः ॥ २४ ॥

[**२५ कालिआहि**]—कालियाहिविषधूमलताभिः कालिकाभिर्गगनमिव करालम्, यामुनाम्बु व्यरचयत्[2] विशुद्धं जातु नन्दतनयः शरदिव[3] ॥ २५ ॥

[**२६ पाढत्तो फणिराअ**]—प्रारब्धः फणिराजपर्वतफणाशृङ्गेषु पादौ समं शीघ्रं निक्षिप्य नर्तितुमयं प्रत्यूषसूर्योपमः, आताम्रातपशोभपीतवसनः सानन्दवृन्दारकश्रेणीनेत्रसरोजरोचनगुणोद्दामः खलु दामोदरः ॥ २६ ॥

[**२७ झणज्झणिअ**]—झणज्झणितनूपुरं चरणपल्लवानोदनानमत्फणिमस्तकं क्रमप्रशिथिलकाञ्चीलतम्, चलच्छिखिपिच्छिकावलयरम्यधम्मिल्लभ्रमद्भ्रमरच्छटम् अनटत्[4] बालगोपालः ॥ २७ ॥

[**२८ गलुलाहि से**]—गरुडादस्मै गलितगर्वशालिने[5] अभयं पुनर् अदिशत्[6] एष भोगिने[7], रुष्टा विषं यद्यपि साधवो जना अमृतं खलु ते तथापि नाम तुष्टाः ॥ २८ ॥

---

१ [व्याहरति]. २ [विरचयति]. ३ T शरदीव. ४ [नटति]. ५ M गव्यशालिने, T शालिनो. ६ [दिशति]. ७ T भोगिनः.

[२९ णाअ-जोव्वअ]—नागयौवतसमर्पितैस्ततो नागहारमिकरैर्भूषितः, एष भाति[1] हरिनीलश्यामलः तारकैरिव शुभो नभःपथः ॥२९॥

[३० सुप्पंतेसुं गोव]—स्वपत्सु गोपगोवृन्देषु दीप्यमानस्ततो निष्पतन् दवाग्निः, सद्योऽनेन अपीयेत[2] विद्युदाभः सर्वापायो भवति लोकोत्तराणाम् ॥ ३० ॥

[३१ गोवाअंतो गोउलं]—गोपायन् गोकुलं कामपालः गोपायमानं कंसभृत्यं दैत्यम्[3], आकांक्षन्तं विप्रलम्भं प्रलम्बं रुष्टो दुष्टं मुष्टया पिष्टवान् ॥ ३१ ॥

[३२ जउणा-सलिले]—यमुनासलिले कदापि या युवतयः किल क्रीडनम् अकुर्वन्[4], हृदयानीव निर्मलानि तासां वसनानि अमुष्णात्[5] वासुदेवः ॥ ३२ ॥

[३३ रण्णे जण्णे]—अरण्ये यज्ञे कुहचिन्माहिते भोजनं याचितैः भूदेवैः किल प्रतिनिराख्यातो दीक्षितैः, भक्ताभ्यः सरसमधुरं सादरं चापि तेषां भार्याभ्यो अलभत[6] तदयं मुक्तिमाभ्यश्च अदात्[7] ॥ ३३ ॥

[३४ एसो खु णंद-पहुदिस्स]—एष खलु नन्दप्रभृतेः पुरन्दरात् भक्तिं निवृत्त्य अकरोत्[8] गिरीन्द्राभिमुखम्, आकृष्य दिवसः कुमुदाकरात् भृङ्गस्य दृष्टिमिव पङ्कजवाटाभिमुखम् ॥ ३४ ॥

[३५ सज्जो गज्जंत]—सद्यो गर्जद्विद्युदुज्ज्वलजलदघटागर्भप्राग्भारस्थूलप्रभ्रष्टां स्पष्टविष्टम्भितभुवनतलां वृष्टिमभ्यापतन्तीम्, गोपाल

---

१ T एषोऽभात्. २ [पीयते]. ३ T भृत्यदैत्यः. ४ [कुर्वन्ति]. ५ [मुष्णाति] ६ [लभते]. ७ [ददाति]. ८ [करोति]. ९ M प्रभ्रष्टस्पष्ट.

एष गोवर्धनमचलवरं तत्क्षणमुत्खनन् छत्रं कृत्वा गृहीत्वा च करकमले डिम्भको अरौत्सीत्[1] एनाम् ॥ ३५ ॥

[३६ णिव्वाण-गव्व]—निर्वाणगर्वशिखिपर्वतवैरिजुष्टं तुष्टं स्वयं स्नुतपयोधरनिःसृतैः, एनं पयोभिः सुरभिरभिषिञ्चन्ती गोविन्द-नाम्ने[2] सुश्लिष्टतरम् अकरोत्[3] ॥ ३६ ॥

[३७ अह खु णं]—अथ खल्वेनमेव काञ्चनकुम्भीविगलितैः किलाभ्रमुवल्लभः, सुरनदीसलिलैः न्यषिञ्चत्[4] प्रमोदशीलो मुदिर इव शारदः ॥ ३७ ॥

[३८ जाउ दाव जउणा]—जातु तावद्यमुनाजलमग्नं वारुणेण हृतं पुरुषेण, अच्युतो बत प्रचेतोनिकेतात् प्रत्युपाहरत्[5] नन्दम-मन्दम् ॥ ३८ ॥

[३९ जोण्हा-विच्छड्ड]—ज्योत्स्नाविच्छर्दप्रत्युन्मृष्टशशिमणि-सान्द्रनिष्यन्दशीते वृन्दारण्ये कलिन्दप्रियदुहितृमहातीर्थरोधःस्थलीषु, वेलाशैलानिलालोलितसरसरसालाग्रलग्नालिवर्गे काले सति वसन्ते अक-रोत्[6] घनमयं केशवो रासक्रीडाम् ॥ ३९ ॥

[४० उवट्ठिअ-तरट्टिआ]—उपस्थितविदग्धस्त्र्यावलिश्लिष्टगोष्ठी-गतः प्रपञ्चितविपञ्चिकामुरलिशृङ्गशृङ्गारितम्, विडम्बितविटक्रमं विमल-मञ्जुसंजल्पितं तरङ्गितसुराङ्गनम् अकरोत्[7] बालकः खेलनम् ॥ ४० ॥

[४१ रास-कीलासु]—रासक्रीडासु व्रीडाविकलव्रजवधूनेत्रेन्दी-

१ [रुणद्धि]. २ [गोपेन्द्र]. ३ [करोति]. ४ [निषिञ्चते]. ५ [प्रत्युपाहरति]. ६ [करोति]. ७ [करोति].

वरमालाप्रालम्बालंकृताङ्गो मृदुहसितसुधासिक्तवक्त्रेन्दुबिम्बः, संगायन्नटन् सरसतरमयं संचरञ्छयानः सर्वासु दिक्षु अदृश्यत सकलजनानन्दनो नन्दनस्ते ॥ ४१ ॥

[४२ सोहग्ग-गव्विर]—सौभाग्यगर्वशीलमनसां नीतम्बिनीनां प्राप्तस्तथा बहुतनुरपि परोक्षभावम्, एष तमःप्रकृतीनां न दर्शनीयः सूर्य इव विस्तृतप्रभोऽपि विभावरीणाम् ॥ ४२ ॥

[४३ विरदे मदे]—विरते मदे विरहिणीनां तासां ततः प्राकटयत्[2] विग्रहमयं कुमारः, प्रशमं गते शिशिरे तत्क्षणं कुसुमं प्रकाशयति हि चूतपादपः ॥ ४३ ॥

[४४ संखोही संखऊडो]—संक्षोभी शङ्खचूडोऽपि स वृषभतनुः किं चारिष्टो गरिष्ठः विष्टो रुष्टेन केश्यपि च तुरगवपुर्ध्वंसितः केशवेन, वामारम्भी स व्योमोऽपि खलु परित्रुटितः शौरे वैरिद्रुमाणां दावाग्निर्नन्दनस्ते किमिह हि बहुना सांप्रतं जल्पितेन ॥ ४४ ॥

[४५ आणाइओ धणुह]—आनायितो धनुर्यज्ञच्छलेनैष कंसेन तेन ध्रुवमात्मनिबर्हणार्थम्, शाखाग्रसंघर्षसंघटितो हि वह्निः शून्यीकरोति तरसैव हि किं न[3] वृक्षम् ॥ ४५ ॥

[४६ अक्कूराणण-सिप्पि]—अक्रूराननशुक्तिगर्भगलितां तां सूक्तिमुक्तावलीं गृहीत्वा अकुरुतां[4] हन्त पितरौ कर्णयोस्तौ मण्डनम्, अत्यारूढहार्दरावनताशिरोन्यञ्चात्पिञ्छाञ्चलं गाढं किं च पर्यस्वजेतां[5] बहुशो मायाग्रजं साग्रजम् ॥ ४६ ॥

---

१ [दृश्यते]. २ [प्रकट्यति]. ३ T कि नु . ४ [कुरुतः]. ५ [परिश्वजेते]

[**४७ पालेआअल-मोलि**]—प्रालेयाचलमौलिघूर्णनशीलमहाकल्लोलहल्लोहलस्फारोड्डामरचारुचारणधुनीस्वच्छाभिर्वत्सौ चिरम्, युवां जीवतं पूर्णिमामृतमयूखोन्निद्रज्योत्स्नाझरीपाण्डित्यच्छिदुरच्छविभिर्महितौ कीर्तिभिर्धात्रीतले ॥ ४७ ॥

[**४८ इअ मुदिअ-मणाणं**]—इति मुदितमनसोस्तयोराशीर्भिस्तात्रच्छरत्समयश्रीभिश्चन्द्रसूर्याविव शूरौ, समधिकमभिरामां रामकृष्णौ प्रसन्नौ सकलजनमनोज्ञां लम्भितौ कामपि लक्ष्मीम् ॥ ४८ ॥

[इति रामपाणिवादकृते कंसवधे चतुर्थः सर्गः]

[[**दुव्वाह-पाअड**]—दुर्वाहप्राकृतपयोनिलये गभीरे बालानां वाहितुमिदं खलु जानीत रोधः, नव्यं हि काव्यमिह कंसवधाभिधानं सर्वेऽपि भव्यमतयः परिशीलयत ॥ ४८*१ ॥][1]

[श्रीगुरुपादयोर्नमः । शुभमस्तु]

[समाप्तमिदं काव्यम्]

---

१ Wanting in MT.

सिलोअसूई

सद्दकोसो

This Glossary is a select collection of words that would be useful to a student of Prākrit vocabulary. Pronouns, pronomina forms, proper names and nouns & roots which have retained their Sanskrit forms are usually ignored. Important roots, primitive and causal, are indexed; but their detailed forms are not given. Some interesting and peculiar forms are noted without giving the meaning. Some unusual and difficult words are included. Only one occurrence, usually the first, is noted.

अअंति, ३·२६, see Notes.

अइ = अयि, २·३४.

अक्खद (अक्षत) १·१२, safe, unwounded.

अक्खर (अक्षर) १·३५, letters, words.

अक्खिव–आक्षिप् (धा.) २·३६, to insult.

अग्ग (अग्र) १·४६, tip, top.

अग्गअ (अग्रज) १·३, elder brother.

अग्गअम्म (अग्रजन्मन्) ३·३०, elder brother.

अग्गओ (अग्रतः) १·३, in front.

अग्गदो (अग्रतः) १·५, in front.

अग्गि (अग्नि) १·२९, fire.

अग्गसर (अग्रसर) १·३२, one who moves ahead.

अच्छरा (अप्सरस्) २·४२, a heavenly nymph.

अच्छेर (आश्चर्य) १·१०, surprise, wonder.

अज्ज (अद्य) १·१७, today.

अज्जुण (अर्जुन) ४·१८, see the Notes.

अट्टहासिअ (–हसित) ३·५९, loud laughter.

–अण (जन) १·५१, also **जण**.

अणंतराअं (अनन्तरायम्, –रागम्) ४·४, see Notes.

अणामअ (अनामय) १·९, health, well-being.

अणुवज्ज–passive base of अनुवद्. १·४६.

अणुसप्पिर (अनुसर्पणशील), २·१२.

अणुसंग (अनुषङ्ग) २·५५, necessary consequence.

अण्णत्तो = अन्यतः, ३·२९, see Notes.

अण्णहा (अन्यथा) २·२२, otherwise.

अण्णाअं (अज्ञातम्) ३·८, unknowingly.

अतुच्छअ (अतुच्छ-क) १·२५, not insignificant, great.

अत्त (आत्मन्) ४·४५.

अत्ति (आर्ति) ३·५३, suffering.

अत्थि (अस्थि) ३·५५, bone.

अदि (अति) २·२०.

अदिहि (अतिथि) २·५०,a guest.

अप्पा (आत्मन्) १·५, self, one self.

अप्फाल (आस्फाल) ३·४७, striking.

अब्भअ (अर्भक) ४·२१, child.

अब्भमु (अभ्रमु) ४·३७, see the Notes.

अब्भहिअ(अभ्यधिक) २·९, more.

अब्भावड–अभ्यापत् (धा.)४·३५.

अभणिज्ज (अभाणितव्य) २·५.

अमअ (अमृत) १·१७, nectar; –मोह (–मयूख), १·१७, the moon.

अम्मक (अस्मादृश ?) १·३७, see Notes.

अम्मेलाव–आम्रेडय् (धा.) ३·१८, to repeat.

अलल्लअ २·५६, see Notes.

अल्लिअ ३·१६,see Notes.

अवच्च(अपत्य)१·१२,issue, son.

अवड (अवट) २·५२, a fountain.

अवदाअ (अवदात) २·९, pure.

अवस (अवश) २·२३, unsupported, helpless.

अवस्सं (अवश्यम्) १·४०, necessarily.

अवसेस (अवशेष) ३·५५, remnant.

अविहा (अविधा) १·३७, see the Notes.

असंभमं (असंभ्रमम्) १·५, without confusion.

अस्सु (अश्रु) १·३५, tears.

अहके = अहं, २·६, see Notes.

अहर (अधर) १·५२, lower lip, also १·५४.

अहरोट्ठ (अधरोष्ठ) ३·११,lower lip.

अहिक्खा (अभिख्या) १·६१, beauty, glory.

अहिणाह (अधिनाथ) १·२२, the supreme master.

अहिप्फुसिअ (अभिमृष्ट) २·१७, anointed.

अहिव (अधिप) १·२४, the ruler, king.

अहिलास (अभिलाष) २·२६, longing.

अहिसारिआ (अभिसारिका) २·४४, see Notes.

अहीर (अधीर) १·५६, nervous.

अहुणा (अधुना) २·२२, now.

अंकण (अङ्कन) ३·१९, a mark.

अंकणत्थली (–स्थली) २·३८, open space of the yard.

अंग, ४·१४, see Notes.

अंगअ (अङ्गज) १·४४, love, passion.

अंगणा (अङ्गना) १·३, woman.

अंगहार २·५४, a gesticulation.

अंकिद (अङ्कित) १·४, marked, imprinted with.

अंचल १·५७, skirt, border.

अंतरा १·७, in the middle.

अंतेउर (अन्तःपुर) २·१५, harem.

–अंद (–चन्द्र) १·३६, moon.

अंधार (अन्धकार) ३·१५, darkness.

अंबुही (अम्बुधि) १·८, ocean.

अंभोअव्वाअ (अम्भोजव्रात) ३·६०, a multitude of lotuses.

आ

आअम (आगम) १·१४, coming, arrival.

आअर (आदर) १·२५ regard, respect.

आअल्लअ (D. आयल्लक ?) २·२०, longing, uneasiness.

आअव (आतप) १·४७, heat.

आअंब (आताम्र) ३·१७, reddish.

आइण्ण (आकीर्ण) १·४३, covered.

आकइ (आकृति) १·४३, figure, shape.

आणाइअ (आनायित) ४·४५, brought, invited.

आमेल (आपीड), ३·२८, see notes.

आमोअ (आमोद), २·५१, fragrance.

आरह–आरभ् (धा.), ३·५४, to begin.

आलव–आलप् (धा.), १·३३, to talk.

आलिद्ध (आश्लिष्ट), १·४४, see notes.

आली, ३·१०, a line, row.

आलोअ (आलोक) ३·६०, splendour.

आविज्झ (आविद्ध) ३·१४, pierced.

आवुण–आवृ (धा.) १·४७.

आसव २·५०, flowery juice.

आसाअ (आस्वाद) १·४७, taste.

आसि=आसीत् ३·४७.

आसी (आशिस्), ४·८, a blessing.

आह (आभ) ४·९, like, resembling.

आहीर (आभीर) १·५६, see Notes.

इ

इअप्पलाव (इतिप्रलाप) १·५५.

इआवित्थ २·३५, see the Notes on २·३५ and १·२८.

इक्ख–ईक्ष् (धा) १·२४, to see, to attend.

इक्खण (ईक्षण) १·५, look, eye.

इत्थिआ (स्त्री) २·१४, a woman.

इदर (इतर), ३·५, other.

इह (इभ) ३·४०, an elephant.

-इंध (चिह्न) २·५४, a sign, signal, see Notes.

ई

ईरिअ (ईरित) १·२५, uttered, pronounced.

ईसर (ईश्वर) ३·२७, lord.

उ

उअर (उदर) १·४७, hollow, stomach.

उक्खद १·३५, see the Notes.

उक्खा–उत्खन् (धा.) ३·३४.

उग्गअम्म (उग्रकर्मन्) ३·३०, one of fierce acts.

उग्गज्जिअ (उद्गर्जित) १·४९, thunder.

उग्गूरिअ (उद्घूर्ण) ३·५८, excited.

उग्घोसिर (उद्घोषणशील) २·५३.

उच्छइअ (अवच्छादित) ४·७, covered.

उज्जल (उज्ज्वल) १·१७, bright, shining.

उज्झिहाण=उजिहान, ३·२०, see Notes.

उज्जुई (ऋज्वी) २·१८, straight.

उट्ठंत=उत्तिष्ठत्, ३·५४.

उड्डामर ४·४७, excellent.

उदअ (उदक) २·५०, water.

उद्दाम ३·४८, wild.

उप्पल (उत्पल) ३·१३, a lotus.

उप्फुसिअ (उन्मृष्ट) २·२९.

उब्भड (उद्भट) २·५२, furious.

उब्भडस्सम (उद्भटश्रम) १·१६, excessive or hard labour.

उम्मिल्लाव–उन्मीलय्, ३·१३, to open.

उम्मुह (उन्मुख) १·२८, looking up or at, following.

उम्मेस (उन्मेष) ३·२१, blooming.

उम्ह (ऊष्मन्) १·४७, heat.

उम्हल (उष्मल) १·६०, hot.

उम्हाणं=ऊष्माणं, ३·१४.

उर (उरस्) ३·१७, chest.

उरोअ (उरोज) २·२७, breast.

उलूहल (उलूखल) ४·१७, mortar.

उल्ल (आर्द्र) १·४४, wet, moist, see Notes.

उल्लास ३·६, flash.

उव (meaning पश्य) २·४०.

उवल (उपल) २·४३, stone.

उव्वंत (उद्वान्त) ३·३१, overflowing.

उव्वरा (उर्वरा) ३·२८, see Notes.

उवासर–उपसर् (धा.) २·६०, to approach.

उस (उषस्) १·५८, morning.

उस्सिट्ठ (उत्सृष्ट) २·५९, discharged.

ऊ

ऊसव (उत्सव) १·१८, festivity.

ए

एइ=एति २·१९.

एक्क (एक) १·१७, one, unique.

एक्कदा (एकदा) १·३, once.

एक्कवारं (एकवारम्) २·६, once.

एण्हिं (इदानीम्) ३·६, now.

एत्थ (अत्र) २·५१, here.

एव्वं=एवं ३·२१.

एरिस (ईदृश) १·२६, such, similar.

ओ

ओज्झर (D. निर्झर), २·५२, a stream; see Notes.

ओणअ (अवनत) ४·४६, bent.

ओलंब–अवलम्ब् (धा.) २·४२, to assume.

ओल्लिर (आर्द्रशील) २·५९.

ओवाहिअ (अपवाहित) २·४०, driven away.

ओसर (अवसर) २·२७, leisure.

ओह (ओघ) २·४२, a stream, a party.

क

कअं (कृतम्) १·१४, enough.

कअंत (कृतान्त) १·३९, the god of death.

कइढव=कैटभ ३·४२, see Notes.

कज्ज (कार्य) १·१९, work, mission, duty.

कट्ठं (कष्टम्) ३·४९, alas.

कड (कट) २·५२, the temples of an elephant.

कडक्ख (कटाक्ष) १·४८, side-glance.

कडप्प (D. समूह) २·४६, cluster, mass.

कड्ढ-कृष् (धा.) १·३८, to drag.

कणिट्ठ (कनिष्ठ) ३·५९, younger brother.

कणीणिआ (कनीनिका) ३·१०, eye pupil.

कण्ण (कर्ण) १·३५, ear.

कण्ह (कृष्ण) १·५२.

कण्हभोई (कृष्णभोगिन्) २·३, a black snake.

कण्हिमाण (कृष्णिमन्) ३·४, blackness.

कत्तअ (कर्तृक) १·२६.

कदि=कति, ३·५१.

कप्प (कल्प) २·२४, similar.

कमणी (कमनीय) २·१९, pleasant.

कमलाअर (कमलाकर) ३·१३, a lotus-pool.

करग्ग (कराग्र) १·३३, finger.

करंबिअ(करम्बित) ३·३२, inlaid.

करंबुअ (कर+अम्बुज) १·८, lotus like hand.

कलअल (कलकल) ३·५७, murmer.

कलअंठ (कलकण्ठ) २·५५, a cuckoo.

कला (कलिका) २·१७, a bud.

कलाव (कलाप) २·४९, a band.

कल्ल (कल्य) ३·३, dawn, morning.

कल्लाणं (कल्याणम्) ३·३, Hail, welfare.

कवलद्धपाणि ४·२१, see Notes.

कवित्थ (कुतर्क ?) १·२८, २·३५, see the Notes.

कवोल (कपोल) १·५२, cheek.

कसणगिरि (कृष्णगिरि) १·६२, see Notes.

कसणाअल (कृष्णाचल) २·२४, dark mountain.

कह=कथम्, ३·४४.

कस्सावि (काश्यपि) १·६१, see Notes.

कंची (काञ्ची) ४·२७, girdle.

कंति (कान्ति) १·४२, radiance.

कंदोट्ट (D. कन्दोत्थ) १·४१, a blue lotus; see Notes.

का-कृ (धा.) १·२९, to do.

काराघर (कारागृह) ४·६, a prison house.

कारिअ (कार्य), १·४८, duty, function.

कालण (कारण) १·१४, reason.

कालिआ (कालिका) ४·२५, a dark cloud.

किणो [प्रश्ने] १.१४, a particle of interrogation.

किर=किल, ३·४४.

किंणर २·५८, see the Notes.

किंदु=किंतु २·२६, see Notes.

कीलण (क्रीडन) १·४५, sport, play.

कीला (क्रीडा) २·५९, sport.

कीलिअ (क्रीडित) २·२९, sport.

कुअ (कुच) ३·१२, breast.

कुअ–कुच् (धा.) २·३७, to contract.

कुअंडस (कोदण्ड-क) १·५७, bow.

कुज्झ–क्रुध् (धा.) ३·२८.

कुट्टिम २·४३, pavement.

कुडिलच्छि (कुटिलाक्षि) २·१३, having crooked glances.

कुण–कृ (धा.) १·३८, to do.

कुणाइ=करोति, २·२२.

कुदुउल्ली (कुतुकवती) २·४९.

कुप्प कुप् (धा.) ३·४६.

कुमर (कुमार) २·२, a boy, prince.

कुमाल (कुमार) ३·२९, a boy, prince.

कुमुइणी (कुमुदिनी) १·६४, a night-lotus.

कुलवालिआ (–पालिआ) ४· ३, highborn girl.

कुलिस (कुलिश) ३·२८, a thunderbolt.

कुविद (कुपित) २·२, angry.

कुहइ=कुहचित् ३·६.

कुहणा(कुहना)३·२५, treachery.

कुंठेअर (कुण्ठेतर) २·५९, impetuous.

कुंडलीकअ (कुण्डलीकृत) ३·३२, formed into a circle.

कुंतल ३·५६, lock of hair.

कुंभि (कुम्भिन्) ३·२७, an elephant.

कूर (क्रूर) १·४०, cruel.

केउ (केतु) १·३५, banner, flag.

केच्चिरं=कियच्चिरम् ३·३६.

केरव (कैरव) १·१०, a kind of lily.

केरविणी (कैरविणी) २·२८, a water lily.

कोइल (कोकिल)१·१३, cuckoo.

कोच्चण (कचन)२·५२, ५५, ५७, somewhere.

कोउहल्ल (कौतूहल्व) २·३१, curiosity.

कोच्चि=कचित्, २·५४, ३·१६, see Notes.

कोडर (कोटर) ३·३९, hollow.

कोडि (कोटि) २·८, point.

कोडुअ (D. कुड्य ?), १·५, something curious or wonderful, see Notes.

कोदुअ (कौतुक) १·२४, curiosity.

कोमुई (कौमुदी) २·१९, moonlight.

कोह (क्रोध) ३·५६, anger.

कोत्थुह (कौस्तुभ) १·३६, see the Notes.

क्खअ (क्षय) १·२९, ruin, destruction.

-क्खल-स्खल् (धा.) १·८, stumble, to clash against.

-क्खुह-क्षुभ् (धा.) १·४४, to rouse, to distutb.

ख

खअ (क्षय) ३·६, destruction.

खण (क्षण) १·५, moment.

खम (क्षम) २·२७, able.

खलण (स्खलन) २·४०, stumbling.

खंभ (स्तम्भ or स्कम्भ) १·७, a pillar, post.

खिप्पं (क्षिप्रम्) ३·५५, suddenly.

खु (खलु) १·२, indeed, in fact.

खुज्जिआ (कुब्जा) २·१८, a humpbacked lady.

खुड-त्रुट् (धा.) २·३४, to break.

खुडिअ (त्रुटित) ३·१९, broken.

खुद्द (क्षुद्र) ३·१४, mean.

खेलण (क्ष्वेलन) ४·४०, sport.

ग

गअ (गज) १·५१, elephant.

गअण (गगन) २·४५, sky.

गइ (गति) ३·४, gait.

गण्ह-ग्रह् (धा.) १·२, to take, to receive.

गत्त (गात्र) २·१४, body, limbs.

गद्दह (गर्दभ) ४·२३, see Notes.

गमइ=गमयति ३·३६.

गव्व (गर्व, गव्य) ४·१६, see Notes.

गस-ग्रस् (धा.) १·२९, to catch.

गहिर (गभीर) २·५४, deep.

गंधव्व (गन्धर्व) २·५८, Gandharva, or a songster.

गरिट्ठ (गरिष्ठ) ३·५९, prominent.

गरुअत्तण=गुरुत्व, ४·१३.

गलुल (गरुड) ३·५६, an eagle.

गवक्ख (गवाक्ष) २·४९, a window.

गिम्ह (ग्रीष्म) १·४७, summer.

गुम्मरोअ (गुल्मरोग) ४·२०, a disease of spleen-enlargement.

गोउर (गोपुर) २·४७, gate.
गोरव (गौरव) १·१९, greatness, importance.
गोव (गोप) १·१, cowherd.
गोवद्धण (गोवर्धन) १·४९, name of a mountain; see the Notes.
गोवायंत=गोपायत्, ४·३१
गोविआ (गोपिका) १·३५, a cowherd lady.

घ

घडा (घटा) ४·३५, a collection.
घर (गृह) १·९, a house.
घरेसअ (गृहेशय) ४·१५ see Notes.
घिणा (घृणा), १·३७, compassion, pity.
घुसिण (घुसृण) २·१३, saffron.
घेत्तूण=गृहीत्वा, ४·१२.
घेप्पंत=गृह्यमाण, ३·४७.
घोल—घूर्ण (धा.) ३·३८.
घोलिर (घूर्णनशील) १·५२, rolling, dangling.

च

चअत्थि—चकास्ति, १·२३, see the Notes.
चक्कवट्टि (चक्रवर्तिन्) ४·६, an emperor.
चक्कवाअ, ४·१५, see Notes.
चक्काअ (चक्रवाक) ३·९, the Cakravāka bird.
चम्म (चर्मन) ३·५४, a shield.
चरमाअल (-चल) २·६०, western mountain.
चलण (चरण) १·२, foot.
चवल (चपल) २·५, unsteady.
चवेडिआ (चपेटिका) ३·३२, a slap.
चंकमिर (चंक्रम(ण)शील) १·३, in the habit of strolling, see the Notes.
चंग (D. सौन्दर्य) १·४३, beauty.
चंचलीअ (चञ्चरीक) ३·३, a bee.
चंदम (चन्द्रमस्) १·५८, moon.
चंदमुही (चन्द्रमुखी) २·४८, a moon-faced lady.
चंदलेहा (चन्द्रलेखा) २·१९, crescent of the moon.
चंदिमा (चान्द्रिका) १·४२, moonlight.
चादईउल (चातकीकुल) १·६०, a flock of cātakī birds.
चाव (चाप) २·३८, a bow.
चावमह (चापमख)१·२७, bow festival.
चारण, २·५८, a bard.
चारित्त (चारित्र) ४·३, conduct.
चिण्ह (चिह्न) ३·४, mark.

चिबुअ (चिबुक) २·१८, chin.

चूद (चूत) ४·४३, the mango tree.

चेट्ठिअ (चेष्टित) १·५४, activity, behaviour.

च्चिअ (एव) १·११.

च्चेअ (एव, च एव) १·११.

छ

छइ (छवि) ३·२४, lustre.

छडा (छटा) ३·९, series.

छत्त (छत्र) ३·२७, an umbrella.

छप्पअ (षट्पद) १·४६, bee.

छिउर (छिदुर) ४·४७, extinguishing.

छिव—स्पृश् (धा.) १·३०, to touch.

छुर ३·१९, to cover see Notes.

ज

जअ (जगत्) १·१३, world.

जइच्छा (यदृच्छा) १·४९, chance

जउणा (यमुना) १·६३.

जउणाड (यमुनातट) १·४५, bank of Yamunā.

जच्चमाण=याच्यमान, २·४.

जढर (जठर) ४·२०, stomach.

जण्ण (यज्ञ) १·२४, a sacrifice, a festival.

जण्हवी (जाह्नवी) २·४३, Ganges.

जम (यम) १·१६, one of the means of attaining Yoga, restraint etc.; see the Notes.

जम्म (जन्मन्) ३·३८, birth.

जम्म (जाल्म) २·५, a wretch.

जर (ज्वर) २·२३, fever.

जव १·३३, speed.

जवा (जपा) ३·२३, Japā flower.

जहिट्ठ (यथेष्ट) १·१५, as desired, desirable, agreeable.

जहिं (यत्र, यस्मिन्) १·४६.

जंत (यन्त्र) २·५३, a waterjet.

जंप—जल्प् (धा.) १·७, to speak.

जाइद (याचित) २·२, begged.

जाउ (जातु) ४·२५, once.

जाउण (यामुन) ४·२५, of the river Yamunā.

जामिणी (यामिनी) १·३४, night.

जाल (ज्वाला) १·३१, flame.

जाला ३·३३, see Notes.

जाहे=यावत् or यदा, २·७.

जिअ (जित) १·१७, conquered.

जिणा=येन, ४·१५.

जिण्णंति=जयन्ति, २·५८.

जिम्ह (जिह्म) ३·५२, deceitful, crooked, curved.

जिंभ–जृम्भ (धा.) २·१४.

जुअ (युग) २·३३, a pair.

जुउच्छ—जुगुप्स् (धा.) १·१३, to detest.

जुग्ग (युग्म) १·१२, a pair.

जुज्झ (युद्ध) ३·१, fight.

जुट्ठ (जुष्ट) ४·३६, resorted to.

जुवई (युवति) १·३८, young girl, maiden.

जुवाण=यूनाम्, ४·४,

जुवाणा=युवानः, २·४८,

जेउं=जेतुम्, ३·४०,

जेट्ठ (ज्येष्ठ) ३·५०, elder brother.

जोअब्भसण (योगाभ्यसन) १·१८, exercise in mental concentration.

जोइरिंगिण (ज्योतिरिङ्गण) ३·५१, firefly, see Notes.

जोण्हा (ज्योत्स्ना) २·२९, moonlight.

जोव्वअ (यौवत) ४·२९, a number of girls.

जोह (योध) ३·४०, a fighter.

झ

झत्ति (झटिति) १·३७, suddenly.

झाण (ध्यान) १·५, thought, meditation.

झीण (क्षीण) ३·९, exhausted.

ठ

ठाण स्थान) २·५८, an abode.

ठाविअ=स्थापयित्वा, ४·१२.

ठिअ (स्थित) १·७, standing.

ड

डज्झ–passive base of **दह्** (धा.) १·२९, to burn.

डज्झइ=दह्यते, २-२२.

डसण (दशन) ३·३३, a tusk.

डंड (दण्ड) ३·२८, staff.

डिंभअ (डिम्भ-क) २·३, a child, boy.

ण

णक्ख (नख) २·८, nail.

णच्च–नृत् (धा.) २·५३, to dance.

णच्चण (नर्तन) २·५५, dancing.

णडण (नटन) २·५९, dancing.

णरसिंघ (नरसिंह) २·३५, Man-lion.

णलिणी (नलिनी) २·२६, lotus plant.

णवरि (अनन्तरम्) ३·४०

णह (नभस्) १·३०, sky.

णहप्पह (नभःपथ) १·४४, sky.

णहप्पहा (नखप्रभा) १·४४, lustre of the nails.

णहोवह (नभःपथ) ४·२९, sky.

णंचंत=न्यञ्चत् ४·४६.

णाअ (नाग) ४·२९, a serpent.

णिअ–दृश् (धा.) २·१, to see.

णिअ (निज) १·९, one's own.

णिअमंत (निगमान्त) १·१६, Vedānta, निगम meaning vedic texts.

णिअर (णिकर) २·९, collection.

णिअल (निगल) २·२०, fetter.

णिअंतणा (नियन्त्रणा) १·१२, shutting up, closure.

णिअंबिणी (नितम्बिनी) १·४५, a beautiful woman.

णिआमं (निकामम्) ३·६०, excessively.

णिउल (निचुल) १·४५, a kind of creeper.

णिउज्झ (नियुद्ध) ३·४३, fight.

णिएद (निकेत) २·१५, an abode.

णिक्कम–निष्क्रम् (धा.) २·३८, to go out.

णिक्खुड (निष्कुट) २·५०, a pleasure-grove.

णिच्च (नित्य) २·५२, ever, constant.

णिज्जए=नीयते, २·२२.

णिज्जर (निर्जर) २·४१, a god.

णिज्झर (निर्झर) ३·३१, stream.

णिट्ठुर (निष्ठुर) ३·४६, hard.

णिद्दअ (निर्दय) १·४५, pitiless, unkind.

णिद्दाण (निद्राण) ३·१६, asleep.

णिबंहण (निबर्हण) ४·४५, destruction.

णिब्भंर (निर्भर) ४·२३, excessive.

णिम्मल (निर्मल) ४·३२, clear.

णिमीलिअ (निमीलित) १·५, closed.

णिरत्थ (निरस्त) १·१६, thrown off, set a side.

णिराचक्खिअ=निराख्यात, ४·३३.

णिरिक्खण (निरीक्षण), १·१८, seeing, observing.

णिरूसहं (निरुत्साहम् ?) १·७, without any movement, see the Notes.

णिलुअ (निर्लून) १·४६, plucked, cut.

णिवट्ट–निवर्त् (धा.) १·२७, to turn back.

णिवत्तिअ=निवृत्य, ४·३४.

णिवर (नृवर) २·१५, a king.

णिव्वाण (निर्वाण) ४·३६, extinguished.

णिसिज्झ–passive base of निषिध् (धा.) १·१८.

णिसेह (निषेध) १·२६, denouncing.

णिस्सण (निस्वन) १·६, sound, noise.

णिहिल (निखिल) ३·४१, all, whole.

णिहुअ (निभृत) ३·४ stealthy.

णिहेल (D. नील) २·५१, sapphire; see Notes.

णितं=निर्यत्, १·४७, २·२६, see Notes.

णितीणं=निर्यन्तीनां, ३·१७.

णिण्हुअ (निह्नुत) २·४४, obscured.

णीसंद (निष्यन्द) ४·३९, trickling.

णेउर (नूपुर) ४·२७, an anklet.

णेत्त (नेत्र) १·५७, eye.

णोल्लिअ (नुन्न) १·२, urged, see the Notes.

ण्हुअ (स्नुत) ४·३६, oozing.

त

तआणि (तदानीं) ३·३६, then.

तइ=तदा, २·६०.

तइ=त्वया, २·२५.

तड (तट) १·४६, bank.

तण्हा (तृष्णा) ४·१४, thirst.

तणुलट्ठि (तनुयष्टि) २·११, the slender body.

तणूअ (तनूज) २·३८, a son.

तप्पज्ज (तात्पर्य) ३·२२, aim, object.

तप्पाविइण्ण (तत्प्रवितीर्ण) २·१७ given.

तमप्पवंच (तमःप्रपञ्च) १·५९, mass of darkness.

तमप्पहाण (तमःप्रधान) १·५९, prominent with तमोगुण; see the Notes.

तामिस्स (तमिस्रा) ४·१९, darkness.

तरट्टिआ (D. विदग्धस्त्री) ४·४०, a bold or clever girl.

तरसा, ४·४५, speedily.

तरंगइल्ली (तरङ्गवती) ४·१२, flooded.

तलवुंड (तालवृन्त) १·४८, fan, see Notes.

तवरत्ति (तपरात्रि) २·४८, summer night.

तवोहण (तपोधन), १·१६, an ascetic, a monk.

तहिं (तत्र or तस्मिन्) १·४, there, in or on that.

तंत (तन्त्र) २·२७, doctrine, 'affair'.

तंब (ताम्र) १·४४, red.

तंबुल्ल (ताम्बूल) ३·२३, betel-chewing.

ताडंक (ताटङ्क) ३·२०, a kind of ear ornament.

तामस, २·४८, dark, gloomy.

तारआ (तारका) ३·५, a star, eye-pupil.

तारतम्म (तारतम्य) ३·४५, relative excellence.

ताला, ३·३३, see Notes

तास (त्रास) १·२०, fear, anxiety.

ताहे=तावत् or तदा, २·७

तिक्खंसु (तीक्ष्णांशु) ३·१५, the sun.

तिक्खरस्सि (तीक्ष्णरश्मि) १·११ the sun (whose rays are scorching).

तिलोईवइ (त्रिलोकीपति) १·२२, lord of three worlds.

तीअ=तृतीय, ३· colophon.

तरिए=तीर्यते, १·३८.

तुइ (त्वयि) १·१९.

तुइत्तो=त्वत्, ३·८

तुज्झण=युष्माकम् , १·२५, see the Notes.

तुट्ठ (तुष्ट) १·१९, pleased.

तुण्हिक्क (तुष्णीक) १·७, silent, closed.

तुमारिस=युष्मादृश, ३·१४

तुल्ल (तुल्य) १·६२, similar.

तुहिणअर (तुहिनकर) ३·६, moon.

तूर—त्वर् (धा.) १·८, to hasten.

तूह (तीर्थ) ४·३९, a holy place, see Notes.

तेअ (तेजस्) १·११, lustre.

तोसिअ (तुष्ट) ४·२८, pleased.

—त्थण (स्तन) १·५३, breast.

थ

थट्ट (D. सार्थ) ३·५८, a party.

थणउम्भ (स्तनकुम्भ) २.२४, jarlike breast.

थणिअ (स्तनित) २·३५, thundering.

थल (स्थल) ४·११, region.

थली (स्थली) ४·३९, spot.

थाणिइल्लभाव, २·५६, see Notes.

थिर (स्थिर) ३·१५, steady, mighty.

थुअ (स्तुत) ४·१६, praised.

थुइ (स्तुति) ३·२१, praise.

थोर (स्थूर) २·२७, big, massive.

द

दइच्च=दैत्य, ३·४४.

दक्खणिज्ज=दर्शनीय, ४·४२.
दक्खिज्जइ=दृश्यते, ४·४१.
दच्छंत=द्रक्ष्यमाण, ३·१०.
दप्पसालि (दर्पशालिन्) १·३१, one who is full of pride.
दर, ३·१०, little.
दवग्गि (दवाग्नि) ४·३०, forest fire.
दंति=ददति, २·५२, see Notes.
दंसण (दर्शन) १·१५, seeing, sight.
दाणिं=इदानीं, २·२१.
दाव=तावत्, २·२८, see Notes.
दिअह (दिवस) १·६१, day.
दिक्खिअ (दीक्षित) ४·३३, ready, initiated.
दिक्खु=दिक्षु, ४·४१, see Notes.
दिग्घं (दीर्घम्) २·४५, long time.
दिग्घाउ (दीर्घायुस्) ४·८, long-lived.
दिग्घिआ (दीर्घिका) २·४५, a lake.
दिट्ठमत्तं (दृष्टमात्रम्) २·२६, just at the sight.
दिट्ठंत (दिष्टान्त) ३·५०, end, death.
दिट्ठिए (दिष्ट्या) १·१६, luckily, fortunately; see the Notes.
दिट्ठिगोअर (दृष्टिगोचर) १·१६, within the range of sight.
दिणंत (दिन + अन्त) १·३, evening.
दिण्ण (दत्त) २·१.
दीहं (दीर्घ) ४·७, long, prostrated.
दीहर (दीर्घ) ३·१०, long, large.
दु=तु, १·४६.
दुअल्ल (दुकूल) ३·८, a garment, see Notes.
दुक्खर (दुष्कर) ३·४४, difficult.
दुग्गाव्विर (दुर्गर्वशील) ४·२३.
दुण्णअ (दुर्नय) ३·४०, wicked.
दुत्थचित्त (दुःस्थचित्त) २·३५, mentally disturbed.
दुरप्पणा=दुरात्मना, १·३९.
दुलह (दुर्लभ) १·५८, rare.
दुवार (द्वार) २·२३, gate.
दुव्वार (दुर्वार) ३·२७, irresistible.
दुव्वाह (दुर्वाह) ४·४८*१, difficult to ford.
दुव्विणीअ (दुर्विनीत) २·२, impolite, obstinate.

दुवे=द्वौ, ३·४५.

दुहा (द्विधा) १·२७, divided, twofold.

दुहिउ (दुहितृ) ४·३९, a daughter.

दूअ (दूत) १·२६, a messenger.

दूसह (दुःसह) १·३५, unbearable.

दे=ते, १·१७

दे–दा (धा.) १·२०, to give.

दो (दोस्) १·५३, arm.

दोग्घट्ट (D. गज) २·५२, elephant; see Notes.

दोहण (दोहन) १·३, milking.

द्धअ (ध्वज) १·४, banner, flag.

-द्धणिअ (ध्वनित) २·३५, sounding, roaring.

ध

धअ (ध्वज) ३·५६, banner.

धण–ध्वन् (धा.), ३·५८

धणु (धनुस्) २·३५, a bow.

धणुह (धनुस्) १·२२, bow.

धत्तिवट्ट (धात्रीपृष्ठ) ३·५०, surface of the earth.

धम्मिलुअ (धम्मिल्लक) ४·२७, a braid of hair.

धंस (ध्वंस) ४·१, destruction.

धाउ (धातु) २·२४, mineral.

धुअ (धुत) २·२०, washed, shaken off.

धुणंत=धूयमान, ३·४८

धुणाइ=धुनाति, ३·५६

धुणी (ध्वनि), ४·४७, sound, words.

धिब्बोल (धिक्कार) ३·४७, words of reproach.

धेणुअं, ४·२४, see Notes.

धोरणी, २·५३, a stream.

प

पअच्छ–प्रदा (धा.) १·९, to give.

पअट्टुल (प्रचटुल) ३·३, unsteady, restless.

पअद–प्रयत् (धा.) ३·२७.

पअब्भ–प्रगल्भ् (धा.) १·३०, to have the power, to dare.

पअलंत, २·५०, see Notes.

पआ (प्रजा) ४·६, subjects.

पआव (प्रताप) ३·६०, valour.

पआस (प्रकाश) १·५९, light.

पआसं (प्रकाशम्) ४·३, openly

पइ (पति) ३·५७, master, lord.

पइदि (प्रकृति) ३·२५, nature.

पएद (प्रचेतस्) ४·३८, see Notes.

पएस (प्रदेश) २·४३, region.

पओ (पयस्) ४·४८*१, water.

पओअ (पयोद) २·३५, a cloud.

पओहि=पयोभिः ४·३६, see the Notes.

पक्किआ (प्रक्रिया) १·४०, etymological formation.

पक्खवाली (पक्षपाली) २·५, a wing.

पगे (प्रगे) १·३४, at dawn.

पग्गह (प्रग्रह) १·३३, rope.

पच्चअ (प्रत्यय) २·५६, see Notes.

पच्चक्ख (प्रत्यक्ष) १·१८, eye to eye.

पच्चहं (प्रत्यहम्) २·५३, day to day.

पच्चाअमण (प्रत्यागमन) १·५८, return.

पच्चुवट्ठा—प्रति+उप+स्था (धा.) १·८, to receive.

पच्चूस (प्रत्यूष) ३·१, morning.

पच्चूह (प्रत्यूह) ३·१६, hindrance.

पच्छा (पश्चात्) २·२९, afterwards.

पज्ज (पाद्य) २·५०, washing the feet etc.

पट्ठ (स्पष्ट) ४·३५, evident.

पट्ठि (पृष्टि) १·३३, side.

पट्ठिअ (प्रस्थित) १·३४, started.

पडाइआ (पताकिका) २·४१, a flag.

पडिट्ठ (प्रतिष्ठ) ३·३९, remaining.

पडिण्णा (प्रतिज्ञा) ३·४०, a vow.

पडिप्पआण (प्रतिप्रयाण) १·५९, return.

पडिबिंब (प्रतिबिम्ब) १·६३, reflection, image.

पडिम (प्रतिम) २·५५, like.

पडिवाल—प्रतिपाल् (धा.) १·५९, to wait.

पडिहा (प्रतिभा) २·२, genius.

पडीघाअ (प्रतीघात) ४·१४, removal.

पढम (प्रथम) २·१९, first.

पढिल्ल (प्रशिथिल) ३·३४, loose.

पणअ (प्रणय) ४·५, love.

पणाइद (पणायित) २·४०, praised.

पणोल्ल—प्रणुद् (धा.) ३·४९, to impell.

पण्ह (प्रश्न) २·५०, inquiry; see Notes.

पत्थाव (प्रस्ताव) ३·१, beginning.

पत्थिव (पार्थिव) ४·५, a king.

पदप्स (पतगेश) १·३५ Garuda, the king among birds.

पदुम (पद्म) १·६१, lotus.

पप्फुज्ज–प्रस्फूर्ज् (धा.) ३·५८, to outburst.

पब्भार (प्राग्भार) ४·३५, large quantity.

पमउलद्दा (प्रमुकुलता) ३·३७, see Notes.

पमद्द (प्रमर्द) १·४५, crushing.

पमल–प्रमृद् (धा.) २·३६, to crush.

पम्मट्ठ (प्रमृष्ट) ३·१७, rubbed.

पम्हल (पक्ष्मल), १·४, hairy, shaggy.

पमुदिर (प्रमोदशील) ४·३७, jubilant.

परप्फर (परस्पर) ३·४७, mutual.

परवंत (परवान्) २·२७, one who is occupied.

परं १·६, greatly.

पराभुव–पराभू (धा) ४·१९.

परिच्चे–परित्यज् (धा.) १·१३, to abandon.

परिधोअ (परिधौत) २·१, washed.

परिपाड–परिपाट् (धा.), २·८.

परिफुस–परिमृज् (धा) ३·७.

परिरंभ–परिरभ् (धा.) २·२७, to embrace.

परिवेढ–परिवेष्ट् (धा.) १·५३, to surround.

परिवेढ (परिवेष) ३·३२, a circle; see Notes.

परिवेस (परिवेष) २·४६, hallo.

परिहा (परिखा) २·४२, a moat.

परुस (परुष) २·३६, harsh.

परोक्खभाव (परोक्ष–) ४·४२, invisibility.

परोस (प्ररोष) २·३६, anger.

पलंबबाहु (प्रलम्ब–) १·२७, of long arms.

पलिज्ज–प्रदीप् (धा.) १·११, to shine.

पलित्त (प्रदीप्त) १·४२, lit up.

पल्लंक (पर्यङ्क, पल्यङ्क) १·४५, bed, couch.

पवट्ट–प्रवर्त् (धा.) १·२७, to start.

पवड–प्रपत् (धा.) ३·५५, to jump.

पवण (प्रवण) ३·२२, intent.

पवंचिअ (प्रपञ्चित) ४·४०, displayed.

पवाल (प्रवाल) ३·१९, coral.

पवाह (प्रवाह) २·४३, stream.

पवित्त (पवित्र) ४·३, pure.

पविसट्ट (D. प्रविकसित) २·४९, opening, blooming.

पवुत्त (प्रवृत्त) २·७, begun.

पव्वअ (पर्वत) ४·२६, mountain.

पसर (प्रसर), २·२८, spread, appearance.

पसव (प्रसव) २·५०, a flower.

पसाअ (प्रसाद) ४·१, satisfaction.

पसुव (पशुप) १·६२, cowherd.

पसूण (प्रसून) २·१७, a flower.

पह–प्रथ् (धा.) २·२९, to extend, spread.

पह (पथ) १·२८, path.

पहरिस (प्रहर्ष) ३·३७, joy.

पहाण (प्रधान) १·३९, chief, important.

पहुदि (प्रभृति) ४·२३, commencing with.

पंकअ (पङ्कज) १·४, a lotus.

पंडिच्च (पाण्डित्य) ३·४२, skill.

पंथअ (पान्थक) १·१६, a traveller, one who follows the path.

पंसण (पांसन) १·२३, a wicked person, a wretch.

पंसु (पांसु) १·४८, dust, pollen.

पाअड (प्राकृत) १·२९, not cultured, ordinary.

पाअड (प्राकृत) ४·४८*१, Prākrit language.

पाअव (पादप) १·४७, tree.

पाइहिमो=पास्यामः १·५४.

पाईण (प्राचीन) ३·२०, eastern.

पाउस (प्रावृट्) ४·२, rain.

पाडल (पाटल) १·५२, pink.

पाडिप्फद्धी (प्रतिस्पर्धि) ३·४४, competition.

पाढत्त (प्रारब्ध) ३·१, begun.

पाणाअ=प्राणाय् (धा.) १·२६, to breathe.

पारिअ (पारित) १·२१, able.

पारुह–प्ररुह् (धा.) १·६१.

पालंब (प्रालम्ब) ४·४१, pendant.

पाली ३·२, a line, row.

पालेअ (प्रालेय) ३·२४, snow.

पाव–प्रापय् (धा.) १·९, to lead.

पावे–प्रापय् (धा.) ३·२०.

पासट्ठिअ (पार्श्वस्थित) १·६, standing nearby.

पासुत्त (प्रसुप्त) ३·२, sleeping.

पिअदंसण (प्रियदर्शन) २·३०, good looking.

पिक्क (पक्व) १·५२, ripe.

पिच्छिल २·५२, slimy.

पिज्ज–passive base of पा (धा.) १·१७.

पिज्जमाण=पीयमान, २·३८.

पिणद्ध (पिनद्ध) १·३८, fixed.

पिदर (पितृ) १·१२, parents.

पिसंगिमाण (पिशङ्गिमन्) ३·१८, tawny colour.

पिहज्जण (पृथग्जन) २·११, an ordinary man.

पिहु (पृथु) २·५१, great.

पिंछ (पिञ्छ) १·१, a feather of a tail.

पिंछिआ (पिञ्छिका) १·४१, feather.

पीअ (पीत) ४·२६, yellow.

पीअंबर (पीताम्बर) १·४३, yellow garment.

पीढमद्दअ (पीठमर्द-क) १·४९, companion.

पुण्ण (पुण्य) १·१९, merit.

पुण्ण (पूर्ण) १·१७, full.

पुण्णभाअ (पुण्यभाज्) २·३१, meritorious.

पुण्णिमा (पूर्णिमा) २·१९, Full-moon day.

पुप्फ (पुष्प) १·५०, flower.

पुप्फवंता ३·१७, see the Notes.

पुरस्सर ३·३, preeminent one.

पुलअ (पुलक) १·६३, horripilation, hair-end.

पुलअ—प्रलोक् (धा.) १·४, to see.

पुलआलि (पुलक+आली) १·४, line of hair-ends.

पुव्वासा(पूर्वाशा) ३·२०, eastern direction.

पुहवी (पृथ्वी) ४·२३, earth.

पेक्ख—प्रेक्ष् (धा.) २·११, to see.

पेच्छ—प्रेक्ष् (धा.) १·२४, to see, attend, visit.

पेच्छणिज्ज (प्रेक्षणीय) २·१३, attractive.

पोण्णिद्द (प्रोन्निद्र) ३·४१, awake.

पोद (पोत) ३·४०, young one.

पोसअ (पोषक) १·१३, one who brings up.

—प्पआम (प्रकाम) १·४३, sufficiently, very much.

—प्पआव (प्रताप) १·३१, strength, power.

—प्पओअण (प्रयोजन) १·१५, occasion, purpose.

—प्पकम (प्रक्रम) १·६१, beginning.

—प्पमुह (प्रमुख) १·२१, leading.

—प्पमोअ (प्रमोद) १·४, joy, delight.

—प्पहिअ (प्रहित) १·५४.

प्फुडं (स्फुटम्) १·२९, clearly.

फ

फलिह (स्फटिक) २·४३, crystal.

फार (स्फार) ३·६०, excessive.

फिड—भ्रंश (धा.) ३·४७.

फिडिअ (D. भ्रष्ट) ३·८, dropped.

फुर—स्फुर् (धा.) १·४२, to shine.

फुल्ल (पुष्प) १·४६, flower; see Notes.

ब

बज्झ—बन्ध् (धा.) ३·२, to construct.

बड्ड (बटु) ३·५२, a boy.

बलिअं (D. गाढम्) २·१४, strongly.

बहुत्तण (बहुत्व) २·६०, abundance.

बंधई (बन्धकी) ३·१७, an unchaste woman.

बंहिअ (बृंहित) ३·५८, increased.

बालचावल (बालचापल) २·६, a boyish prank.

बाह (बाष्प) ४·७, tears.

बाहिर (बाह्य) १·६, external.

बाहुजंत (बाहुयन्त्र) ३·४७, armlock.

बाहोल्ल (बाह+उल्ल—बाष्पार्द्र) १·४, wet with tears; see Notes.

बिब्भाण—विभ्राण ३·५३.

बिब्भंता—बिभ्य : ३·५१.

बीअ (द्वितीय) २ colophon.

बीमंता—बिभ्यतः, ३·८.

बुज्झ—बुध् (धा.) ३·२, to wake.

बुड्ड—मज्ज् (धा.) १·६३, to dive, to sink.

बेण्णि—द्वौ, ३·४१.

—ब्भुमआ (भ्रू) १·५७, eye brow.

भ

भग्ग (भग्न) ४·१८, destroyed.

भण्ण—Passive base of भण् (धा.) १·२८.

भणाइ—भणति २·२०, see Notes.

भत्त (भक्त) ४·३३, devoted.

भत्ति (भक्ति) ४·३४, devotion.

भत्तु (भर्तृ) ३·४१, master.

भमण (भ्रमण) ३·४८, movement.

भवं (भवान्) १·१४, your honour.

भव्व (भव्य) १·१४, a pious or virtuous person.

भव्वमदि (भव्यमति) ४·४८*१, a man of pious intention.

भंगअ (भङ्गद) १·४३, defeating, surpassing.

भंड (भाण्ड) १·३२, a pot.

भाअ (भाग) ३·१२, region.

भादर (भ्रातृ) १·२७, see the Notes.

भिच्च (भृत्य) २·२, servant.

भिद (भृत) २·१२, filled.

भिंग (भृङ्ग) ३·९, a bee.

भिंगउल (भृङ्गकुल) १·३८, a swarm of bees.

भुअ (भुज) १·३१, arm.

भुअंग (भुजङ्ग) १·४३, serpent.

भुअंतर (भुजान्तर) १·५३, chest.

भुआलआ (भुजालता) १·४३, arm-creeper.

भुव–भू (धा.) १·१०, to be, to become.

भूअधत्ती (भूतधात्री) २·४९, the earth.

भूअल (भूतल). १·४, surface of the earth.

भूदेव ४·३३, a priest.

भूरि १·१४, much.

भूवइ (भूपति) १·३२, king.

भूवट्ठ (भूपृष्ठ) ३·५४, surface of the earth.

भूसा (भूषा) ३·२०, an ornament.

भोअ (भोग) १·४३, hood or the body of a serpent.

भोइ (भोगिन्) ४·२८, a serpent.

म

मअ (मद) १·७, hilarity, vanity.

मअ (मृग) १·५०, deer;—लंछण, १·५०, moon.

मइलदम ३·३९, see the Notes.

मइले–मलिनय् (धा.) १·३०, to darken.

मइंग (मृदङ्ग) २·५४, a tabor.

मउ (मृदु) २·२, gentle, mild.

मउअ (मृदुक) २·२२, tender.

मउंद (मुकुन्द) १·४७, a name of Kṛṣṇa.

मऊर (मयूर) २·५३, a peacock.

मग्ग (मार्ग) २·३१, path.

मच्छर(मत्सर) ३·५८, jealousy.

मज्झ (मध्य) २·४२, centre;—वट्टिणी (वर्तिनी), standing in the centre.

मण्ण–मन् (धा.) १·४०, to think, to consider.

मणिपत्त (मणिपात्र) २·१२, a jewelled pot.

मणिप्पहा (मणिप्रभा) १·४३. lustre of jewels.

मण्णे=मन्ये, २·२२.

मणोज्ज (मनोज्ञ)१·४४,pleasing.

मणोरह (मनोरथ) १·५१,desire.

मत्तंड (मार्तण्ड) ३·५१, sun.

मसधारण ३·२९, see Notes
मसुं=मर्तुम्, ३·२९.
मत्थअ (मस्तक) १·३६, head.
ममार्सिस=मयि, १·१४.
मरगअ (मरकत) ३·१२, emerald.
मल्लअ (माल्यक) २·३३, a flower, a garland.
मल्लिअक्ख (मल्लिकाक्ष) २·२६, goose.
मलिज्जमाण (मृद्यमान) १·५३, being crushed.
मसार ३·२६, an emerald.
मसिण (मसृण) २·१३, glossy, soft.
महणिज्ज (महनीय) २·३१. glorious.
महं (महत्) १·१९, great.
महाअण (महाजन) १·१३, a great person.
महाघर (महागृह) १·२४, a big hall.
महिअ (महित) २·३३, worshipped, decked.
महिसक्खअ (महिषाक्ष-क) २·३२, bdellium.
महुगोट्ठी (मधुगोष्ठी) २·५५, a liquor-club.
मंच १·२२, sofa, dias.
मंजु ४·४०, sweet.
मंजुल ४·९, lovely.
मसल (मांसल) १·४८, fleshy. heavy, loaded.
माआ (माया, मातृ) ४·१७.
माउरा (मातृ) ३·२५, mother.
माउल (मातुल) १·१८, maternal uncle.
माणिणी (मानिनी) २·२७, a proud lady.
मादा (मातृ) १·१३, mother.
मालभारी (मालभारिन्) २·१, bearing or wearing a garland.
मालिअ (मालिक) २·१, a garland-maker.
मि (मां, मे) २·२३.
मिअच्छी (मृगाक्षी) २·२०, a fawn-eyed lady.
मिट्ठ (मृष्ट) १·९, dainty, sweet.
मिदक्खरं (मिताक्षरम्) १·१४, in measured words, in short.
मिस (मिष) ४·२३, pretended appearance.
मिहिर (मिहिर) २·३७, the sun.
मिहुण (मिथुन) २·५१, a couple.
मिहो (मिथः) ३·५८, mutually.

मुउल (मुकुल) ३·१३, a bud.
मुउंद (मुकुन्द) १·५५, a name of Kṛṣṇa.
मुच्छा (मूर्च्छा), २·२२, infatuation.
मुट्ठि (मुष्टि) २·३३, fist.
मुण–मन् or ज्ञा (धा.) १·११, to think, to understand.
मुत्ति (मूर्ति) १·४०, form.
मुत्ति (मुक्ति) ४·३३, release.
मुद्ध (मुग्ध) १·३६, see the Notes.
मुदिअ (मुदित) २·३०, happy.
मुदिर ४·३७, a cloud.
मुल्ल (मूल्य) ४·१३, price.
मुसिणाइ=मुष्णाति २·४७.
मुसिणाउ=मुष्णातु, ४·१६.
मुह (मुख) १·१७, mouth, face.
मुहल (मुखर) २·५७, noisy.
मुहा (मुधा) १·५६, in vain.
मुहत्तअ (मुहूर्त-क) १·५२, a period of time.
मेहला (मेखला) १·४३, girdle.
मोअ–मोच् (धा.) ४·६.
मोक्ख(मोक्ष) २·२८, liberation.
मोत्ता (मुक्ता) १·८, pearl;–गुण, pearl-string.
मोलि (मौलि) २·६०, head, the top of anything.
मोलिभुव (मौलिभू) २·६०, top-region.
मोर (मयूर) १·४१, peacock.
मोह (मयूख) २·१०, a ray of light.
मोह २·४५, delusion.
म्ह=स्म २·२५, see Notes.

र

रअ (रजस्) १·४, dust.
रअअ (रजक) २·१, a washerman.
रअणी (रजनी) २·४५, night.
रइ (रति) २·४८, love sport; –स्सम, exertion of....
रइ (रवि) २·४६, the sun.
रक्खित्तर (रक्षितृ) ४·६, a protector.
रक्खिभड (रक्षिभट) २·३६, a soldier on guard.
रण्ण (अरण्य) ३·४०, a forest.
रत्त (रक्त) ३·४८, blood.
रद्णाअर (रत्नाकर) २·४९, ocean.
रम्म (रम्य) २·११, attractive.
रसाल ४·३९, the mango tree.
रस्सि (रश्मि) २·४३, a ray.
रह (रथ) १·४, a chariot.
रह (रहस्) १·२३, secrecy, privacy.

रहस (रभस) २·८, haste.

रहंगणाम (रथाङ्गनाम) २·४५, a Cakravāka bird.

राअ (राग) २·२४, glow, hue.

राई (राजि) १·६१, a line, row.

राअमग्ग (राजमार्ग) २·१, the royal road.

राअहाणी (राजधानी) २·३०, royal residence.

रामा ४·४, a beautiful damsel.

रासि (रश्मि, राशि) ३·१७, a ray, a heap or mass.

रिक्ख (ऋक्ष) ३·१५, a star.

रीइ (रीति) १·१३, course, way, method. –गामिणो (–गामिनः) १·१३, those that follow the course or way.

रुइ (रुचि) २·४४, light, glow.

रुक्ख (वृक्ष) २·२२, a tree

रुग्ग (रुग्ण) २·८, injured, broken.

रुव–रुद् (धा.) १·६, to weep, to cry.

रुंभ–रुध् (धा.) ३·२७, to stop.

रुसिअ (रुष्ट) ४·२८, angry.

रूढ (रोधस्) ४·४८*१, dam; see Notes.

रेहा (रेखा) १·४, a line.

रोआणिज्ज (रोचनीय) १·६१, pleasing.

रोह (रोधस्) ४·३९, bank.

ल

लक्खण (लक्षण) २·५६, see Notes.

लग्ग–लग् (धा.) १·३७, to stick, to follow.

लच्छी (लक्ष्मी) २·३१, wealth, glory.

लट्ठि (यष्टि) २·८, stick.

लदा (लता) १·५४, creeper.

लहु (लघु) २·९, light.

लहुइद (लघूकृत) २·४१, humiliated.

लंघीअ ४·१२, see Notes.

लंभ (लम्भ) १·१२, obtaining, finding.

लंभ–लभ् (धा) ४·१४.

लित्त (लिप्त) २·४५, besmeared.

लुह–मृज् (धा.) २·२४, see Notes.

लोअ (लोक) १·५९, world.

लोअण (लोचन) १·५१, eye.

व

वअण (वचन) २·३६, a word.

वअंगण (व्रज+अङ्गन) १·३, yard of the cowpen.

वअंगणा (व्रजाङ्गना) १·३६, the cowherd woman.

वइत्थिआ (व्रजस्त्री) १·६०, a Vraja lady.

वएस (व्रजेश) १·३२, the cowherd chief.

वओ (वचस्) १·२८, speech, statement; see the Notes.

वणिआ (वनिता) १·६४, woman

वरिल्ल (D. वस्त्र) २·१, a garment; see Notes.

वलही (वलभी) २·४७, a turret.

वलआमुह (वडवामुख) ३·१८, submarine fire.

वलिअ (वलित) २·१८, turned.

वले १·२, a term of address; see the Notes.

वउ (वपुस्) ४·४४, body.

वसण (वसन) २·९, a garment.

वसहि (वसति) २·६०, an abode.

वसंवअ (वशंवद) १·५६, obedient, devoted.

वहू (वधू) ४·४१, a maiden.

वक्खाइ=व्याचष्टे १·४०.

वग्ग (वर्ग) ४·२३, group.

वच्च—व्रज् (धा.) १·२३, to go.

वच्छ (वक्षस्) १·४२, chest.

वच्छ (वत्स) ४·८, a boy.

वच्छल (वत्सल) १·१३, loving, affectionate.

वच्छलंछण (वत्सलाञ्छन) १·४२, see the Notes.

वच्छलिज्ज (वात्सल्य) २·६, affection.

वज्ज (वज्र) ३·३५, thunderbolt.

वज्झ—वधु (धा.) ३·५२.

वड्ढाव—वर्धापय् (धा.) ४·८, to congratulate.

वण्ण (वन्य) १·५३, wild.

वत्त (वक्त्र) ३·३९, face.

वत्थि ३·५५, see Notes.

वत्थु (वस्तु) १·६, object, thing.

वप्प (वप्र) २·४६, a rampart.

वम्मह (मन्मथ) २·२१, god of love.

वय्याअरण (वैयाकरण) २·५६, a grammarian.

वल्लव (बल्लव) ४·१६, a cowherd.

वल्लह (वल्लभ) २·५९, a beloved.

वंक (वक्र) ३·५३, crooked.

वंकदा (वक्रता) २·२, crookedness.

वंझ (वन्ध्य) २·६, barren.

वाअ [वा—म्लै (धा.)] ३·३९, to fade.

वाअ (वाद) २·५६, disputation.

वाअ (व्याज) ४·२३, disguise.

वाअ (वात) २·४७, wind.

वाअ (वाक्) १·५५, speech.

वाआलिअ (वाचालित) ३·५७, noisy.

वाड (वाट) २·५०, a garden.

वाडिआ (वाटिका) १·१, enclosure, settlement.

वाणिर (वानीर) १·४६, cane creeper.

वाम २·५९, refractory, unfavourable.

वामच्छि (वाम+अक्षि) ३·२५, left eye.

वामदा (वामता) १·१८, perversity.

वामा २·५९, a beautiful woman.

वामिआ (वामिका) २·१४, adverse.

वारिअ (वारिद) १·६०, a cloud.

वारिवाह ३·२४, a cloud.

वावुड (व्यापृत) १·३, engaged.

वाहर–व्याहर्, २·२५.

विअअ (विकच) ३·२३, blooming.

विअड्ढ (विदग्ध) ४·५, clever.

विअप्पह (वियत्पथ) ३·२२, the path of the sky.

विअल–विगल्, ३·१५.

विअल (विकल) ४·४१ destitute of.

विअस–विकस् (धा.) १·१०, to bloom.

विअस्सर (विकस्वर) ३·६०, blooming.

विअंभ–विजृम्भ (धा.) १·१८, spread.

विआस (विकास) १·६१, shining.

विइण्णंति–विचिन्वन्ति, १·१६, see the Notes.

विओअ (वियोग) १·३५, separation.

विक्कअ (विक्रय) ४·१३, exchange.

विक्कंति (विक्रान्ति) ३·४८, feat of valour.

विक्खण (वीक्षण) १·२५, seeing, meeting.

विक्खद (विक्षत) ३·१५, wounded.

विक्खा (वीक्षा) ३·३, seeing.

विक्खोह (विक्षोभ) ३·१५, mangling.

विग्गह (विग्रह) १·४, the body, figure.

विघट्ट ३·४६, impact.

विच्छड्ड (विच्छर्द) ३·१४, display.

विच्छाईकअ (विच्छायीकृत) ३·४, rendered pale.

विज्जंति=विद्यन्ते, २·५८.

विज्जाहर (विद्याधर) २·५८, a Vidyādhara, or one who has Vidyās.

विजिम्ह (विजिह्म) १·५७, curved, bent.

विज्जुली (विद्युत्) १·४९, lightening.

विज्जुलिल्ल (विद्युत्वत्) ३·२४, possessed of lightening.

विट्ठरस्सव (विष्टरश्रव) ३·५९, a name of Kṛṣṇa.

विट्ठ (विष्ट) ४·४४, spreading.

विट्ठंभिअ (विष्टम्भित) ४·३५, pervaded.

विट्ठि (वृष्टि) २·५९, rains.

विड (विट) ४·५, a voluptuary.

विड्डिरिल्ल (D. भयंकर) २·३६, fierce; see Notes.

विढत्त (विधृत) ४·५, see Notes.

विणम्म (विनम्र) १·१५, bent down.

विणिउंजिओ=विनियोजितः, ३·४३.

विणिद्द (विनिद्र) ३·२१, awake.

विण्हि (वृष्णि) ४·७, see Notes.

विणीअ (विनीत) २·१५, modest, polite.

विण्हु-वच्छअ (विष्णुवक्षस्) १·३६, chest of Visnu.

विणोअण (विनोदन) १·४९, removal.

वित्थर-विस्तृ (धा.) २·५१, to spread.

वित्थर (विस्तर) २·३९, extension, prolixity.

वित्थिण्ण (विस्तीर्ण) ३·५५, extensive.

विदालुण (विदारुण) १·३७, cruel, pitiless.

विप्पलंभ (विप्रलम्भ) ४·३५, trechery.

विप्पलंभण (विप्रलम्भन) १·२६, deceipt, trechery.

विमअ (विमद) १·३०, great vanity.

विमअ (विमत) ३·६०, an enemy.

विम्हअ-विस्मय् (धा.) १·६२.

विम्हर-विस्मर् (धा.) १·४५, to forget.

विरामइल्ली (विरामवती) ४·४, terminable.

विलंबिअ (विलम्बित) १·४९, hanging.

विलोव (विलोप) ४·३, loss.

विवक्खिद (विवक्षित) २·२५, expressed.

विवंचिआ (विपञ्चिका) ४·४०, sport, amusement.

विवुद (विवृत) ३·१०, opened.

विस (विष) २·२२, poison.

विसअ (विषय) २·६०, topic, territory.

विसअ (विषद) ३·११, bright.

विसज्ज–विसृज् २·३०, to take leave.

विसज्जिअ (विसर्जित) १·१९, sent, despatched.

विसट्ट (D. विकसित) १·१०, bloomed.

विसम ३·४९, uneven, unfair.

विसमट्ठिअं ३·५३, see Notes.

विसमेसु (विषमेषु) २·२२, the god of love.

विसिट्ठ (विशिष्ट) १·१५, special, specified.

विसिह (विशिख) २·२२, an arrow.

विसूरणा (D. वेदना) ३·७, sorrow.

विसोह (विशोभ) ३·७, pale, contracted.

विसोहण (विशोधन) २·९, washing away, purification.

विहड–विघट् २·४५.

विहणासि=विहंसि, ४·२४.

विहल (विफल) २·५६, inoperative.

विहव (विभव) २·२१, wealth.

विहाअ=विहाय १·३७, having abandoned.

विहाइ=विभाति ३·४३.

विहावरी (विभावरी) ४·४२, night.

विहि (विधि) १·२६, a positive instruction.

विहि (विधि) १·१८, fate, destiny.

विहु (विधु) १·१०, moon.

विहुल्ल (विफुल्ल) १·४, blooming.

विहूइ (विभूति) २·४१, prosperity.

विहूसाव–विभूषय् (धा.) १·१, to adorn.

वीसंभरा (विश्वम्भरा) ३·५८, earth.

वीससिमो=विश्वसिमः, ४·२४.

वीहल (विह्वल) १·५६, perturbed.

वीला (व्रीडा) ३·५, shame.

वीहिआ (वीथिका) २·४४, street.

वीही (वीथी) ३·२६, road.

वीहीगाही (वीथीगाही) १·६४.

वुंत (वृन्त) १·४६, stalk.

वुंद (वृन्द) १·६४,party, group.

वुंदर (वृन्द) २·५७, a group.

वुंदारअ (वृन्दारक) ४·२६, a god.

वुंदावण (वृन्दावन) १·५०, name of a park; see Notes.

वेर (वैर) ३·२९, hatred.

वेला १·६२, bank.

वोल–अपक्रम् (धा.) २·७, to pass, to proceed.

स

सअ–शी (धा.) ४.४१, to lie down.

सअ (शत) २·३५, hundred.

सअं (स्वयम्) १·२९, himself.

सअड (शकट) १·२२, a cart.

सअण (स्वजन) २·३०, one's own people.

सअलुण (सकरुण) ३·९, compassionate.

सइ (सदा) २·५१, always.

सइप्पआस (सदाप्रकाश) २·९. see Notes.

सउ (शयु) ४·२०, a boasnake.

सक्कए=शक्यते, २·३.

सक्कवि (सत्कवि) २·२९, a good poet.

सक्कुण–शक् (धा.) ३·३३, to be able.

सक्खिणी (साक्षिणी) १·४६, witness.

सग्ग (स्वर्ग) २·४७, heaven.

सच्च (सत्य) १·१२, true, surely.

सच्छ (स्वच्छ) ३·२२, clear, brilliant.

सच्छंदं (स्वच्छन्दम्) ३·१३, voluntarily.

सच्छहं (D. सच्छायम्) १·१७, similar to, like.

सज्जिअं (सज्यं [धनुः]) २·३३, with a string.

सज्जो (सद्यस्) १·१०, immediately.

सणिअं (शनैः) २·१२, slowly, gradually.

सण्णद्ध (सन्नद्ध) ३·४५, ready, prepared.

सण्णह–सन्नह् (धा.) १·२१, to be ready, to prepare.

सत्ति (शक्ति) २·१४, power.

सत्तु (शत्रु) ३·२५, an enemy.

सत्थअ (सार्थ-क) १·६, collection, multitude, range.

सद्द (शब्द) १·४०, word.

सद्दूल (शार्दूल) ३·४९, a tiger.

सम—शम् (धा.) २·५१, to pacify.

समत्त (समाप्त) ४· colophon, ended.

समत्थ (समस्त) १·५९, whole, all.

समल्लअ ३·२५, see Notes.

समाल्लिअ (समालीन) १·२, see the Notes.

सम्हर ४·१२, memorable.

समाअण्ण—समाकर्ण् (धा.) १·३५, to hear.

समाअम (समागम) २·१६, meeting.

समाउर (श्रमातुर) १·४८, exhausted.

समाउर (समातुर) ३·२५, anxious, afflicted.

समाउल (समाकुल) १·२०, disturbed, agitated.

समाकड्ढ—समाकृष् (धा.) २·३१, to pull.

समारंभ—समारभ् (धा.) १·२२, to begin, to undertake.

समावड—समापत् (धा.) २·१२.

समिंधे—समिन्ध् (धा.) १·३१, to burn, to enkindle.

समीर २·५१, breeze.

समुट्ठिअ (समुत्थित) १·२९, rising up.

समुवट्ठिअ २·३९, see Notes.

सर (शरत्) ४·४८, autumn.

सर (सरस्) २·५१, a lake.

सरअ (शरत्) ४·२५, autumn.

सरण (शरण) ४·२१, a shelter.

सरास (शरास) १·२४, a bow.

सरिस (सदृश) २·१६, similar, like.

सरीर (शरीर) २·१०, body.

सरीरि (शरीरिन्) १·१२, the embodied being, people.

सरोअवाड (सरोजवाट) ३·२१, lotus-plantation.

सरोइणी (सरोजिनी) १·५९, lotus plant.

सरोरुह २·५१, a lotus.

सलह (शलभ) १·२९, moth.

सल्ल (शल्य) २·२०, an arrow, dart.

सलाहा (श्लाघा) २·५७, praise.

सव (श्रव) ३·२०, ear.

सवइ (सपदि) १·६१, at once.

सवस (स्ववश) २·२३, self-dependent.

सस (शश) ३·४९, a hare.

ससि (शशिन्) २·१०, moon.

सहल (सफल) २·५६, operative, effective.

सहस्स (सहस्र) ४·१८, thousand.

सहस्सरस्सि (सहस्ररश्मि)१·५९, the sun.

सहा (सभा) २·२९, an assembly.

सहाजिअ (सभाजित) १·३२, honoured, respected; see Notes.

संकंत (संक्रान्त) २·२४, reflected.

संख (शङ्ख) १·४ couch.

संखोहि (संक्षोभिन्) ४·४४, oppressive.

संघरिस (संघर्ष)४·४५, rubbing.

संछिव–संस्पृश्, २·१७.

संझा (सन्ध्या) २·१७, evening.

संझाराअ (सन्ध्याराग) ३·१५, glow of twilight.

संत (शान्त) ३·९, pacified.

संतदि (सन्तति) ३·९, a line, array.

संता=सन्तः ३·९.

संद (सान्द्र) २·५५, vehement; ४·३९, copious.

संदण (स्यन्दन) १·६१, chariot.

संपअं (सांप्रतम्) १·१९, now.

संपआ (संपद्) १·२०, wealth, glory.

संपआस–संप्रकाश् (धा.) १·३१, to shine.

संपइ (संप्रति) १·२·१, now.

संपक्क (सम्पर्क) १·४८, contact.

संपत्त (संप्राप्त) ३·७, reached.

संपमद्द–संप्रमर्द् (धा.) १·२१, to crush.

संपुण्णदा (संपूर्णता) २·१९, fullness.

संभर–संस्मर् (धा.) १·५, to remember, to meditate.

संभराव–संस्मारय् (धा.) २·४३, to remind.

संभरावअ (संस्मारक) ३·२३, reminiscent.

संभव १·१९, origination, accrual.

संभार ३·६०, wealth.

संवग्गिअ (संवल्गित) १·३३, rolling, moving.

साअरं (सादरम्) १·५५, respectfully.

साडोवं (साटोपम्) ३·४२, proudly.

साम (श्याम) २·४४, dark.

सामल (श्यामल) १·४१, dark.

सारअ (शारद) ४·३७, autumnal.

सारच्छवि (शारच्छवि) २·२३, variegated skin.

सारसेक्खणा (सारसेक्षणा) २·१८, a lotus-eyed lady.

साहसिक (साहसिक्य) २·२५, audacity.

साहं (सार्धम) १·६४, with.

साहा (शाखा) ४·४५, a branch.

साहिट्ठ (साधिष्ठ) १·१५, the best, excellent.

सिअ (सित) २·१०, white.

सिअअ (सिचय) २·१०, a garment.

सिणिद्ध (स्निग्ध) १·१, attached, affectionate, loving.

सिणेह (स्नेह) ४·७, love, affection.

सिर (शिरस्) २·८, head.

सिरी (श्री) १·१, Lakshmī, the goddess of wealth and prosperity.

सिलिट्ठ (श्लिष्ट) ४·४०, united, attended.

सिलोअ (श्लोक) २·५७, a verse.

सिसु (शिशु) ३·४९, young one.

सिहर (शिखर) ४·२२, peak.

सिहा (शिखा) २·३२, flame.

सिहि (शिखिन्) ४·३६, fire.

सिहि (शिखिन्) १·१, peacock.

सिक्क (शिक्य) १·३२, see the Notes.

सिट्ठ (श्लिष्ट) ३·११, touched.

सित्त (सिक्त) ३·५६, sprinkled.

सिप्पआरिआ (शिल्पकारिका) २·१५, an artisan.

सिप्पि (D. शुक्ति) ४·४६, a pearl-oyster.

सिंखरा (शृङ्खला) ३·३१, chain.

सिंचाव—सेचय् (धा.), ४·१.

सिंग (शृङ्ग) २·१०. a peak; ४·४०, a horn, lute.

सिंघ (सिंह) ३·४०, a lion.

सीअ (शीत) ४·३९, cold.

सीअर (शीकर) २·५१, mist, spray.

सीअल (शीतल) १·६०, cool.

सीस (शीर्ष) २·४, head.

सीसअक्क (शीर्षचक्र) ३·३५, multitude of hoods.

सुअ (शुक) १·४६, parrot.

सुअण (सुजन) २·२९, a good man.

सुअंति=श्रूयन्ते, २·३४.

सुइरं (सुचिरम्) ३·८, for a long time.

सुउमार (सुकुमार) २·१६, tender.

सुऊढ (सुगूढ) १·४६, hidden.

सुक्क (शुष्क) १·४७, dry.

सुज्ज (सूर्य) ४·४२, the sun.

सुज्जकंद (सूर्यकान्त) ३·१४, sun-stone.

सुण–श्रु (धा.) १·२०, to hear.

सुत्तहार (सूत्रधार) ३·१, the stage manager.

सुत्ति (सूक्ति) ४·४६, a well-spoken word.

सुप्पंत=स्वपत् ४·३०.

सुब्भु (सुभ्रू) २·२५, having lovely brows.

सुमण (सुमनस्) २·५८, a good man, or god.

सूर (शूर) ४·४८, heroic.

सुरद्दु (सुरद्रु) ३·५७, a celestial tree.

सुरहि (सुरभि) २·१६, fragrant; ४·३६, the celestial cow.

सुवण्ण (सुवर्ण) १·४३, gold.

सुव्व–श्रु (धा.) १·६, to hear.

सुह (शुभ) १·६१, auspicious.

सुहअ (सुभग) ३·३, fortunate, blessed.

सुहा (सुधा) १·२, nectar.

सुहावे–सुखय् (धा.) १·६०, to appease.

सुहीअण (सुधीजन) १·२, men of intelligence; see the Notes.

सुंडा (शुण्डा) ३·३२, trunk.

सुंदेर (सौन्दर्य) १·१७, loveliness, beauty.

सूर (सूर्य) २·४०, the sun.

सूरकण्णा (सूर्यकन्या) १·६२, the river Yamunā.

सेअ (स्वेद) २·४७, perspiration.

सेच्छं (स्वेच्छम्) ३·५८, voluntarily.

सेज्जा (शय्या) १·५०, bed.

सेणी (श्रेणी) ४·२६, a line, row.

सेरं (स्वैरं) ३·५६, according to pleasure.

सेहर (शेखर) a chaplet, crest.

सोअ (शोक) १·६०, sorrow, grief.

सोच्छिइ=श्रोष्यति २.६.

सोणिअ (शोणित) ३·१५, blood.

सोणिमंडल (श्रोणिमण्डल) १·४३, the region of hips.

सोमाल (सुकुमार) १·४३, tender.

सोरह (सौरभ) १·३८, fragrant.

सोह (शोभ) २·४२.

सोह (सौध) २·४२, palace.

सोहग्ग (सौभाग्य) ३·१९, loveliness.

सोहा (शोभा) २·२१, beauty.

सोहिद (शोभित) ४·१०, charming.

ह

हकार—आह्वे (धा.) १·२३, to call.

हढ (हठ) ३·५४, force.

हत्थिव (हस्तिप) ३·२९, the elephant driver.

हदास (हताश) ३·२५, wretched.

हम्मिअ (हर्म्य) १·३४, palace.

हरि ३·१५, lion.

हरिद (हृत) २·२५, carried.

हरिम्मणि (हरिन्मणि) १·४१, an emerald.

हलब्बोल (D. कोलाहल) २·५९, loud noise.

हव्ववाह (हव्यवाह) २·५, fire.

हिअअ (हृदय) २·१४, heart.

हिरण्णरेअ (हिरण्यरेतस्) १·३१, fire.

हिरी (ह्री) ४·४६, modesty.

हु=खलु २·३.

हुत्तो (अभिमुख) ३·२३, towards.

हेला ३·३२, sport.

हो—भू (धा.) १·३२, to be, to become.

होदु=भवतु २·६.

TRANSLATION

CANTO ONE

1. The Lord (Viṣṇu), the spouse of Lakṣmī, who has a chaplet of peacock-feathers, who is honoured by the side-glances of loving Gopīs and who has himself become the [adopted] son of Yasodā, adorns the settlement of cowherds.

2. O wise people, do you receive the story of his slaying of Kaṁsa, which, in fact, is pleasing like nectar and which I narrate ever clinging to the feet of teachers, [and being] urged by the quality of devotion.

3. Now, once upon a time, when the elder brother of Gada (i. e., Krsna), accompanied by his elder brother (i. e., Balarāma), was strolling in the yard of the cowpen where there were ladies engaged in milking the cows in the evening, he sees the son of Gāndinī (i. e., Akrūra) approaching him in front.

4. [Akrūra] who was paying homage there seeing the (particles of) dust on the ground marked with [the signs of] lines, chariots, conchs, lotuses and banners; whose body was covered with horripilation, was wet with tears of joy and was blooming;

5. who was blinking his eyes at every moment in meditation; who had placed his folded hands on his head that was bending; and who was coolly meditating on the flashing self that was in front of him and that possessed infinite wonders.

6. Nothing from outside disturbs an individual who greatly experiences the happiness [of the realization] of the great Brahman, who does not see the range of objects round about him, who does not hear the loud noise that is set out [round about him],

7. who is weeping for a moment and laughing now and then, who is standing breathless like a pillar for a moment and who is

walking about for a moment, and who is talking aloud for a moment and who is [standing] with the mouth closed as if through vanity.

8. That ocean in the form of Acyuta, who was adorned with circles of foam in the form of strings of pearls that were heaving and clashing as he was happily strolling with hurried steps, rises up to receive him (i. e., Akrūra) who was like a river flowing towards him.

9. Taking him by the lotus-like hand, the son of Devakī (i. e., Kṛṣṇa) leads him home, inquires about his health, offers him dainty meals, and further speaks something [thus]:

10. "O Akrūra, looking at you (who are) an affectionate relative (of mine), my mind has become bloomed [with joy]. Ah! is this surprising that the Kairava-lotus immediately blooms when the moon has arisen?"

11. [Akrura addresses Krsna:] "I think, strong as you are, you live somehow with (your) splendour eclipsed, in fact, by the outshining lustre of the king of Bhojas (i. e., Kaṁsa) like lamps by day (with their light eclipsed by the outshining lustre) of the sun."

12. [Krsna says:] "Inasmuch as those parents of ours are undergoing imprisonment, though [we] the two sons are safe [here], people are saying: 'Surely, to have no son is better than having a bad one'."

13. "How can we abandon even these [foster-]parents who nourish our bodies and who are affectionate like our mother and father? Will not great men detest those that follow the way of the cuckoo in this world?"

14. "Or there is no need of too much talk. Will you tell [us] what is the occasion for [your] arrival?" After saying this, Mādhava (i. e., Krsna) stops, for pious men talk in measured words.

15. Hari (i. e., Kṛṣṇa) is addressed thus by Kaṁsa's messenger whose character is pure and whose head is bent [respectfully] : 'To have an excellent and agreeable audience with yourself is the special purpose of our arrival'.

16. You whom search for long even the great ascetics that have cast off [worldly] attachment, that travel along the path of the Vedānta [philosophy] and that labour hard in the practice of Yoga-exercises such as self-restraint etc., have been visible to me (lit., have come within the range of my sight) through my good luck.

17. Victorious are my eyes by which is being tasted (i. e., seen) your face which is an unique abode of the qualities of well-formed beauty, which is similar to the lucid full-moon and which is sparkling with a smile.

18. O Mādhava, that the festival of seeing thy face eye to eve is prohibited by your maternal uncle who is, as it were, a mass of sin spreading out, is indeed a perversity of fate.

19. Indeed, fate is pleased with me now; indeed, there is a great accrual of merit to me that today I have been despatched to you on an important mission by that very king of Bhojas.

20. O Mādhava, listen what that maternal uncle of yours, who is ever agitated by fear, aims at : now he wishes to cheat even you who bestow on the world very great prosperity indeed.

21. Verily that miscreant prepares himself now to crush you to destroy whom, of long arms, Pralamba, Keśin and others were not able.

22. O Lord of the three worlds, that wicked king, seated on the dais, conspires with Kumbhirāja and the Mallas to kill you [after inviting you] with the pretence of bow-festival.

23. Whatever that wicked king told me in private, having called me [to himself], you hear that as well : "O Akrūra, quickly go to Gokula and further talk to those boys, Rāma and Keśava [thus]

24. In a big hall at Mathurā, guarded by the arms of the king

of Bhojas, the consecration of a bow is being celebrated; if you have any curiosity to see that, then come along and attend the festival.

25. Let that Nandagopa also, accompanied by friends and relatives, come quickly to my abode; I have great eagerness to see you [all]" : thus it was all pronounced by him.

26. Such is the (outward) form (lit., body) of this affair wherein, indeed, breathes the [spirit of] fraud. O son of Nanda, you may or you may not go: it is not for the messenger to persuade or dissuade.

27. The son of Rohiṇī (i. e., Balarāma) speaks to him (i. e., Krsna) thus: 'O brother, [my] curiosity gets excited (lit., starts), because there is a bow-festival; and it gets damped (lit., vanishes), because it is an occasion for treachery: [so] the fixity of my mind is divided'.

28. [Then] these words are uttered by Vanyamālin (i. e. Krsna): " O destroyer of Pralamba (i. e., Balarāma), away with (this) meaningless conjecture; it is only for the ill-behaved (lit., those that are ready for unworthy acts) that there are enemies. Whence is [there] any fear for us who are following the path of duty?

29. Well, if an ordinary man were to act rashly, indeed he would himself come by his ruin. Is not a swarm of moths, which is out to swallow a burning flame (lit., enkindled fire), burnt down?

30. No one, whose ways are crooked and full of vanity, can dare touch us who are of pure character. Tell (me), can the darkness of night darken the brilliant clusters of stars in the sky?

31. The strength of arms of one who is full of the pride of his arms becomes manifest only in the midst of enemies. Does even the multitude of the flames of fire burn by itself without fuel?

32. Now, we will all set out together taking the lead of the chiefs of Vraja without being confused, with poles and pots, and mounted-on carriages; let the king of Bhojas (i. e., Kaṁsa) be honoured."

33. [After] speaking thus, the son of Devakī (i. e., Krsna) gets into the chariot with Balarāma (lit., one who has a plough in his hand); and suddenly by his side the son of Gāndinī (i. e., Akrūra), with reins between his fingers [gets into the chariot].

34. Happily spending the night, himself sleeping in the palace-like chariot itself, Mādhava started [on his journey] early in the morning accompanied by Nandagopa and others that had gathered together [there].

35. Then, hearing the report of Kṛṣṇa's (lit., one whose banner is marked with the eagle) departure, unbearable to the ears, the Gopīs, who are afraid of separation, begin to lament with their words broken by the water of tears trickling as for as necks.

36. Alas! doubly cursed are we, the cowherd ladies! What grace is there in Nanda's home without Nanda-prince, as on the head of Sambhu without the crescent moon (lit., young or not fully grown moon) and as on the chest of Visnu without the Kaustubha (jewel)?

37. Alas! verily ridiculous is our heart which even now follows that cruel person who suddenly went away ruthlessly renouncing us who have no other patron.

38. What shall we do here, [inasmuch as] the heart of young girls is fixed on a meritorious person? [For] it is not possible to drag away a swarm of bees [settled] on a tree fragrant with fine flowers.

39. Really Janārdana is our vital life; the wicked person, by whom he was led away far off, came [here] verily as a messenger of the god of death and not as a messenger of Kaṁsa: thus you [should] understand, O Gopīs.

40. The etymological formation of the word Akrūra is necessarily [made] thus in is case: 'No one other than he is cruel (*krura*)' Just as the word A-ghora (i. e., non-terrible) denotes Īśvara of terrible form, so we think [with regard to Akrūra as well].

41. O (Gopīs), you remember [hereafter] only Hari's figure

which has dark and delicate radiance like that of an emerald; which has peacock feathers adorned by his glossy hair; which has large eyes like blooming lotuses;

42. which has the lunar orb [in the form] of its perfectly beautiful face (attended) with moonlight [in the form] of brilliant radiance of the flashing teeth; whose chest is ablaze with the lustre of the Kaustubha and the strings of bright pearls; which has a distinct mark of (Śrī-)Vatsa (on the chest);

43. which is distinguished with extremely tender and creeperlike arms that surpass the beauty of the body of a serpent; whose hips are covered with a yellow garment which is hanging down from a golden belt that is overspread with the lustre of jewels;

44. whose lotuslike feet are overspread with the lustre of the nails, are clear like the brilliance of the sky, and are red and radiant like coral; and which, for a moment, rouses the passion of cowherd girls by its side-glances lit up (lit., moist) with the pleasing smile.

45. O beautiful girls, let not the various novel sports, which were indulged in by Janārdana on the banks of Yamunā and which were vigorous on account of the crushing of beds made of fresh leaves of Nicula creepers, be forgotten.

46. Where, in fact, stands as a witness that cane-creeper, growing on the bank, whose clusters of flowers are plucked, which is full of bees hovering round on the tips of bending stalks and in which are concealed the echoed notes of parrots.

47. Where, as a matter of fact, the forest-trees, which have put forth (their) sprouts by [reason of their] tasting the nectar of the pleasant notes issuing from the hollow of Mukunda's flute, ward off the summer heat for us, though [they are] withered by the heat of conflagration.

48. Where the sylvan breezes, which are moist and cool on account of the contact with the waves of Yamunā (lit., the

daughter of Kalinda) and which are loaded with the pollen of lotuses, act the part of fans for us who are sick with fatigue.

49. Where the clouds hanging on the slopes of the mountain Govardhana and possessed of thunder and lightening are like companions who have accidentally come and who are bent on chasing away the vanity of us here.

50. Where, for us, Vrndavana was an unique rendezvous; the moon himself, a jewel-lamp; the heap of the leaves of trees, a fresh bed; and the vernal flowers, the [various] ornaments.

51. O young ladies (walking gracefully like elephants) that time is gone; let us bid farewell to [our cherished] desires, because the person, who was the root-cause of all the happiness and who was like a salve to the eyes of people, has gone away.

52. When, indeed, shall we see, for a moment, Krsna's lotuslike face which is shining with earrings that are dangling on the cheeks and have a clear hallo of light and whose pink lower lip is like a fully ripe Bimba fruit ?

53. Surrounding [him] by these arms, when, indeed, shall we embrace his broad chest so as to crush the brilliant garland of wild flowers by the impetuous pressure of [our] swelling breasts?

54. Rushing forth with speed and behaving according to our desire, when, indeed, shall we drink the nectar of the lower lip of him (i. e., Kṛṣṇa) who is standing fearlessly in the heart of the rendezvous-bower and who is waiting (for us)?

55. Then that son of Gāndinī (i. e., Akrūra), who came (back) at the instance of Mukunda, respectfully spoke something to those ladies who were lamenting thus and who were suffering from excessive sorrow at the separation from their beloved.

56. O Ābhīra ladies, verily you are lamenting in vain being nervous and perturbed. How can that Hari, who is devoted to you, forsake you, [who are] of tremulous eyes, even for a moment ?

57. Being nailed by the arrows [in the form] of the side-glances discharged from the bows [in the form] of your arching eyebrows, how can he waver [in his devotion] ? Now you should patiently bear his rash departure on an important mission.

58. Does not the moon, that sinks in the ocean [early] in the morning, come up [again] in the evening? No more sorrow; for you, who are graceful, the return of a person who has gone away is not a rarity.

59. Like lotus plants (waiting) for the sun who illumines the whole world and who expells the spreading mass of darkness, you wait for the return of him (i. e., Kṛṣṇa) who bestows the light (of knowledge) on all the people and who removes the mass of ignorance.

60. That cloud [in the form] of the messenger of Mādhava appeases with extremely cool showers of water [in the form] of words the flock of Cātakī birds [in the form] of the party of Vraja ladies that was tormented by the hot summer [in the form] of the misery of separation.

61. Then, at the dawning of the day, the son of Gāndinī (i. e., Akrūra), immediately mounting the chariot occupied by Hari, acquires a rare and auspicious beauty pleasing to the rows of lotuslike eyes of men, just as Kāśyapi (mounting the chariot occupied by the sun acquires a rare and auspicious beauty which is pleasing to the beds of lotuses).

62. Accompanied by the cowherd chiefs, Mādhava, driving (lit., going) in a chariot that surpassed the wind by its speed, reaches the bank of Yamunā (lit., the daughter of the sun) where the Tamāla trees on the slope are struck by series of waves similar to the rows of the peaks of Krsna-giri.

63. That son of Gāndinī (i. e., Akrūra), bathing in the waters of Yamunā, had his body bristling with hair-ends through surprise after seeing Vāsudeva even [in the waters] there like a reflection.

64. Then, after crossing that [river Yamunā], that slayer of Madhu (i. e., Krsna), who is pleasing and sweet to the young minds, enters the town, Mathurā by name, accompanied by his party; and there, passing through the streets, he gives excessive pleasure to the ladies just as the moon to the night-blooming lotuses.

Thus (ends) the First canto in the [poem] Kaṁsavaho composed by Rāma Pānivāda.

CANTO TWO

1. Now, Vanamālin (i. e., Krsna) who was wearing a garland given by a florist and Musalin (i. e., Balarāma) see a certain washerman going by the royal road and carrying a load of washed clothes.

2. He was asked for clothes by the princes whose faces were charming with a gentle smile, [but] the vile servant of Bhojarāja, who was obstinate with excessive vanity, gets angry and speaks [thus]:

3. "O boys, why are you thus talking about this (matter) which, indeed, cannot even be thought of? What would not the black snake, which indeed bites even when threatened [from a distance], do when touched [actually]?

4. Not only that these clothes of Bhoja king, asked for [by you] will not be obtained, but also you [should] know that verily this itself would become, Alas, the cause of even your decapitation.

5. Evidently the wretches invite (lit., experience) their own ruin by uttering unspeakable words. Do not the moths die in the fire by [reason of their] possessing (wantonly) fluttering wings?

6. Well, let it be, only once I [may] put up with your boyish pranks; [but] the king, who is devoid of [any] affection, would not tolerate these, if he hears them.

7. After speaking thus bitterly, when he began to proceed simply laughing, all of a sudden the clothes were taken away by the slayer of Madhu (i. e., Krsna) from his hands.

8. Then the lord of Laksmī, suddenly injuring it (i. e., the head) by the points of his nails, knocks down the head of him (i. e., of the washerman) who was thinking of attacking him and who, with excessive anger, had hurriedly raised his hand armed with a stick.

9. The soul of the washerman, becoming lighter than ever and having become pure on account of the washing away of its sins, enters into eternal light; and [at the same time] the pile of

clothes, becoming lighter than ever and having become pure on account of the washing away of its dirt, enters into [the possession of] Vāsudeva.

10. With white robes put on, his body, which is blue like the Tamāla tree and which is attractive with a shining girdle of gold, shines brightly, as does the peak of the Blue-mount, beautiful with its slopes bright with gold, on account of the rays of the moon.

11. Then he sees a certain humpbacked lady whose appearance was attractive to the eyes though her slender body was bent and who was as it were the (bent) bow of Cupid.

12. Going nearer, Hari asks her who was gradually coming (to him) carrying in her hand a jewelled pot, full of saffron, that was followed by bees.

13. " O young girl of crooked glances (lit., eyes), whence do you come, [and] how is it that your body is bent [like this]? O (you) of beautiful form, to whom are you slowly proceeding to give this soft saffron ?

14. Then she speaks [in reply]: "On me strongly works the adverse power of fate that has produced even in my body (that) crookedness which is known [to exist] in the heart of women.

15. O handsome one, [just] hear, I am a modest artisan residing in the king's harem; and I am going to the mansion of king Kaṁsa in order to give him [this] saffron.

16. Tender is this your body and [quite] fragrant is this saffron-paste; so let your honour alone accept this, because the meeting of the like leads to happiness."

17. Thus Kṛṣṇa and Rāma, with (their) limbs fully anointed with the saffron given by her, glitter like Sinduvāra tree with flowers and buds lit up (lit., being touched) by evening twilight.

18. Slowly catching that lotus-eyed (woman) at her chin with his tender hand, Krsna then made that humpbacked lady straight with her moonlike face turned aside with obvious bashfulness.

19. Just as the crescent of the moon, though curve in the

beginning, becomes full on the full-moon day; so she became at once full of the moonlight [in the form] of pleasant and delicate loveliness.

20. After saluting Nanda-prince that had come too near her, the fawn-eyed lady, who was carrying [in her heart] the dart of love's uneasiness, addresses (him) with words that had shaken off the fetters of bashfulness.

21. "O illustrious one, can it be that the god of love, who has conceived hostility towards you, thinking that he is vanquished by this your superb physical beauty, is tormenting me because I am compassionated by you now ?

22. I think, the god of love (lit., the god with an odd number of arrows) nowadays prepares (his) arrows with the flowers of poisonous trees; otherwise, how is it that with mild ones (i. e., arrows) my heart would be tormented (lit., burnt) and be led to infatuation by him ?

23. O you of lovely form, with [your] side-glances, which are speckled [black and white] like the variegated skin of a spotted antelope, oblige me whose mind is tormented by the terrible fever of Cupid and who have been made helpless though a mistress of my own self.

24. Your delightful image is reflected in (my) heart which [consequently] possesses a glossy and lovely grace of yellowish blue; with my jarlike breasts I [would fain] wipe off the saffron that resembles the glow of minerals on the Kṛṣṇa-mountain."

25. Then Vāsudeva spoke [thus]: "O you with lovely brows, it is a very great audacity on your part; [for] you have taken away [from me, i. e., you have anticipated] whatever words I wanted to say.

26. Does the goose wait for courting words [from the lotus plant] under the semblance of the humming notes of bees issuing from [its] blooming lotus-mouths? But [on the contrary] he [makes] advances towards the lotus plant as soon as he sees it.

27. O proud lady, I, who am occupied with an important business, have no leisure to embrace your jarlike massive breasts: it is only a man of leisure that can afford to indulge in love affairs.

28. I shall come (back) as soon as I am free from the shackles of the king's service: even that moon, whose appearance is screened by clouds, is not able to touch the water lily.

29. And thereafter, let the sports desired by [our] hearts extend over the nights bathed in moonlight like the utterances of gifted poets in the assemblies of appreciative people."

30. Thus addressing that pleasant-looking lady and bidding good bye to her who was really satisfied [by his assurance], Krsna accompanied by his elder brother proceeded with his people, and gradually enters the royal residence.

31. There, even the common people, whose curiosity bloomed at the sight of the dignity of the splendour of [their] glorious and extremely shining bodies, point out the path to him: whom do the meritorious not attract?

32. [Then] the enemy of Madhu (i. e., Kṛṣṇa) enters the gymnasium for archery which was lit up by the flames of jewel-lamps, in which clusters of garlands were hung on golden pillars, and which was full of the fragrance of bdellium and insense.

33. Taking the bow that was decked with manifold fragrant flowers by (his) tender hands and stringing it immediately, he pulls it clasping it by the fist.

34. No sooner the words of the servants, "O boy, do not, do not touch that bow honoured by the king" are heard, than the bow is broken by the slayer of Madhu (i. e., Krsna).

35. Is this thunder? [But] whence [can there be] a cloud? Or is it indeed the roaring of the Man-lion that has returned? Kaṁsa had his mind thus disturbed with hundreds of thoughts by [hearing] the sound of the crashing of the bow.

36. Then Rāma and Kṛṣṇa fierce with anger, crush in a battle, with broken pieces of the bow, the soldiers on guard that were assailing and insulting [them] with harsh words.

37. When Vanamālin (i. e., Kṛṣṇa), like the sun, is shining, the minds of good people, like day-lotuses, bloom (with joy); while those of wicked people, like night-lilies, are contracted.

38. Then the son of Devakī (i. e., Kṛṣṇa), coming with Rāma out of the gymnasium for archery and being gazed at (lit., drunk) by the eyes of young ladies, moves about visibly in the open space of the yard.

39. Coming to the capital of the Bhoja king and looking with gratification at the royal residence, he gradually addresses Rāma in detailed words and in a pleasant manner.

40. Behold the sweetness of our town Mathurā which is praised by the world and which drives away the chariot of the sun due to its stumbling against the domes of the series of jewelled palaces.

41. With fingers [in the form] of fluttering flags on the hands [in the form] of lofty banners raised aloft, this [town], full of pride, browbeats as it were the city of gods which is humiliated by its prosperity.

42. This [town], in which hosts of Apsarās in the form ot town-ladies are playng on the open flats on the tops of palaces which possess the beauty of the golden mountain (i. e., Meru) and which (town) stands in the midst of the ocean [in the form] of the moat, itself assumes the glory of Jambūdvīpa.

43. The region of the pavement, inlaid with crystal stones and blended with the rays of yellowish blue dwellings, reminds us here now of the streams of Jāhnavī (i. e., Ganges) joined by Yamunā.

44. Here [in this town], without any apprehension, lovelorn ladies proceed [to meet their lovers], even by day, along the streets that are obscured by the splendours, black like darkness, flashing from pleasure-mounts made of black precious stones.

45. Here, the sky being lit up (lit., besmeared) by the lustre of golden palaces, the Cakravāka-couples in the lakes, mistaking it (i. e., lustre) for the rays of the rising sun, do not get separated even pretty late at night.

46. Here the masses of the splendour of the jewels on the ramparts, which emanate in the form of a circle and touch the sky, brighten for a while the luminous hallo of light of the sun and the moon.

47. The heavenly breeze steals the pearls under the guise of the drops of perspiration on the moonlike faces of lovely women, loitering in the round enclosures on the turrets of gates.

48. Here [in this town], the youths, cohabiting with the moon-faced ladies in the interiors of moon-stoned dwellings, do not, indeed, experience the exhaustion of love-enjoyment even on the gloomy summer-nights.

49. This [town of Mathurā], with its head [in the form] of lofty palaces lifted up and with its eyes [in the form] of circular windows dilated, is, as it were, looking eagerly at the earth which has a girdle-band [in the form] of the ocean.

50. Here, the young trees in the pleasure-grove perform the function of washing the feet of guests with the water [in the form] of the trickling juice of flowers and make an inquiry about (their) well-being with the notes of cuckoos.

51. Here, the breezes, loaded with the moisture of the lakes and charged with the delicious fragrance of lotuses, are indeed ever ready to allay the increasing sexual exhaustion of the couples.

52. Here, in some places, the bees, which are swarming on the ground that is slimy with streams [oozing] from the fountains of the temples of constantly infuriate elephants, create the illusion of a pavement of (blue) sapphire stones: is it not so?

53. Here, the peacock dances, day to day, in some shelter which is constantly sprinkled over by streams of water splashing with a rustling sound as they issue forth from the channels of water-jets without any hindrance.

54. Here, somewhere, is heard the sweet and loud sound of a tabor which is deep and [therefore] resembling the thunder of clouds and which is a signal to the gesticulations of actors in the

midst of musical concerts that are displayed with the observance of tempo.

55. Do you hear, somewhere in the liquor-clubs, at the time of dance, the singing of maidens from the eastern countries which is vehement due to the effect of intoxication, which is charming, and which resembles the sound [issuing] from the throat of a cuckoo.

56. Yonder [you] hear the sound of the disputations of grammarians like this : [some maintaining] 'the sūtra (*anaci ca*), which defines the (retrospective) influence of a following letter (in duplicating the immediately preceding), is inoperative, because the substitute-letter has the same value as that of the original one'; [while others argue] 'it is operative in the matter of changes due to any letter'.

57. This town of ours, which is (rendered) resonant in some places by hosts of bards that are uttering panegyrics (lit., glorificatory verses), though seen for a long time, does not, indeed, [permit us to] divert (our) eyes elsewhere.

58. Are there no Gandharvas <songsters> here? Are not the Vidyādharas <men possessed of various vidyās>, indeed, found (here)? Is there not the fine party of Cāraṇas <bards> (here)? Are not the Kiṁnaras <different people> triumphant (here)? Is this not an abode of the gods <good people>? Is not the great Indra <the king> the lord of it? This charming abode of wealth which is glorious with the possession of religion is heaven itself (which is an abode of gods that is glorious with the Sudharman hall).

59. Here, the beautiful ladies, whose passion is excited by the loud shrieks of the violently dancing peacocks that are full of eager longing on account of the splashing sound of rain-showers discharged by massive and thundering clouds that are clinging to the peaks of pleasure-mountains, and who are affectionate (lit., wet) with great attachment, though refractory in love, embrace (lit., cling to the necks of) [their] beloveds, closely and impetuously, bringing together (i. e., pressing) the golden jars [in the form] of their swelling breasts.

60. Thus, when that son of Vasudeva (i. e., Kṛṣṇa), after personally summing up <drawing together>, at ease, hundreds of utterances <rays> detailed <far spreading> on account of the abundance of topics <vastness of regions>, approaches his residence, at that time the sun as well [approaches] the peak of the western mountain.

Thus (ends) the Second Canto in the [poem] Kaṁsavaho.

CANTO THREE

1. The sound of the drum, which is begun early in the morning and which is the Sūtradhāra that comes forth first at the commencement of the wrestling fight which is like a dart to the heart of adversaries, announces, as it were, to the parties of bards, the passing of the [appointed] time of awaking.

2. The bardic party, constructing poetic compositions with words full of sentiment [and hence] resembling (*iva*) the waking genius of a wise poet, gradually proceeds to wake up the sleeping lotus-eyed (Kṛṣṇa).

3. Hail! O blessed one, may the dawn, which is indeed the occasion for a happy waking and which is attended by restless swarms of bees that are [as it were] the side-glances darted by the lotus-beauty, bestow good fortune on you, the preëminent one.

4. This lord of night (i. e., the moon), seeing the prospect of the loveliness of your face outshining by the beauty of its eyes the darkness of his spot, has stepped away with stealthy steps [even] before your waking up.

5. O descendent of Yadu, these stars of your eyes (i.e., pupils), on [your] waking, will favour all the people; and behold, on account of them, those other stars [in the sky] (will) indeed quickly grow pale through [a sense of] shame.

6. In the light of the moon the masses of darkness remain, indeed, somehow sheltered by the shade of trees; [but] now, in

the flash of the light of your moonlike face, they disappear suspecting their destruction.

7. O blessed one, the sun has arrived hastily in order to touch with his rays *(kara)* the contracted lotus-face of the lotus plant which (face) is pale with the pangs of separation, even as you go to caress with your fingers the contracted lotuslike face of Rādhā haggard with the pangs of separation.

8. O Mukunda, the rays of the moon, with their garments [in the form] of pleasantness dropped away unknowingly, have disappeared somewhere being afraid of the sun who has been for a long time preparing (himself) to rise, just as the soldiers of the enemy, being afraid of you who have been for long preparing (yourself) to rise, (have disappeared somewhere with their garments dropping down unknowingly through fear).

9. Now that the night, the cause of separation, has vanished, the Cakravāka birds meet their mates, just as the good people meet the series of your compassionate glances when their array of sins is pacified.

10. Seeing a swarm of bees hovering within the slightly opened calices of lotuses, Oh, we remember your eye-pupil which is moving unsteadily within [your] large eyes that are gradually opening as you wake up.

11. This cluster of the rays of the dawn, which is reddish like the Bandhūka flower and whose glow is slightly blended with moonlight, captures our attention like your lower lip which is touched by the lustre of (your) very bright teeth resembling a string of pearls.

12. O Kṛṣṇa, the emerald pavement, suffused with the reddish rays of the sun, shines like the (dark) region of your chest imprinted with the saffron from the massive and jarlike breasts of the cowherd girls.

13. O Vāsudeva, waking up (i. e., as you wake up) you too make the lotuses of your eyes bloom, [even] before the lotus-pool voluntarily opens (its) eyes in the form of [lotus-] buds.

14. These sun-stones, pierced by the rays of the sun, begin to emit heat: even the insignificant do not tolerate the display of others' lustre, then what of great men like you?

15. This red glow of twilight, [which is indeed] a stream of blood, flows forth from the frontal region of the mighty elephant [in the form] of darkness, which (frontal region) is wounded by the claws of the fierce (*sphuṭa*) lion [in the form] of the sun and from which pearls [in the form] of stars are falling down on account of the mangling.

16. The bee, leaving immediately the night-lotus bed which is closing (lit., sleeping), resorts to the day-lotus bed which is blooming (lit., waking up), because, for one who has many beloveds, there is no hindrance anywhere in the matter of ever new love-sports, as in your case.

17. The reddish mass of the sun's rays causes the saffron-paste, (which was painted) on the large jarlike breasts of unchaste women coming out from [their] lovers' houses and which has been rubbed off by the chests of their beloveds, to look as if it has been applied once again.

18. And further, this (mass of the sun's rays), appearing in contact with the water of the (eastern) ocean, causes the suspicion of the bright submarine fire; and on the heads of elephants it intensifies the reddish hue of the vermillion powder.

19. Surely, let this lustre of the sun, which looks like a piece of broken coral, freely flash on your sapphire-blue chest, so as to acquire the loveliness of the saffron mark left [there] by the massive breasts of that Lakṣmī.

20. Behold this orb of the rising sun which is an ornamental coral ring on the ear of the lady [in the form] of the East, which is a thousand petalled lotus in the lake of the sky, and which is a dome on the jewelled palace [in the form] of the eastern mountain.

21. Janārdana, who is awake even before the out-pouring of suchlike eulogies of theirs, [then] leaves his bed: [for] the

lotus-plantation blooms first, and then indeed spreads out the cackling of the royal swans.

22. Early in the morning, he, like the sun that pervades the region of the sky with the exuberance of the splendour of his brilliant body, becomes visible to all the people whose minds are intent on the aim of serving his feet.

23. Then he proceeds towards the city-gate [after] saluting the twilight which is red like a blooming Japā flower, which looks like a maiden's lower lip red with betel-chewing, and which is reminiscent of the moonlike face of Rādhā.

24. That Kṛṣṇa, whose chest is beautiful with a dangling necklace, (while) following Balarāma whose body has a snowy lustre, looks very well like a fresh blue cloud shot with [a streak of] lightening following the moon.

25. Then throbs the left eye of his mother, who was afflicted with sorrow over many a day, and [so also] of the enemies like Kaṁsa and others who had resorted to trechery and of the athletes who were wretched by nature.

26. Rāma and Kṛṣṇa, who shone with the splendour of their costumes and with their manifold graces, gradually pass along the road which is decorated with glistening emeralds [in the form] of the continuous brilliance of the side-glances of town-ladies standing on the turrets of palaces.

27. At the gate, according to the king's command, Ambaṣṭha tries to stop by means of an elephant that lord (Kṛṣṇa) of irresistible valour like a person trying to screen the revered sun with the umbrella [in the form] of his hand.

28. That crooked-minded (Ambaṣṭha) urges on the eminent elephant, Kuvalayāpiḍa by name, whose huge tusks were hard like thunderbolt and who looked as if he were Airāvata himself sporting on the earth.

29. "O naughty (lit., unrestrained) boys, why do you rush into the presence of this rutted elephant, that is the very yard of Yama's

house, to court (your) death? Get aside immediately:" thus speaks the elephant-driver with vanity.

30. "If you do not turn aside the elephant, then he would not remain alive even for a moment:" after speaking thus, Hari, who is fierce in action, accompanied by his brother, began to overpower him.

31. Dragging him (i. e., the elephant) with his arms, Mukunda disports turning round and round the elephant who was wet with streams of rut overflowing from his wounded temples and who had a snakelike chain fastened round his waist, as [it was done] formerly [with] the mount Mandara (which was wet with torrents of water rushing from its broken sides and which had a snake passing round its middle part).

32. Then knocking down that enraged elephant who was indulging in useless sport [in the form] of circular movement with his trunk formed into a ring, he (i. e., Kṛṣṇa) strikes him with violent slaps on the temple that was swarmed with bees.

33. When, in [course of] the sport, Hari clings to the earth, that great elephant, which pierces the ground [in order to strike him] with the pair of tusks, is not able to pull out the same as it sinks there.

34. Then Kṛṣṇa, with his mind enraged, stepping within half a moment on the temple [of the elephant] with the left foot, pulls out with both hands the pair of his tusks with [their] root-bonds broken and loosened.

35. When the great elephant falls down like the Black mountain that was tossed away with the wings broken by the thunderbolt, verily the globe of the earth trembles as if dislodged from the multitude of the hoods of Śeṣa.

36. How long does the great elephant move voluntarily along the path trodden by Ambaṣṭha? Thinking thus Vāsudeva sends, at that moment, [that] wicked Ambastha, indeed, along the path trodden by the great elephant.

37. Then Rāma and Kṛṣṇa, roaming in the residence [of Kaṁsa], like sun and moon in the firmament, characterised by excessive heat and gentleness, bestow on some the blooming due to joy and on others fading [due to sorrow].

38. All the people immediately achieve, according to their desire, the purpose of the existence of [their] eyes, after seeing, to their satisfaction, those [Rāma and Kṛṣṇa] whose chests have rolling and brilliant sylvan garlands and who are sporting carrying the tusks of the great elephant in their hands.

39. The faces of those, who bear hatred smouldering (lit., standing) in their hearts, become completely faded at that time: the forest-fire, present in the hollows of trees, ever fades (their) flowers.

40. Then those well-accoutred athlete-fighters, who had pledged themselves to conquer the Yadu princes and who were directed by the vile king, go forth rapidly to attack them like wild elephants (that go forth to attack) the lion-cubs.

41. Then both Cāṇūra and Muṣṭika, who were awake and who shone with the sprouts of vanity as though sprinkled over by the shower of the glances of their master seated on an elevated platform, personally protect the entire army of Mallas.

42. Cāṇūra, advancing towards the slayer of Kaiṭabha (i. e., Kṛṣṇa), proudly speaks thus: "O son of Vraja chief, the king of Bhojas (just) waits here wishing to see your skill in the art of fighting.

43. It is the king alone that is skilled in the science of archery, and it is the cowherd (i. e., yourse) alone that is expert in the technique of fight. In whatever (department) one makes excessive efforts in that one becomes adept.

44. How, indeed, can this competition with the wrestlers of great valour be difficult for you? As a matter of fact, were not the Daitya heroes such as Pralamba, Keśi and others killed by you, [when you were] just a child?

45. Verily, therefore, both of you fight a duel, according to the regulations [of the duel], with two wrestlers; let the Bhoja king, who is full of curiosity, know for himself the relative excellence of the strength of arms of us [the fighting parties]."

46. Hearing his words thus, Kṛṣṇa, being pleased, gets prepared and occupies himself with him [in a duel]; and Balarāma (lit., the pestle-bearer) also, being enraged, [occupies himself in a duel] with Muṣṭika by means of his fists hard like the impact of the thunderbolt.

47. Theirs was a duel in which there was a mutual exchange of words harsh with reproach, in which arm-locks were being adopted, unfastened and dropping down, which was terrible on account of the clear and shrill sounds of [mutual] striking, and which agitated [all] the three worlds.

48. These [fighters], who drag with the pair of their hands the knees and shanks [of the opponents], whose limbs are broken and besmeared with blood in course of the conflict and by whose wild movements the circle of the earth was made to tremble, begin to display manifold feats of valour.

49. "Alas! what hard-hearted (person) would impell the tigers to fight with the youngs of hares? Let us go away, this is an unfair duel not to be witnessed": so speak the good people at that time.

50. Holding Cāṇūra by both of his feet, Kṛṣṇa dashes him with a crash on the ground; and similarly, in fact, his elder brother [strikes down] that wicked Muṣṭika: [thus] both the wrestlers met their end.

51. In fact so many wrestlers, that were fighting, were killed by the elder brother of Gada (i. e., Kṛṣṇa); and so many, that were frightened, took to their heels: when the sun is distinctly arisen, even the planets are wiped (out of sight), then what of the swarms of fireflies?

52. "Let these boys, that are bitter by nature, be imprisoned per force, and let even these cowherd parties be killed violently;

know that these deceitful ones would destroy you, if they are let loose": thus speaks the king of Bhojas at that time.

53. That Kṛṣṇa, who destroys the sufferings of those that are devoted to him *(vinata-arti-bhañjana)*, assails that Kaṁsa who possessed a wicked intention, who was crooked by nature, who was terrible like a black serpent and who was seated on a platform, just as the lord of birds (i. e., Garuḍa), who destroyed the sufferings of Vinatā, attacks a terrible black serpent that has excessive poison and that is crooked by nature.

54. No sooner Kaṁsa gets up holding the sword and shield in both of his hands and begins to strike him, than the destroyer of Madhu (i. e., Kṛṣṇa) forcibly makes him fall on the ground from the elevated seat within a moment.

55. Jumping on his chest which was moist with the sandal-paste on the broad region of the breasts, that Kṛṣṇa, sword in hand, quickly so cuts the bone and fat that the king becomes [merely] a legendary remnant.

56. Pitilessly dragging his body, which is sprinkled with blood coming out of the mouth, that eagle-bannered (Kṛṣṇa) attains, according to his pleasure, the pacification of [his] enmity at that moment: verily anger agitates the hearts of even the great.

57. At that time a shower of flowers from the celestial trees (viz., Kalpavṛkṣa), which is noisy with the murmers of series of hovering bees and which is let down by the hands of gods, falls from heaven on the head of the lord of Lakṣmī (i. e., Kṛṣṇa) which is decorated with peacock feathers that are flashing in the glossy and thick locks of hair.

58. Apparently the heavenly nymphs, with mutual jealousy. dance voluntarily in the firmament; celestial drums, excited by heavenly breezes, sound deeply; and the earth is full of loud sounds of the furious, outbursting and joyful trumpeting of the party of quarter-elephants with the streams (of rut) from the fountains of their temples let loose (lit., burst).

59. Then the eight youngest brothers of (that) king, who were uppermost in harsh horselaugh etc., though wicked and enraged in thought, joined the company of gods on account of their being killed by Viṣṭaraśrava (i. e., Kṛṣṇa).

60. Thus, the sun [in the form] of Mukunda, whose splendour is beneficial, who has driven away the darkness [in the form] of enemies by the sunshine [in the form] of the excessive valour of the wealth of his arms, who is a [great] hero, and who is preëminent in spotless virtues, makes the multitude of lotuses [in the form] of the minds of wise people fully blooming in this world.

Thus (ends) the Third Canto in the
[poem] Kaṁsavaho.

CANTO FOUR

1. And afterwards, the cloud [in the form] of Kṛṣṇa verily sprinkles with the showers of (his) beautiful (lit., the wealth of) side-glances the living world that was being burnt by the pressure of the summer-heat [in the form] of the valour of arms of the Bhoja king.

2. When the king Kaṁsa went to destruction, great satisfaction pervades the minds of people, just as a party of swans (occupies) the beds of lotuses, when the rain-cloud has fallen down (in the form of rain).

3. Then the highborn (and virtuous) girls move about openly and freely without any fear of (their) pure conduct being molested, just as the moon's rays being free from (the tyranny of) darkness spread out openly and freely.

4. Then, though pleasant in the evening, the night, terminable as it is, causes pain to youths, because they are desirous of enjoying themselves with beautiful damsels without any interruption and without an end to their passion.

5. It is the amorous glance of clever ladies, which possesses passionate love, which is very crooked and which has the lustre of

a blooming lotus, that falls on the voluptuaries, but not the king's sword which possesses a passion for blood, which was curved and which had the lustre of a blooming (blue) lotus.

6. Then, having appointed Ugrasena as the emperor of Bhojas and Andhakas and as the protector of the subjects, that consort of Kamalā (i. e., Kṛṣṇa) releases (his) mother and father from the prison-house.

7. The hero among the Vṛṣṇis (i. e., Kṛṣṇa), accompanied by his elder brother, approaching them (i. e., the parents) whose eyelids were fringed with affectionate tears and mentioning his name, offered a prostrated salutation.

8. Indeed that Ānakadundubhi (i. e., Vasudeva), along with Devakī, congratulated these (Rāma and Kṛṣṇa) with blessings consisting of words hindered by tears: "O boys, may you be long-lived for long".

9. Crushing the shining garland of wild flowers, the father embraces their chest which was shining like clear crystal in the case of one and which had the lovely appearance of powdered collyrium in the case of the other.

10. Then, having arrived (there) and offering salutations, the son of Gāndinī (i. e., Akrūra) utters pleasing words, which are arranged in the form of narrative and which are charming on account of their order (of events), concerning the princes.

11. This is he whose body, blue like sapphire, having a garland of wild flowers rolling on the chest and equipped with four arms, and hence (a sight) to be seen, you are surely beholding as he appears in front [of you].

12. And while you were crossing (the river Yamunā) taking him (with you) on that cloudy midnight, that flooded river (lit., the daughter of Kalinda), though overflowing the banks by its waters, became fordable with legs at that time.

13. Having put him on the bed of the cowherdess, her daughter was brought by you, O Śauri: considering the gravity of the

occasion, people do not mind, in fact, the heaviness of the price [paid] in [a transaction of] exchanges.

14. Verily this is that same naughty (boy) who, failing to get the satisfaction of (his) thirst, drank, merely by sucking her breast, even the life of Pūtanā that suckled him.

15. Indeed this is he by whom, (when) staying in Nanda's house, the Daitya hero, Tṛṇāvarta (by name), was made nonexistent; and [thus] that [Tṛṇāvarta who had assumed the form of a whirlwind or] Cakravāta (was made to be) a Cakravāka bird in the lake of Yama's realm.

16. Indeed here is he, the thief of cow-products, who was praised thus by jocular gods: "Let him steal (i. e., put down) all the vanity (*gavva = garva-*) of the enemies: but why does he steal the dairy-products (*gavva = gavya*) of the cowherds who are his relatives?"

17. It is that very person who releases from bondage the people that are bound down by illusion, he himself, the noble one, was fastened to a mortar by his mother: indeed here he is.

18. O Śauri, formerly it was only one Arjuna, possessing one thousand arms, that was routed by Bhārgava (i. e., Paraśurāma); [but] by this (Kṛṣṇa) a pair of Arjunas, that had more than one thousand arms [in the form] of long branches, was broken down.

19. In fact Bakāsura, that tried, as it is said, to overpower him who was grazing his hundreds of cows, perished himself like a mass of darkness (that tries to overpower) the thousand-beamed sun (who spreads his hundreds of rays in the space).

20. That wretched Aghāsura, that was himself lying assuming the form of a boa snake, was killed by him who, standing in (its) stomach, enlarged himself, just as a person of Karmic flaw (is killed) by the disease of spleen-enlargement (which arising in the stomach becomes developed).

21. He who began (lit., begins) to swing round this boy on the strength of māyā (i. e., miracle) was himself deceived; in fact

Viriñca (i. e., god Brahman), who fell in the deep ocean of māyā, sought shelter of Kavaladdha-pāṇi (i. e., Kṛṣṇa).

22. Indeed many days were spent by him in fondling sports with parties of cowherd boys at Vṛndāvana, on the pleasant banks of Yamunā and on the peak of Govardhana mountain which resembles a palace.

23. By this Bala-(rāma) was forcibly shaken the proud heart itself of groups of demons like Dhenuka (who assumed the form of a) Gardabha and others under the disguise of palm-grove; under the disguise of the copious water of its fruits the cause of the people's sorrow was drunk up; and under the disguise of the lives of the enemy the burden of the earth was removed effectively.

24. It is reported that Kṛṣṇa jocularly addressed Rāma thus: "Well, while grazing the dhenuka (i. e., cattle) in order to protect them, why do you kill Dhenuka (i. e., the demon by that name)? How can we rely on you?"

25. On one occasion, the Nanda prince, like the autumn, makes pure the water of Yamunā which was dreadful with the columns (lit., creepers) of the poisonous exhalations of the snake Kāliya like the sky with the (masses of) dark clouds.

26. Indeed this Dāmodara, who is comparable to the morning sun, who has put on the yellow garment that looks like reddish sunlight, and who is extraordinary with the merits of enlightening the lotuses [in the form] of the eyes of the series of jubilant gods, began to dance quickly by simultaneously putting (both) the feet on the peaks [in the form] of the hoods of the mountain [in the form] of that great serpent.

27. The boy Gopāla dances producing a tinkling sound of the anklets, bending the hood of the serpent by the pressure of (his) sproutlike feet, with the creeperlike girdle becoming gradually loose and with swarms of bees hovering round the hair which was attractive with a circle of waving peacock feathers.

28. Moreover, this (Kṛṣṇa) bestows shelter from Garuḍa on the serpent (Kāliya) whose vanity was completely gone: though good people, when displeased, are (dangerous like) poison, still they are indeed (beneficial like) nectar, when pleased.

29. Then this (Kṛṣṇa), who is dark like sapphire, being decorated with clusters of Nāga garlands that are offered to him by a party of Nāga girls, looks like the clear sky with the stars.

30. Further, when bands of cowherds and cows were asleep, the lightening-like blazing forest-fire that was breaking out is drunk by him at once: every danger is possible in the case of the eminent (people) of this world.

31. Kāmapāla (i. e., Balarāma), who was guarding the flock of cows, getting angry, crushed with the fist [that] wicked Pralamba, a Daitya, a dependant of Kaṁsa, who feigned to be a cowherd and who intended [to play some] trechery.

32. It is said, whenever any maidens sport in the waters of Yamunā, that Vāsudeva steals their clothes, as if they were their clear hearts.

33. When, at a celebrated sacrifice (held) in a forest, he was turned off by the sacrificial priests who were asked for food, he gets tasteful and sweet food, along with respects, from their devoted wives; and he bestows liberation on them.

34. Diverting the devotion of Nanda and others from Purandara (i. e., Indra), he directs (it), in fact, towards the great mountain (Govardhana), just as the day turning away the attention of the bees from the bed of night-blooming lotuses (directs it) towards the plot of day-blooming lotuses.

35. Immediately digging up the great mountain Govardhana, making an umbrella [of it], and taking (it) in his lotuslike hand, this boy Gopāla stops at once the rushing shower which falls down in great abundance from the interior of the array of clouds that are thundering and ablaze with lightening and which clearly pervades the surface of the earth.

36. Sprinkling this (Kṛṣṇa), who was resorted to by Indra (lit., the enemy of the mountain) whose fire of vanity was extinguished and who was pleased, with [the streams of] milk flowing from her sponteniously oozing udder, the heavenly cow makes his title Govinda (i. e., Gopendra) all the more appropriate.

37. Then, indeed, the jubilant beloved of Abhramu (i. e., Airāvata), like an autumnal cloud, sprinkles him with the waters of the celestial river poured down from golden pitchers.

38. Well, on one occasion, Acyuta at once brings back, from Varuṇa's abode, [that] Nanda who had dived in the waters of Yamunā and who was carried away by a dependant of Varuṇa.

39. In the vernal season, when the swarms of bees sticking to the tops of juicy mango trees are disturbed by the breezes from the mountains on the shore, this Keśava performs the steady Rāsa sport in the park of Vṛndā which is cool on account of the copious trickling down of moon-stones that are touched by the effusion of moonlight and in the extremely holy localities on the banks of Yamunā (lit., the beloved daughter of Kalinda).

40. The boy (Kṛṣṇa), frequenting the assemblies attended by parties of clever girls that had come there, performs a sport in which [various] amusements are displayed, which is ornamented with the Muralī lute, in which the ways of a voluptuary are mocked, in which there are clear and sweet conversations, and which thrills the heavenly nymphs.

41. In the Rāsa sports, this your son, whose body is decked with a pendant garland of lotuses [in the form] of the eyes of Vraja maidens that are overwhelmed with bashfulness, whose moonlike face is besmeared with the nectar of sweet smiles, and who gladdens all the people, is seen in all the directions singing, dancing, moving and lying in a most charming manner.

42. Though possessing manifold bodies like that, he became invisible to beautiful ladies whose minds are proud of their beauty: this (Krsna) is not visible for persons of malignant nature, just as

the sun, though of far spreading lustre, (is not visible) to the nights (which are full of darkness).

43. When the vanity of those ladies in separation subsided, this prince manifests his body: well, when the winter has passed away, the mango tree suddenly exhibits blossoms.

44. Even [that] oppressive Śaṅkhacūḍa, that mighty Ariṣṭa who had a bull's body and also that all-spreading Keśi who has a horse's body: (every one of them) was destroyed by Keśava who was enraged; in fact, even that Vyoma, whose enterprises were wicked, was crushed by him. O Śauri, your son is a forest-fire to the trees [in the orm] of enemies: what is the use of saying anything more now?

45. This (Kṛṣṇa) was invited by that Kaṁsa with the pretence of the bow-festival, indeed, for his own destruction. Is it not that the fire enkindled by the rubbing of the branches speedily reduces the tree to nonexistence?

46. Having taken that series of pearls [in the form] of well-spoken words dropping from the interior of a pearl-oyster [in the form] of the mouth of Akrūra, those parents make an ornament (of them) for (their) ears to the joy of all; and moreover [they] closely and repeatedly embrace Kṛṣṇa (lit., the elder brother of Māyā), whose peacock-feathers were directed downwards when his head was bent a little due to excessive modesty, along with his elder brother.

47. O boys, on this earth [may] you live long decked with fame which is shining on account of the excellent and agreeable utterances of bards that are loud like the roaring of lofty waves [of rivers] rolling down the peaks of Himālayan mountain and which possesses the brilliance that extinguishes the skill of (i. e., puts to shame) the stream of moonlight spread by the moon of the full-moon night.

48. Then, by these blessings of those [parents] whose hearts were delighted, the heroic Rāma and Krsna, who looked pleasant,

were endowed with an indescribable lovely glory which charmed the minds of all people, like the moon and the sun (who become endowed with a charming glory) on account of the beauty of the autumnal season.

Thus (ends) the Fourth Canto in the [poem] Koṁsavaho composed by Rāma Pāṇivāda.

48*1. Well, know this new poem, called Kaṁsavaha, to be a [veritable] dam for novices to take (them) through the deep ocean of Prākrit (language) which is difficult to ford: may you all [people] of pious intentions study (it) frequently.

Salutation to the feet of the revered master.

May there be happiness.

THIS POEM ENDS.

48*2. O Lakṣmī's consort, O you whose lotus like feet are worshipped by Brahman and other gods who are desirous of the expiation of their sins, O master, O lord of Lakṣmī, protect me soon.

NOTES

[Besides the usual ones the following abbreviations are used in these Notes: भाग० 10.5.9=श्रीमद्भागवतम् (निर्णयसागर ed.) स्कन्ध, अध्याय, श्लोक; Hc. or Hema.=Prakrit Grammar of Hemacandra (Poona 1936); Mk.=प्राकृतसर्वस्वम् of मार्कण्डेय (Vizagapatam शाक १८४८); Trivikrama=प्राकृतशब्दानुशासनम् (Ms..); Pischel = references are to the sections of his Grammatik der Prakrit-Sprachen (Strassburg 1900); Vr., Vara., or Vararuci=प्राकृतप्रकाश of वररुचि (London 1868); वृ० वा०=वृत्तवार्तिकम् of राम पाणिवाद (Trivandrum 1937). For the explanations of mythological details given in these Notes the following works are mainly consulted: श्रीमद्भागवतम् (निर्णयसागर ed. Bombay); A Classical Dictionary of India by J. Garret (Madras 1871) and its Supplement (Madras 1873); A Classical Dictionary of Hindu Mythology etc. by J. Dowson (London 1879); Vedic Mythology by A. A. Macdonell (Strassburg 1897); Epic Mythology by E. W. Hopkins (Strassburg 1915); भारतवर्षीयप्राचीनचरित्रकोश by सि. चित्राव (Poona 1932).]

CANTO ONE

1. The poet begins the poem with an auspicious word सिरी as in किरातार्जुनीयम् and शिशुपालवधम्. सिरीअ णाहो is primarily विष्णु of whom कृष्ण is the eighth incarnation. If we read सेहरं and अंचिअं, then they would qualify तणअत्तणं; see also iii. 57 below. अंचिअ is a p. p. p. from अंच् I U. or अर्च् I P. to honour. My emendation अंचिओ etc. is supported by the छाया in Ms. T. यशोदा is the wife of cowherd नन्द. It was to her bed that कृष्ण, at his birth, was conveyed by वसुदेव in exchange of her new born infant

योगनिद्रा that was brought to देवकी. Till he killed कंस, कृष्ण remained with यशोदा who, therefore, became his foster-mother. त्तण is the termination for abstract nouns (Vr. iv. 22). It may be noted that the Sanskrit छाया often changes the tense of verbal forms. सिहिपिंछसेहरो indicates how कृष्ण used to wear peacock-feathers in his childhood to which माघ also refers in शिशुपाल-वधम् iii. 5.

2. Apparently the forms कंसवहं and कहं agree in प्राकृत, but they may be construed कंसवधं नाम कथां. कंस is the son of उग्रसेन and the cousin of देवकी, the mother of कृष्ण. He deposed his father and became notorious as the tyrannical king of Mathurā. He married two daughters of जरासन्ध, the king of Magadha. As it was foretold that he would die at the hands of a son of देवकी, he tried to destroy all the children. When बलराम, the seventh son, was born, he was carried away to गोकुल where he was nurtured by नन्द as a child of रोहिणी. The eighth child कृष्ण too was taken to गोकुल. कंस tried without any success to destroy these two boys, but at last met his end at the hands of कृष्ण. The present work narrates how कंस was slain by कृष्ण. वले or बले is a term of address in conversation (Vr. ix. 12); it expresses specification or assertion (Hc. ii. 185); or it is simply a term of address (Mk. viii. 26) as it is here. Its etymology is not certain. Three Sanskrit words attract our attention: अबले (Voc. sg. of अबला) >वले, with the supposition that it was first meant for ladies; वरं, taking into account Hemacandra's meaning; or उत रे > उव ले>वले, उत being represented by उव, see ii. 40 below. सुहीअण=सुधीजन, सुखीजन or सुहृज्जन. समल्लिअ p. p. p. of the धात्वादेश, समल्ली, but it may be traced back to सम-आ-ली. णोल्लिअ p. p. p. from णोल्ल usually equated with नुद्.

3. इर is a Prākrit suffix showing 'habit' corresponding to Sk. शील (Vr. iv. 24): चंकमिरो=चंक्रम(ण) शीलः. The second line qualifies वअंगण. The author's style is so much influenced by Sanskrit that I find it necessary to put अवग्रह, otherwise we will have a form like हिसरंत. गदाग्रज is a name of कृष्ण, as he had a younger brother गद by name. This name is used in शिशुपालवध also ii. 69. To explain दक्खइ Pischel postulates a form *दक्षति (§ 554). गान्दिनी was a princess of काशी. She was the wife of श्वफल्क and the mother of अक्रूर who, therefore, gets the names गान्दिनेय, गान्दिनासुत etc., He was sent by कंस to invite कृष्ण to attend some sports at मथुरा.

4. बलराम and कृष्ण have auspicious marks of royalty on their soles; and their imprints, when they are moving in the yard, are seen on the ground. अक्रूर respectfully bows down to them. रेहा- 'lines etc.' or we may take 'conchs etc. consisting of lines'; compare भागवत 10. 38. 25-6 and 34: पदानि तस्याखिललोकपालकिरीट-जुष्टामलपादरेणो : ॥ ददर्श गोष्ठे क्षितिकौतुकानि विलक्षितान्यब्जयवाङ्कुशाद्यैः ॥ २ ॥ बाहोल्ल=बाह+उल्ल=बाष्प+आर्द्र (Vr. iii. 38, Hc. i. 82). पुलऊण gerund from पुलअ to see (Vr. viii. 69) from प्रलोकृ (Pischel § 104, 130).

5. निमीलित+ईक्षणं, in such a manner that his eyes were closed in meditation. अक्रूर began to reflect, in meditation, on the flashing परमात्मन्, viz., कृष्ण who was just before him. कोड्डअं, also कुड्डं or कुड्डअं, is a देशी word meaning आश्चर्य; Sk. lexicons note a word कुड्य with that sense; and we have in Marathi कोडकौतुक.

6. In an ecstatic state of meditation, a साधक has all his faculties fully concentrated on परमात्मन्; and as such he is not amenable to external disturbances for the time being.

7. अक्रूर has approached कृष्ण who is परमात्मन् incarnate, so his joy knows no bounds; and in that jubilant and ecstatic mood he is behaving like one who is almost out of his senses. क्षणं may be as well rendered by 'now' instead of 'for a moment'. If the reading is correct, णिरूसइं=निरुत्साहम्; णिरूससं would be a better reading standing for निरुच्छ्वसन् of the छाया.

8. In this verse we have both the figures of speech रूपक and उपमा.

9. देवकी is the wife of वसुदेव, mother of कृष्ण and cousin of कंस. Compare भाग. 10. 38. 36-39.

10. अक्रूर is the son of श्वफल्क and गान्दिनी. He belonged to the यादव family and was an uncle of कृष्ण. कंस sent him to invite कृष्ण and राम to मथुरा He is famous as the possessor of श्यामन्तक gem. The figure of speech here is दृष्टान्त. कैरव is a kind of white lotus which blossoms at moon-rise.

11. भोजराज is a name of कंस, as he is the king of Bhojas. पलिज्जमाण is the present passive p. from the root प्रदीप (Hc. i. 221). The figure of speech here is उपमा.

12. This verse can be put in the mouth of अक्रूर as well with equal propriety, and in that case णो is honorific plural and पिदरा means elders. Thus अक्रूर would be taunting राम and कृष्ण just to enkindle their wrath against कंस. compare भाग. 10. 39. 6 etc. The figure of speech here is अर्थान्तरन्यास.

13. The bird कोकिल or cuckoo, it is said, lays its eggs in the nest of a crow which warms and guards them. When the young ones come out and have the wings, they fly away caring little for the crow that nourished them all along. In the light of this, कोइल-रीइ-गामिणो means 'those that follow the way of the cuckoo',

i. e., those that behave ungratefully towards their foster-parents. In the last line कइं merely introduces interrogation. परिन्चेमु is taken as the Imperative 1st p. sg. by the छाया possibly according to Vr. vii. 18, but I have taken it as Present 1st p. plural.

14. Compare the second half with शिशुपाल. ii. 13–यावदर्थपदां वाचमेवमादाय माधवः। विरराम महीयांसः प्रकृत्या मितभाषिणः ॥ The figure of speech here is अर्थान्तरन्यास.

15. अक्रूर explains his mission. His foremost intention is to have a glimpse of the excellent and agreeable personality of कृष्ण who is an incarnation of God. व्व stands for emphatic एव. Verses 15–16 remind us of शिशुपाल. i. 31 etc. नारद addresses कृष्ण by saying त्वमेव साक्षात्करणीय इत्यतः किमस्ति कार्यं गुरु योगिनामपि, and then goes on to explain how परमात्मन् is to be realized by saints.

16. The first two lines mention the essential qualifications for God-realization. णिअम=निगम means Veda, so णिअमंत=वेदान्त. निगमान्त-पान्थाः or -पान्थकाः 'those that follow the course of वेदान्त'. The word वेदान्त primarily stands for the group of Upanishadic texts which come last in the enumeration of the four branches of Vedic literature (संहिता, ब्राह्मण, आरण्यक and उपनिषद्), which chronologically form the last compositions, and which form the culminating point of Vedic thought so far as their contents are concerned. यम, नियम, आसन, प्राणायाम, प्रत्याहार, धारण, ध्यान and समाधि (पातञ्जलयोगसूत्राणि २-२९): these are the eight अङ्गs or means of attaining Yoga or mental concentration. विइण्णंति is a direct corruption of the Sk. form विचिन्वन्ति. दिट्ठिए=दिष्ट्या, Inst. sg. of दिष्टि f. 'good fortune'.

18. अक्रूर complains that it is really unfortunate that he is not able to come and see कृष्ण now and then due to the prohibition of कंस who is enemical towards कृष्ण. कंस is as it were a heap of sin spreading on all sides. Here the figure of speech is उत्प्रेक्षा. It may be आक्षेप as well, if we render व by 'nay.'

19. Note the form तुइ, Loc. sg. of युष्मद्, which is frequently used in the प्राकृत portions of the Sanskrit plays. अक्रूर congratulates himself on his good luck that he has been sent to कृष्ण by कंस himself.

20. We have यमक at the close of the *a* & *b* and *c* & *d*. कं पि etc. कामपि अवर्णनीयां संपदम्. The very existence of कृष्ण, the incarnation of divinity, adds glory to the world.

21. कृष्ण is called here प्रलम्बबाहु. To have long and pendant arms is a sign of perfection and merit. We have यमक at the beginning of *a* & *b* and *c* & *d*. प्रलम्ब was an Asura dependant of कंस Disguised as a गोप he joined the play of boys with a view to devour बलराम and कृष्ण. When he took बलराम on his shoulders, as the rules of the play required, he expanded his form and began to run away. कृष्ण came to his rescue and challenged the demon. बलराम beat प्रलम्ब on his head with his fist till his eyes were knocked out and his brain forced through the skull, so that he fell to the ground and expired. From this बलराम gets the name प्रलम्बसूदन (see i. 28, also iii. 44, iv. 31). केशिन् was a Daitya who assumed the form of a horse and attacked कृष्ण, but was killed by that hero who rent him asunder by thrusting his arm into his jaws (see below iii. 44 and iv. 44). अप्पणा=आत्मना, personally, him self. According to the popular exposition of the सांख्य doctrine, सत्त्व, रजस् and तमस् are the constituents of everything in creation in various proportion. कंस is called तमप्पहाणो–तमोगुणप्रधानः, because he is preeminently characterised by तमोगुण which is the cause of heaviness, ignorance, illusion, lust, anger, pride, sorrow, dullness and stolidity. Does the last हि stand for additional emphasis? Or should we read सण्णहेहिइ, Fut. 3rd p. sg., which would indicate his wish.

22. कुम्भराज (in our text कुम्भि–) was an Asura chief perhaps the same as the son of प्रह्लाद and the brother of निकुम्भ who was slain by कृष्ण because of his immoral behaviour. मल्ल is the name of a clan of people, perhaps the professional wrestlers in the service of कंस There is nothing special in saying that the king was seated on a dias (मंचमाढिओ), but we can understand its use for the sake of alliteration with the opening syllables of the fourth line. In भाग. 10. 42. 35 कंस is described as seated on राजमञ्च.

23. गोकुल is also known by the names व्रज, महावन, पुराणगोकुल etc. where कृष्ण was brought up. It is at a distance of six miles from मथुरा and contains spots associated with the early life of कृष्ण. A new गोकुल is founded by वल्लभाचार्य; and it is at a distance of one mile to the south of महावन on the eastern bank of यमुना.

24. चअत्थि is directly corrupted from the Sk. form चकास्ति. In this text कंस is variously mentioned as भोजाधिप, भोजभूपति, भोजपति, भोजराज, भोजेश etc. The छाया reads मधुरा, perhaps a South Indian spelling of मथुरा. सरासजण्णो–शरासयज्ञः refers to a festival of consecrating the bow.

25. नन्द or नन्दगोप is the cowherd नन्द, the foster-father of कृष्ण. The form तुज्झण, Gen. pl. of युष्मद्, perhaps stands metris causa for तुज्झाण which is recorded by grammarians (Pischel §420)

26. As a messenger अक्रूर thinks that his duty is merely to deliver the message. It is not for him to say whether कृष्ण should go or should not go to मथुरा. He would neither ask him to go nor prohibit him from going. It is a point which is to be decided by बलराम and कृष्ण That he should come to attend the festival is the body' of the present business, and it is animated by the spirit of treachery. In disclosing जहिं खु पाणाअइ विप्पलंभणं, अक्रूर has not gone out of his way, for कंस had plainly disclosed his intention to him (भाग. 10. 36. 27–39).

27. On वले see i. 2 above. भादर is the normal base from भ्रातृ in शौरसेनी of the dramas especially in Nom., Acc. and Inst. रोहिणी was one of the wives of वसुदेव, the father of कृष्ण. Her son was बलराम. She is to be distinguished from the wife of कृष्ण of the same name.

28. Note इदं वओ. वओ is a direct corruption from वचः, neuter, though it appears like a mas. form. वन्य or वनमालिन् is a name of विष्णु-कृष्ण, as he wears a garland of forest flowers. कवित्थ appears to be some corrupt word the counterpart of which, viz., अवित्थ, is used at ii. 35. The Sk. छाया renders them by कुतर्क and वितर्क. Are we to connect it with कदर्थ, useless, meaningless ? The देशी word उप्पित्थ, meaning 'mental disturbance' also attracts my attention; it occurs in रावणवहो १५-८३. There is a crop of enemies only for the wicked, while the dutiful and virtuous have to fear from none.

29. In the light of Vararuci iii. 50 and 57, there is no justification for forms like प्फुडं, क्खअं etc. which show an initial conjunct consonant. This can be explained only on the basis of the author's habit of thinking in Sanskrit and then corrupting a string of words (here अथ-स्फुटं, यदि-क्षयं) into Prākrit. This tendency of keeping the initial conjunct in a word is seen to a great extent in this text. काहिइ, जाहिइ, Fut. 3rd p. sg. forms from the roots कृ to do and या to go. This verse reminds us of शिशुपाल. xvi. 35 –महतस्तरसा विलङ्घयन्निजदोषेण कुधीर्विनश्यति । कुरुते न खलु स्वयेच्छया शलभानिन्धनमिद्धदीधितिः ॥. The figure of speech here is दृष्टान्त.

30. ताराणियरे समुज्जले Acc. pl. The figure of speech here is दृष्टान्त.

31. जालसंचओ=ज्वालासञ्चयः. Here also the figure of speech is दृष्टान्त.

32. वएसग्ग–व्रजेशाग्रसराः 'leading the representatives of the व्रज country'. व्रज is the name of a district around आग्रा and मथुरा. नन्द, the foster-father of कृष्ण, lived there; and it formed the scene of कृष्ण's juvenile adventures. शिक्य is a balance-like mechanism consisting of a bamboo pole with rope-nets hanging on both the sides in which are put milk-pots and carried to distant places on shoulders. सहाजिओ p. p. p. from the root सभाज् to honour, to serve, to visit. Compare भाग० 10.39.10 etc. Note the ring of the syllable स in the last two lines.

33. सीरपाणिः is a name of बलराम, because he carried a plough in his hand as a weapon. पड्ढि=पृष्ठिः side; so अक्रूर takes his seat in the chariot by the side of कृष्ण, and has the reins of horses in his hands.

35. पतगेशकेतुः is कृष्ण, as his banner is emblazened with the eagle. जलुक्खद etc. is equated with जलोक्षताक्षरम् by the छाया; but I have taken जलोक्षिताक्षरम्, i. e., 'with their words sprinkled by the water of tears'. We may even taken जलावक्षताक्षरम्, i. e., 'with their words broken or hindered etc.'. अस्सु from अश्रु for which grammarians usually give अंसु. Their tears, it appears, were flowing as far as their necks. For the lamentations of गोपीs, see भाग. 10.39.13 etc.

36. In the phrase अमुद्ध–अंदम्मि, the word चन्द्र loses its initial consonant, because the initial of a second member of a compound may be optionally treated as noninitial (Hc. on i. 177). मुग्ध is to be understood as distinguished from पूर्ण. कौस्तुभ is the famous jewel worn on by विष्णु or कृष्ण on his chest. It was obtained at the time of the churning of the ocean. नन्द being the foster-father, कृष्ण is called नन्दज. व्रजाङ्गनाः are the cowherd ladies from व्रज-मण्डल, a territory of some eighty miles round about मथुरा. Compare this verse with रावणवहो iv. 20–सग्गं अपारिजाअं कोत्थुह-लच्छिरहिअं महुमहस्स उरं। सुमिरामि महणपुरओ अमुद्धअंदं च हरअडापब्भारं ॥ In this verse the figure of speech is मालोपमा.

37. अविहा may stand for अपि हा or अविधा, the latter being an interjection expressing sorrow and expecting help. The Sk. छाया takes the former, though the latter is equally suitable. तहिं=तस्मिन् (Vr. vi. 7). तमम्हआणं would have been a better reading, अम्हआण= अम्हाणं with स्वार्थे क-suffix. Or is it that he uses अम्मक in the sense of अस्मादृश ?

38. किमम्मकाओ for किमेत्थ अम्हे appears to be a genuine reading, as the छाया also correspondingly differs in the two Mss. The figure of speech here is दृष्टान्त.

39. कृष्ण is the very life of गोपीs; अक्रूर came there and led कृष्ण away; thus he took away their very life : so verily he is the messenger of यम and not of कंस. That is how the गोपीs argue. प्राणाः always Mas. pl. in Sanskrit; here it is pl. but Neu.

40. There is no doubt that the author is thinking in Sanskrit, though he is writing in Prākrit. According to his wording the etymology of अक्रूर stands thus : अस्मात् क्रूरः न परः इति अक्रूरः. Usually we have न विद्यते क्रूरतरः यस्मात् स अक्रूरः, i. e., 'No one is more cruel than he.' This idea is found in भाग० also, 10. 39. 21 and 26. अघोर (=शिव) is the name of ईश्वर who is often identified with रुद्र, भैरव etc. As a भूतेश्वर he haunts the cremation ground, wears serpents round his head and skulls for a necklace, indulges in revelry, and being drunk deep dances ताण्डवनृत्य with his wife and tramples on rebellous demons. With these details in view, he is really घोर, fierce or terrible, but still he is called अघोर. माघ also has expressed a similar idea that भौमदिन, though अप्रशस्त, is called by the name मङ्गल–तव धर्मराज इति नाम कथमिदमपष्ठु पठ्यते। भौमदिनमभिदधत्यथवा भृशमप्रशस्तमपि मङ्गलं जनाः ॥ xv. 17.

41. We may read हरिस्सरूवं or हरिस्स रूवं, and accordingly it may be rendered हरिस्वरूपं or हरे रूपं. Upto the close of verse 44 we have the adjectives of रूवं. Third line may be thus dissolved: सिणिद्धेहि केसेहि अंचिआ मोरपिंछिआ जस्स. कंदोट्ट, a blue lotus, is usually considered as a देशी word. I think, it comes from कन्दोत्थ (कन्द+उत्थ) which is a Sk. word. Various words like कन्दट, कन्दोट etc., noted by lexicographers, are mere back-formations from the Prākrit कंदोट्ट.

42. Construe समग्रं सौन्दर्यं यस्य etc. It appears that the reading, according to the Sk. छाया, was पलित्त-वच्छप्फुड–, i. e., 'the श्रीवत्स mark was clearly visible on account of the shining chest etc.' वत्स or श्रीवत्स is a particular mark or curl of hair on the breast of विष्णु or कृष्ण and of other divine beings. It is said to be white and represented in pictures by a symbol resembling a cruciform flower. To explain the form चन्दिमा, which the grammarians derive from चन्द्रिका by a special rule, Pischel postulates a form *चन्द्रिमन् (§ 103). The word चन्द्रिका would give us चंदिगा or चंदिया which might have been misread as चंदिमा due to orthographical confusion at a pretty early stage of Prākrit literature.

43. भोग usually means the hood, but it is also used in the sense of the body of a serpent. The girdle is holding up the garment which therefore is hanging from the girdle. From the word आकृति Vararuci has a form आइदि (ii. 7), Hemacandra has आकिइ (i. 209), while our text has आकइ.

44. I have construed thus: णहप्पहालिद्धं णहप्पहामलं पवालतंबुजलं च पाअपङ्कअं. आलिह is given as a substitute for स्पृश् (Hc. iv. 182), and आलिद्ध is equated with आश्लिष्ट by a special rule (Hc. ii. 49). Just as मुद्ध goes back to the root मुह् and दुद्ध to दुह्, it is not unlikely that आलिद्ध comes from आलिह्. Pischel (§ 303) postulates a word like *आलिब्ध. In explaining the etymology of उल्ल Pischel has in view Vedic words like उद्र 'water', उद्रिन् 'abounding in water' (§ 111).

45. जउणाड=यमुनातट, a case of internal Sandhi (Pischel § 165). Of course the author is referring to their amorous sports.

46. जहिं=यत्र or यस्मिन् यमुनातटे. The cane-creeper is standing there as a witness to their love-sports enjoyed in the past. फुल्ल, a blooming flower, has been treated undoubtedly as a Sanskrit word of much antiquity; and the root फुल्ल is recorded even by धातुपाठ. But the root फुल्ल itself has a Prākrit appearance, and I think that it might go back to the Sk. root स्फुट्.

47. णित Present parti. from इ with नि (Pischel § 493), but according to the Sk. छाया it is from इ with निर्. It appears from the छाया there was a various reading बंधुरस्सरामआसाअ etc. Here the figure of speech is विषमालङ्कार.

48. समाउराणं=श्रमातुराणाम्. The known forms for तालवृन्त are तालविंट, –वेंट, –वोंट and even –वुंट; for ताल° we may have तल° as well (Pischel § 53). Our form appears to be a further deduction from तलवुंट.

49. The mountain गोवर्धन is situated at a distance of eighteen miles from वृन्दावन in the मथुरा district. It is this mountain which

कृष्ण is said to have taken on his little finger to protect the people from the heavy rains poured down by Indra. The clouds remove the vanity of proud ladies that are averse to their lovers. The clouds enkindle their passion whereby they become submissive. Compare मेघदूत ३: मेघालोके भवति सुखिनोऽप्यन्यथावृत्ति चेत: and the com. विरहिणां मेघसंदर्शनमुद्दीपनं भवतीति भाव:.

50. वृन्दावन was their meeting place where they sported in moon-light on the beds of fresh sprouts wearing various kinds of vernal flowers as ornaments. Different opinions are held about the exact identification of the ancient site of वृन्दावन. It was situated in the मथुरा district and served as a meeting place for कृष्ण and गोपीs. It is interesting to note that the metre is preserved even in the Sanskrit छाया.

51. कुणिमो तिलंजलिं–the desires of गोपीs to meet कृष्ण etc. are not likely to be fulfilled now; so they are offering as it were, by way of good bye to their cherished desires, two handfuls of water with sesamum seeds that constitute the customary libation to the departed. जणल्लोअणंजणो–collerium is dark, a decoration for the eyes, an object of attraction to ladies and has a soothing effect: so is कृष्ण's personality as well.

52. कृष्ण is the son of वसुदेव and देवकि. He is an अवतार of विष्णु. There was a good deal of supernaturalness about his birth. With the fear that कंस might kill him, he was taken to गोकुल and brought up there as a cowherd boy in the house of नन्द. कंस finding that he was outwitted and that his enemy was living at गोकुल tried various ways to kill कृष्ण, but all his efforts failed against divine कृष्ण. Most of these incidents are referred to in the fourth canto of this book. With a view to overpower and kill him कंस

invited him with the pretext of a bow-festival. This plan also failed, and eventually कृष्ण killed कंस as described in this work.

53. कृष्ण has a garland of wild flowers which would be crushed when he is violently embraced by गोपीs. दोहिं=दोर्भ्याम्, by both the arms. विशालं भुजान्तरम्–the extensive space between the arms, i. e., the chest.

54. मग्ग°–literally, whose eye is set on our path of arrival, i. e., who is eagerly waiting for our arrival.

55. मुउंदवाआउ Inst. sg. It appears that it is कृष्ण that sends अक्रूर to console the गोपीs.

56. Originally आभीर was the name of a nomadic clan that settled in Northern India and Gujerat; later on it is often used in the sense of cowherds.

57. In giving the etymology of भुमआ, Pischel postulates a stage like *भुवका (§ 123). अक्रूर's main argument of consolation is that कृष्ण has gone away to achieve an important mission, a duty, so गोपीs should try to put up with his separation which is temporary.

58. Apparently the moon plunges into the western ocean early in the morning and emerges out of the eastern ocean in the evening. Further अक्रूर consoles the गोपीs that their coquettish grace is tempting enough to attract कृष्ण back though he has gone away for the time being. The figure of speech in this verse is प्रतिवस्तूपमा.

59. The first two lines are to be construed with कृष्ण, for whom the गोपीs are waiting, as well as with the sun whose arrival the lotuses await: the former, as an incarnation of विष्णु, bestows the light of religion and dispels the darkness of अविद्या or तमोगुण for the benefit of all the people, while the latter is a source of light for the whole world and dispels the darkness of night. We have an उपमा here.

60. The figure of speech here is परम्परितरूपक. By reading this verse one is reminded of रघुवंश x.48 –रावणावग्रहक्लान्तमिति वागमृतेन सः । अभिवृष्य मरुत्सस्यं कृष्णमेघस्तिरोदधे ॥

61. काश्यपि is the name of अरुण or Dawn who drives the chariot of the sun. हरिसणाहं is to be construed both ways: occupied by हरि or कृष्ण and secondly by हरि or the sun.

62. कृष्णगिरि is the Karakorum or the Black mountain. सूरकण्णाउ Gen. sg. from सूर्यकन्या. गाहए, reaches.

63. कृष्ण वासुदेव is omnipresent. When अक्रूर was taking his bath plunging himself in the stream of यमुना, he was simply thrilled with surprise to see कृष्ण even there. Compare भाग० 10.39.40 etc.

64. तं=तां यमुनाम्. There is some play of sound in the first line. The figure of speech is उपमा. Note साहं=सार्धम्, with, accompanied by.

In this canto verses 1–60 are composed in वंशस्थ metre which is four times ⏑ – ⏑ | – – ⏑ | ⏑ – ⏑ | – ⏑ – ॥ (जतौ जरौ च वंशस्थम् । वृ० वा० १९); Nos. 61–62 are in मालिनी metre which is four times ⏑ ⏑ ⏑ | ⏑ ⏑ ⏑ | – – – | ⏑ – – | ⏑ – – ॥ (ननौ मयौ मयौ यकारश्च मालिनी वसुवाजिभिः । वृ० वा० ३३); No. 63 is in वसन्तमालिका (also called मालभारिणी) metre which is double ⏑ ⏑ – | ⏑ ⏑ – | ⏑ – ⏑ | – –, ⏑ ⏑ – | – ⏑ ⏑ | – ⏑ – | ⏑ – – ॥ (विषमे ससजा गौ च समे सभरया यदि । वसन्तमालिका नाम वृत्तमेतदुदाहृतम् ॥ वृ० वा० ५०); and No. 64 is in शिखरिणी metre which is four times ⏑ – – | – – – | ⏑ ⏑ ⏑ | ⏑ ⏑ – | – ⏑ ⏑ | ⏑ – ॥ (ऋतुरुद्रैः शिखरिणी यमौ नसभला गुरुः । वृ० वा० ३४).

CANTO TWO

1. For the details about the washerman's incident see भाग० 10. 41. 31–42. Though the details are there, the situation is made quite dramatic by our author. मुसलिन् is a name of बलराम

who is armed with a club. वरिल्ल is considered as a देशी word meaning 'a garment'. Either it goes back to उपर on the analogy of उत्तरीय or it comes from the root वृ to cover, with the suffix इल्ल.

3. To entertain the idea of getting the clothes belonging to कंस is to invite his wrath, and to demand them openly is indeed a fatal calamity. कंस is compared with a black serpent. It bites even when it is simply threatened from a distance, then what tc say when it is actually touched. It will do all that is within its power to do. Here the figure of speech is प्रतिवस्तूपमा. सक्कए, a direct corruption of शक्यते.

4. If they do not get the clothes demanded, there is no positive loss; but the washerman warns them that they would lose their heads for this demand. जच्चमाणं is a direct corruption of the Sk. form. We may note that there is यतिभङ्ग at the end of the third line.

5. वअ+उग्गमेण=वउग्गमेण. The figure of speech here is अप्रस्तुत-प्रशंसा supported by दृष्टान्त.

6. In the form होदु we see that the termination is softened into दु and not that the consonant is lost; see also in 8 below. The other reading for अहके is अहहे. Should we read अहए possibly derived from *अहक: which is postulated by Pischel (§ 142, 194, 417)? The form अहके, however, is recognised by Vararuci (xi.9) for the मागधी dialect. For तुज्झाण see i. 25 above. सोच्छिइ Fut. 3rd p. sg. (Var. vii. 17).

7. जाहे and ताहे in the sense of यदा and तदा (Var. vi. 8). मधु was a demon killed by कृष्ण, and therefore कृष्ण is known by the names मधुमथ(न), मधुसूदन, मधुवैरिन् etc.

8. Compare with this verse भाग॰ 10. 41. 37 etc.—एवं विकत्थ-मानस्य कुपितो देवकीसुतः। रजकस्य कराग्रेण शिरः कायादपातयत्॥ तस्यानु-जीविनः सर्वे वासःकोशान्विसृज्य वै। दुद्रुवुः सर्वतो मार्गं वासांसि जगृहेऽच्युतः॥

9. The adjectives are to be construed both with रअअस्स अप्पा and वसणाणं णिअरो. The washerman was haughty, but he had the good luck of being killed at the hands of lord कृष्ण; so his आत्मन्, with all modesty and with all its sins washed away, enters into the realm of eternal light, namely, the person of divine कृष्ण. Simultaneously with the departure of his spirit, the clothes which were clean with their dirt washed away came into the possession of कृष्ण with all modesty. For the idea of the spirit entering into कृष्णपरमात्मन् see शिशुपाल॰ xiv. 64 and xx. 79. The spirit of शिशुपाल, who was killed by कृष्ण, enters the body of कृष्ण. The figure of speech here is तुल्ययोगिता.

10. कृष्ण has a blue body decked with a shining girdle of gold, and he has put on the white garments; so he looks like the Blue mountain having golden slopes covered with moonlight. Note the play of the syllable स in the first line and partly in the second line. We have an उपमा here.

11. Compare the details of the following incident with भाग॰ 10. 42. 1 etc. According to छाया, णं=एनाम्. The name of this lady is त्रिवक्रा as given in भाग॰. According to बालचरित of भास, her name is मदनिका.

13. Now and then the author shows the tendency of repeating some syllable or the other in a melodious manner.

14. She says that Fate has been adverse to her, with the result that it has put even in her limbs crookedness which is to be found usually in the heart of women. Here the figure of speech is अतिशयोक्ति.

15. Compare भाग॰ 10. 42. 3 etc.–दास्यस्म्यहं सुन्दर कंससंमता त्रिवक्रनामा ह्यनुलेपकर्मणि। In this way our text has got some common words etc., with भाग॰ in corresponding contexts.

16. The copulative particle च is used twice in the first half: it means that it is put to each of the members connected. चिएअं=चिअ+एअं. The author happily expresses a common idea which we come across so often in Sanskrit literature. Compare कुलेन कान्त्या वयसा नवेन गुणैश्च तैस्तैर्विनयप्रधानैः। त्वमात्मनस्तुल्यममुं वृणीष्व रत्नं समागच्छतु काञ्चनेन ॥ रघु॰ vi. 79; साधारणोऽयमुभयोः प्रणयः स्मरस्य तप्तेन तप्तमयसा घटनाय योग्यम् ॥ विक्रमोर्वशीयम् ii. 16; स धर्मराजः खलु धर्मशीलया त्वयास्ति चित्तातिथितामवापितः। ममापि साधुः प्रतिभात्ययं क्रमश्चकास्ति योग्येन हि योग्यसंगमः ॥ नैषधीय॰ ix. 56. The figure of speech here is अर्थान्तरन्यास.

17. The flow of the phrases clearly indicates that the author first thinks in Sanskrit and then a Prākrit line is mechanically produced.

19. Note the form पुण्णिमाअं, a direct corruption of पूर्णिमायां Loc. sg. of पूर्णिमा. There is alliteration in the last two lines. कमणी appears to be a contraction of कमनीय.

21. मदन is already enemical towards कृष्ण, because he feels that he is surpassed by the physical beauty of कृष्ण. कृष्ण has become a partisan of त्रिवक्रा by compassionating her. मदन is tormenting her now; and this can be due to the fact that she is sided by कृष्ण with whom मदन is not on good terms. Here we have the प्रत्यनीकालङ्कार.

22. Usually the arrows of मदन are made of अरविन्द, अशोक, चूत, नवमल्लिका and नीलोत्पल flowers which obviously are incapable of burning and infatuating, and hence the need of her conjecture that his arrows nowadays are made of flowers of poisonous trees. In this text we come across forms like मणाइ, कुणाइ etc. Elsewhere we get भणासि also. Either they are formed on the analogy of मणामि or contaminated with the forms of the ninth class (Pischel § 514). Here the figure of speech is उत्प्रेक्षा arising out of विरोध.

23. She is her own mistress; but as मदन is tormenting her now, she has become helpless; so कृष्ण should come to her rescuse at this moment: that is her line of argument. Note the form मि Acc. sg. of अस्मद् (Pischel § 415).

24. कृष्ण is compared with the Black mount; there is saffron on his chest just as there is mineral colour on the mountain: त्रिवक्रा proposes that she would rub it off with her breasts by closely embracing him. लुइ is given as an आदेश for मृज्. Can we not connect it with रूक्ष्, to make dry?

25. वाहरइ म्ह–Note the use of the particle स्म to give the sense of the past. So far as I know, it is unprecedented in Prākrit. कृष्ण says that it is for him to make advances, and he did intend to that effect. He mildly complains, with a bit of taunt to her audacity as well, that she has really anticipated him by speaking as above. How it is for him to court first is made clear by an illustration in the next verse. He does intend to court her, but due to the important mission on hand he is forced to adjourn his love affairs. तइ=त्वया.

26. What is true of the goose should have also been true in his case but for the urgent and pressing duty on hand to which he has to attend. The form किं दु is found in some Mss. of the dramas. but it is considered as a wrong reading for किं तु. (Pischel § 185).

27. The mission on hand is so pressing that कृष्ण admits that he is not the master of himself (परवान्). The figure of speech is अर्थान्तरन्यास.

28. The form दाव for तावत् is met with in some of the Mss. of गाथासप्तशती 90, 168, 503 etc. (and Weber accepts that reading) and in रावणवहो 3.26 etc. The figure of speech here is प्रतिवस्तूपमा.

29. Compare the idea in the first two lines with मेघदूत ii. 47– पश्चादावां विरहगुणितं तं तमात्माभिलाषं निर्वेक्ष्यावः परिणतशरच्चन्द्रिकासु क्षपासु ॥. सुजनानां–of good people who are capable of appreciating the poetic merits. Perhaps the author has in view the sessions of epic or bardic singers which are continued late at night. The figure of speech here is उपमा.

30. विसए–Prākrits do not admit the distinction of पदs, परस्मैपद and आत्मनेपद; and there is only one set of terminations. Now and then some relics of Sk. आत्मनेपद are inherited. विश् is परस्मैपद in Sanskrit; still our author uses विसए; so perhaps it is metri causa.

31. तहि-तत्र (Var. vi. 7; Hc. ii. 161). Here the figure of speech is अर्थान्तरन्यास.

33. सज्जिअं=सज्यम् 'accompanied by the string'. With Nos. 33-36 compare भाग० 10. 42. 16 etc.

34. Perhaps the author accepts the form इत्ति=इति. Of course we can read मा छिव त्ति without violating the metre. सुअंति=श्रूयन्ते, a case of direct corruption.

35. After hearing the crashing sound of the bow, कंस had his mind crowded with various thoughts to get some reasonable explanation of the occurrence. The incarnation of Man-lion or नरसिंहावतार was an event of the hoary past; so he asks whether it has come back again. इह+अवित्थ see i. 28 above; the reading is obscure, and hence my suggestion in the light of what I have said at i. 28. Here the figure of speech is संदेह.

36. विड्डिर+इल्ल; इल्ल is a possessive termination (Hc. ii. 159) put to विड्डिर, a देशी word meaning terror.

37. The figure of speech here is समुच्चय.

38. अंकणत्थलीअं=अङ्कणस्थल्याम्, a case of direct corruption. Note the opening conjuncts of प्पआसमाणे in 37 and of प्फुड here.

39. I have taken समुवट्ठिअ as a Gerundive form on the analogy of ठाविअ=स्थापयित्वा (iv. 12 below), though the छाया equates it with समुपस्थित. There is rhyme at the close of lines *a* & *b* and *c* & *d*. We can see how the author is finding out an opportunity to give a description of the town of मथुरा which follows in the subsequent verses. In this very context भाग॰ also has a description of मथुरा (भाग॰ 10. 41. 19 etc.), but beyond a few words there is nothing particularly common. Some ideas and words remind us of the description of द्वारका in शिशुपाल॰ iii. 33 etc. Just to avoid the repetition of sense I have taken राजधानी once as 'a capital' and a second time 'a royal residence'.

40. भुवणप्पणाइदाए=भुवनपणायिताया:, thus the doubling of प is either euphonic or for the sake of metre.

41. If the reading was सगव्वं, then it would have qualified णयरिं. The town of मथुरा threatens as it were the celestial town of अमरावती which it has already surpassed by its prosperity. The figure of speech is उत्प्रेक्षा.

42. जम्बुद्वीप is one of the seven islands of which the world is made up. It stands surrounded by the ocean. In its centre stands the mountain मेरु with its golden peaks on which the heavenly nymphs are sporting. This town is metaphorically identified with जंबुद्वीप whose dignity it possesses, because it stands surrounded by a moat and on its shining terraces of lofty palaces beautiful ladies are sporting. The figure of speech is निदर्शना.

43. जाह्नवी, the daughter of जह्नु from whose ear गंगा is said to have issued. At their confluence, it is said, the rivers Ganges and Jumna give a wondeful scene due to the blending of their whitish and darkish streams. This idea is quite a favourite one with Sanskrit writers. Compare रघुवंश vi. 48, xiii. 57; मेघदूत i. 51; शिशुपाल॰ iv. 26; and गउडवहो 1053. The figure of speech here is स्मरणालङ्कार.

44. Note the forms णिण्हुआअं वीहिआअं which are the corruptions of निह्नुतायां वीथिकायां। Even by day there is darkness in the streets which are obscured by the dark hue of the pleasure mounts. So quite fearlessly the love-lorn go to their lovers even by day. अभिसारिका is defined thus: मदेन मदनेनापि प्रेरिता शिथिलत्रपा। योत्सुकाभिसरेत् कान्तं सा भवेदभिसारिका ॥ कुलजां गणिकां प्रेष्यां यथार्हैर्वेषचेष्टितैः। रागातिशयसंपन्नां वर्णयेदभिसारिकाम् ॥

45. चक्रवाक couples get separated at night. But here, as the sky was flooded with the glow of the golden palaces, they remained together even late in the evening thinking that it was the light of the rising sun. रअणीअं=रजन्याम्, a case of direct corruption.

46. The masses of light emanating from the jewels on the ramparts were so bright that now and then they added their mite to the hallos of light of the sun and moon.

47. मुसिणाइ a corruption of मुष्णाति This reminds us of शिशुपाल॰ iii. 79–उत्सङ्गिताम्भःकणको नभस्वानुदन्वतः स्वेदलवान्ममर्ज etc.

48. The houses, being fitted with moonstones, are quite cool even in the summer-nights; so young people do not feel any sexual exhaustion there. समअं=सम(क)म्.

49. इअं महुरा etc. The figure of speech here is उत्प्रेक्षा. कुडुअ+उल्ली, उल्ल being the possessive suffix.

50. सुहपण्हिं=सुखप्रश्नम्, the vowel change in पण्हिं appears to be irregular. सुहपण्हं would be allright metrically. पअलंत=प्रचलत् or प्रगलत्. The guests are offered water to wash their feet and then follows a cordial inquiry about their welfare. This verse reminds us of शिशुपालवध viii. 14–उत्क्षिप्तस्फुटितसरोरुहार्घ्यमुच्चैः सस्नेहं विहगरुतै-रिवालपन्ती । नारीणामथ सरसी सफेनहासा प्रीत्येव व्यतनुत पाद्यमूर्मिहस्तैः ॥

51. Note the play of sound in the first two lines. वित्थरंतं qualifies रहस्समं.

52. दोग्घट्ट is treated as a देशी word meaning an elephant. Sometimes it is differently spelt as दुग्घुट्ट, दुग्घोट्ट; and Trivikrama (II. i. 30) gives its etymology thus: दुग्घोट्टो दोग्घोट्टो द्विपः। पिबतेर्घोट्टः। द्वाभ्यां पिबतीति. The elephant has two frontal globes, so it may be called द्विघटः to which word I would trace back दोग्घट्ट. Pischel traces ओज्झर from a postulated word *अवक्षर (§ 326). Note the form दंति, the usual form from the root दा being देंति (Pischel § 474). Our author regularly uses णिहेल in the sense of इन्द्रनील jewel (iii. 19, iv. 11 below). Note the form वसुहम्मि Loc. sg. of वसुहा. The author is describing the various scenes in the town of मथुरा. In some places the ground is slimy with the rut of elephants; thereon the bees are settling down; and so it gives the appearance of a pavement of इन्द्रनील jewels.

53. The reading पंचमं also would be equally significant indicating the musical note guiding the dance.

54. The compound may be thus dissolved: णिव्वहंतो तालो जेसुं ताणि फुडाणि संगीआणि तेसुं जो णडाणं अंगहारो तस्स चिंधं. चिंध=चिह्न, here इंध, च् being lost, as that word becomes noninitial in a compound. कोच्चि =कचित्. Though the छाया equates कोच्चि with क्वचित्, it is rather difficult to justify this equation grammatically. I would suggest that कोच्चि might stand for कश्चित्. Note मइंग for मृदङ्ग, usually we have मुइंग, also मिइंग (see Pischel § 51).

55. Though the author is describing the scenes from मथुरा, after all he belongs to the western coast; so possibly he refers to the female singers from the East.

56. The author depicts a scene of grammarians' debate at मथुरा. They are discussing a point of Sanskrit grammar. The case in issue is the Sandhi between two words like सुधी+उपास्य. According to the rule of Pāṇini इको यणचि (vi. i. 77), the ई at the end of सुधी is changed to य्. Thus we get सुध्य्+उपास्य. Now according to the सूत्र, अनचि च (viii. iv. 47), the consonant ध्, which is preceded by the vowel उ and followed by the consonant य् is to be doubled optionally: सु ध् ध् य्+उपास्य. But in view of the fact that the substitute letter has the same value as the original (स्थानिवद् आदेशो), i. e., the consonant य् is as good as the vowel ई and should not therefore have the effect of duplicating the preceding ध्. This means that the rule अणचि च should become inoperative. But this objection is set at rest by the सूत्र which adds अनल्विधौ 'not when a rule of letter is to be applied.' The rule is not inoperative, because of the अल्विधि, i. e., at the time of the application of the letter-rule like अणचि च. I may quote here the relevent portion from सिद्धान्तकौमुदी–इको यणचि ।६।१।७७। इकः स्थाने यण् स्यादचि संहितायां विषये। सुधी उपास्य इति स्थिते। स्थानत आन्तर्यादीका-

रस्य यकारः । सुध्य् उपास्य इति जाते । अनचि च ।८।४।४७। अचः परस्य यरो द्वे वा स्तो न त्वचि । इति धकारस्य द्वित्वम् । स्थानिवदादेशोऽनल्विधौ ।१।१।५६। आदेशः स्थानिवत्स्यान्न तु स्थान्यलाश्रयविधौ । अनेनेह यकारस्य स्थानिवद्भावेनाच्त्वमाश्रित्यानचि चेति द्वित्वनिषेधो न शंक्योऽनल्विधाविति तन्निषेधात् (pp. 12-3, निर्णयसागर ed. Bombay 1908)

57. कृष्ण is visiting the town of मथुरा after a long time; and he is not tired even though he has seen it for a long while. It is attracting him all the more, and he feels not in any way inclined to divert his attention anywhere else.

58. The town of मथुरा is heaven itself, and this identity is described in terms of double meaning which can be made applicable to मथुरा as well as to heaven. The first set of words describes heaven and the second set (put in the angular brackets in the translation) describes the town of मथुरा. वसु means 'god' also 'wealth'. Heaven is an abode of gods and मथुरा that of wealth. Once we read किण्णरा and a second time किं णरा. इणमो is possible in Nom. sg. neuter (Vr. vi. 18). If the reading was सुहम्मुज्जलं, it could have given us two convenient qualifications: i) सुधर्मोज्ज्वलं 'glorious with the Sudharman hall' and ii) सुहर्म्योज्ज्वलं 'glorious with excellent mansions'. There is some repetition of the same syllable here and there in the first two lines. Here the figure of speech is रूपक arising out of श्लेष.

59. Young ladies, who were first averse to meet their lovers, have their passion now enkindled by the natural phenomena round about, and immediately and violently embrace their beloveds. See i. 43 above. The author achieves some sound effect by repeating the syllables. It is equally possible to read वल्लहाणं कंठे गण्हंति. as in the Sk. छाया. If we take कंठे Acc. pl., we violate the usage;

and if we take कंठे Loc. sg., then गण्ह is being used intransitively. So in view of the Sanskrit idiom I have taken वामा वल्लहा (Acc. pl.) णं कंठे (Loc. sg. collectively) गण्हंति. Compare iii. 50 below: चाणूरं चलणजुअम्मि गण्हमाणो.

60. As it is evening now, कृष्ण retires to his residence, and the sun to the western horizon. The first two lines are to be construed with both, so some words are used with double meaning. The meanings of words to be construed with the sun are put in the angular brackets in the translation. Note the form उवासरेइ for उवसरेइ. तइ=तदा (Var. i. 11). Here the figure of speech is तुल्ययोगिता. We may not take गो in the sense of cow, because कृष्ण is in मथुरा now on an important mission. He should not be painted as a cowherd here; and moreover the context shows that he summed up his description of मथुरा which he began in verse No. 39.

In this canto verses 1–57 are composed in वसन्तमालिका metre (see p. 179 above); No. 58 is in शार्दूलविक्रीडितम् which is four times – – – | ⏑ ⏑ – | ⏑ – ⏑ | ⏑ ⏑ – | – – ⏑ | – – – | – ||, and it is thus defined: अतिधृत्यां तु सूर्याश्वैर्विरामो यत्र दृश्यते । मसौ जसौ तः शार्दूलविक्रीडितमिदं तगौ ॥ वृ० वा० ३८; No. 59 is in स्रग्धरा metre which is four times – – – |– ⏑ – |– ⏑ ⏑ | ⏑ ⏑ ⏑ | ⏑ – – | ⏑ – – | ⏑ – – |, and is thus defined: प्रकृत्यां मुनिशैलाश्वैर्विश्रमो यत्र विद्यते । मरौ भनौ यत्रयं च स्रग्धरा नाम सा भवेत् ॥ वृ० वा० ४१; and No. 60 is in कटक metre (also called अवितथ) which is four times ⏑ ⏑ ⏑ | ⏑ – ⏑ | – ⏑ ⏑ | ⏑ – ⏑ | ⏑ – ⏑ | ⏑ – |, and is defined thus: नजभा जो जो लगौ च कटकं विदुः । वृ० वा० ३५.

CANTO THREE

1. वोलंति qualifies पबोहवेलं. सूत्रधार is the first to come on the stage either to perform the preliminary rites of पूर्वरङ्ग or to open the conversation at the close of नान्दी. Here the drum-sound is compared with सूत्रधार. आदत्त (here पादत्त with the preposition) is usually equated with आरब्ध by the grammarions. Pischel however postulates a form *आचत्त (§ 286) to explain it. Here the figure of speech is उत्प्रेक्षा based on रूपक This opening reminds us of शिशुपाल० xi. 1 etc.

2. पद्मलोचन or –विलोचन is कृष्ण himself who is being addressed by the bardic party. We may note the alliteration here and there in this verse. Compare माघ's comparison of poets with kings शिशुपाल० xi. 6.

3. Verses 7–20 form the address of the bards. The first कल्लाणं is exclamatory 'Hail'. Early in the morning bees are hovering everywhere and some of them issuing forth from the lotuses that are just opened. They are compared with the side-glances darted by the beautiful lady in the form of the lotus.

4. Construe तुह होस्संतिं मुहलच्छि of which अच्छि ... कण्हिमाणं is an adjective. Because कृष्ण was rising up from the bed, the moon feared that his face would be thrown into the background by that of कृष्ण and went away at once. The blue eyes of कृष्ण are more than a match for the dark spots on the moon. The moon sets in the morning and on this the author bases his fancy.

5. The author takes advantage of the double meaning of तारका= 'eye-pupil' and 'star'. Early in the morning the stars in the sky grow pale, and that, the author fancies, is due to their being humiliated by the brilliance of the pupils of कृष्ण's eyes which are opened as he leaves the bed. Compare a similar situation in शिशुपाल० xi. 24.

6. जोण्हाअं=ज्योत्स्नायां. The way in which the word is used indicates that darkness is personified. ओसरंते, note the आत्मनेपद.

7. Some of the words are to be construed with राहाए as well as सरोइणीए. करंचल–points of rays and also fingers. राधा was the favourite mistress of कृष्ण when he stayed at वृन्दावन as a गोपाल among the cowherds. In later poetry some symbolical and mystical character is seen in राधा that she represents the human spirit attracted to the God or the pure divine love flowing towards the divinity. तुवं=त्वम्. We have here समासोक्ति and उपमा.

8. What the sun is to the moon's rays कृष्ण is to the soldiers of the enemy. दुइत्तो Abl. sg. दुकूल gives the form दुऊल also; but दुगुल्ल in अर्धमागधी (Pischel § 90).

9. Note the forms झीणाअं, णिसाअं, संतदीअं etc. It is when the sins of mundane beings are exhausted that lord कृष्ण bestows his favours on them.

10. The lotuslike eyes of कृष्ण with their dark and unsteady pupils remind one of the calices of lotuses in which there are dark bees hovering. So we have here the figure of speech स्मरणालंकार.

11. The figure of speech here is उपमा.

12. If कण्ह-वच्छ-भाओ, then we may render 'the dark region of your chest'.

13. कृष्ण is compared with a lotus-pool and his eyes with the lotuses therein.

14. Note आविज्झा=आविद्धा, perhaps due to contamination with such forms as विध्यते=विज्झइ. सुज्जकंद=सूर्यकांत, on the change of न्त to न्द see Pischel § 275. The figure of speech is अर्थान्तरन्यास. This verse reminds us of शाकुन्तलम् ii. 7–शमप्रधानेषु तपोधनेषु गूढं हि दाहात्मकमस्ति तेजः। स्पर्शानुकूला इव सूर्यकान्तास्तदन्यतेजोऽभिभवाद्वमन्ति ॥

15. The sun is a lion, and the darkness an elephant. The former is mangling the latter with the consequence that the stars in the form of pearls (which the elephant carries in its head according to कविसमय) are scattered and that there is the twilight in the form of blood. The figure of speech is परंपरितरूपक. This reminds us of शिशुपाल० xi. 49–परिणतमदिराभं भास्करेणांशुबाणैस्तिमिरकरिघटायाः सर्वदिक्षु क्षतायाः। रुधिरमिव वहन्त्यो भान्ति बालातपेन छुरितमुभयरोधोवारितं वारि नद्यः ॥

16. The छाया renders अल्लिएइ by आश्रयति; we should better connect it with आली, to settle down upon. Note the opening conjunct in प्पडिणव. As to the figure, there is अर्थान्तरन्यास in the third supported by उपमा in the fourth line. Such a combination is called by the name विकस्वर.

17. The morning sun is spreading his red rays on the breasts of unchaste women that have the saffron therefrom rubbed away by the chests of their beloveds whom they visited; so this twilight here is like fresh saffron on their breasts. This reminds us of शिशुपाल० xi. 55.

18. अम्मेलावइ=आम्रेडयति, repeats and hence intensifies. The red hue of the vermillion on the heads of elephants is intensified, as it is lit up by the rays of the morning sun. पिसंगिमाणं Acc. sg. पिशंगिमन् in the sense of पिशंगत्व. This verse reminds us of शिशुपाल० xi. 43–45.

19. छुर to cover, फुरउ would have been more appropriate. The saffron mark left by लक्ष्मी's breasts on the chest of कृष्ण is so bright that it would lend some loveliness even to the rays of the morning sun.

20. Note the form उज्जिहाण directly corrupted from Sk. उज्जिहान pres. p. from उद्–हा to rise up. The figure of speech is मालारूपक. The illustrative quotation given by साहित्यदर्पण (x. 30) may be compared with this verse: मनोजराजस्य सितातपत्रं श्रीखण्डचित्रं हरिदङ्गनायाः। विराजते व्योमसरःसरोजं कर्पूरपूरप्रभमिन्दुबिम्बम्॥

21. कृष्ण is awake even before the bards pour out their eulogistic songs, just as the blooming of the lotus plant precedes the cackling of the swans. Here the figure of speech is दृष्टान्त.

23. The twilight lustre was like a red जपा flower; cf. मेघदूत i. 36–सान्ध्यं तेजः प्रतिनवजपापुष्परक्तं दधानः। The brilliant twilight with its reddish hue reminds कृष्ण of the moonlike face of राधा from whom he is now separated. हुत्तं=अभिमुखम् (Hc. ii. 158). Here the figure of speech is स्मरण.

24 The figure of speech is उपमा, and the imagery is finely projected by the author.

25. बहुदिअहे, Acc. pl. This we might call Acc. of time, 'for or over many days'. The throbbing of the left eye is considered as auspicious in the case of females but inauspicious for males: what was a happy prospect for कृष्ण's mother was a fatal calamity for कंस and others. For the various omens at that time see भाग. 10. 42. 27 etc. स-माउराए=स्वमातुः the use of स्व is not quite appropriate, but it was perhaps necessary for rhyme seen at the end of *a* & *b* and *c* & *d*. In the light of author's own usage (i. 2, iii. 16) rather समल्लिआणं, but perhaps he has used समल्लआणं for rhyme.

26. Perhaps the author imagines that the streets are speckled with reflections of the glances of ladies who are standing on the mansions. अअंति=अयन्ति, Pres. 3rd p. pl. of इ I P, to go.

27. अम्बष्ठ is the keeper of the elephant कुवलयापीड belonging to कंस. His attempt to overpower कृष्ण with the help of his elephant was as ill-advised as that of a person who wishes to shelter himself from the sun by his hand. For this event see भाग० 10. 43. 1 etc.

28. आमेल=आपीड (Vr. ii. 16), but Pischel postulates a word *आपीड्य from which he derives आमेल (§ 122). **आपीडं कुवलयपूर्वे** i. e., आपीड prefixed by the word **कुवलय**, which amounts to **कुवलयापीड** the name of an elephant belonging to **कंस**. In **शिशुपाल०** we have हिरण्यपूर्वं कशिपुं=हिरण्यकशिपुं i. 42. **अभ्रमु** is the wife of ऐरावत who therefore gets the name **अभ्रमुनाथ.** Cf. शिशुपाल० i. 52 सलीलयातानि भर्तुरभ्रमोः

29. मत्तवारणं, in the first line, means the fence round the mansion (of यमगृह), while in the second line a rutted elephant viz. **कुवलयापीड.** The form **अण्णत्तो** may be explained from **अन्यद्+तः,** and on the analogy of this we get **सव्वत्तो** etc.

30. Here too we have *a* & *b* and *c* & *d* rhyming. **सजीवो=** सजीवः, the duplication of the second member is perhaps due to the metre. The first two lines constitute the reply of **कृष्ण** who is **उग्रकर्मा**, i. e., whose acts are fatally fierce. Cf. भाग० 10. 43. 4 etc.

31. खुडिअ=खण्डित or त्रुटित, wounded, cut or bursting open. मंदरं व पुव्वं–here is a reference to the mythological churning of the ocean for nectar. On that occasion the mountain **मन्दर** was used as a churning stick and the serpent **वासुकी** as a rope. The normal Prākrit form is **सिंखला** for **शृङ्खला**, but here we have **सिंखरा.** There are a few Prākrit words which show र for the ल of the Sanskrit words: **किर** (iii. 44) =**किल, फरअ=फलक, सामरी=शाल्मली** (Pischel § 259). Here the figure of speech is **उपमा.**

32. From the छाया it appears that the original reading might have been **परिवेसमूढहेलं**; the author has already used **परिवेस** at ii. 46. First **कृष्ण** leads that elephant round and round, so that it might get exhausted; and when it takes circular movements with its trunk gracefully bent, he fells it and strikes on its temples.

33. जाला and ताला are used like यदा and तदा (Hc. iii. 65). Pischel derives them from * यात् कालात् and * तात् कालात् which are postulated stages. Note the form महिम्मि from मही f. for loc. sg. तं stands for इसणजुअं. The elephant strikes the ground with the idea that कृष्ण is there, but as he has slipped away with his adroit movements the elephant, due to its heavy stroke, stands there with its tusks sinking in the earth. It is pinned in that position, and कृष्ण takes advantage of further attack. अहो=अथो, now.

34. For the detailed description see भाग० 10. 43. 9 etc., especially verse 14.

35. The similes here have in view certain mythological references. Once upon a time the mountains, which had formerly wings, grew very refractory and troublesome; so Indra cut off their wings with his thunderbolt, and they fell finally in their present positions. We have a vivid and elegant description of the flying mountains in गउडवहो (verses 224–235). The elephant कुवलयापीड falls like कृष्णगिरि when its wings were cut by Indra's thunderbolt. शेष is the king of नागs, the serpent race, dwelling in पाताल. He has thousand heads or hoods that are said to carry the globe of the earth. When the elephant fell, the earth shook as though it was dislodged from the heads of शेष.

36. अम्बष्ठ being the keeper, the elephant followed him and his instructions all these days. Now कृष्ण wanted to reverse this order, and he made अम्बष्ठ follow the elephant. The elephant was first killed and अम्बष्ठ was made to follow it to the grave. Note that the alternative lines begin with similar words.

37. पुप्फवंता=पुष्पवन्तौ, usually 'those that are decorated with flowers'; but in view of the qualifications उम्हसोम्मसीला and गअणतलं व गाहंता it is more appropriate to take that word to mean 'sun and moon'. It is better that the simile should stop with the second line. The reading प्पमइलदं would stand for प्रमलिनतां. The arrival of राम and कृष्ण was a matter of joy to some and a matter of sorrow to others. *a* & *b* and *c* & *d* rhyme at the beginning.

38. After killing the elephant कुवलयापीड, राम and कृष्ण are carrying the tusks as trophies in their hands; compare भाग० 10. 43. 15–16. People saw these brothers to their heart's content, and felt that their eyes were fruitful today. In early Kannaḍa, Tamil and Malayalam poetry the second letter of all the lines of a verse is the same. Our author shows such a tendency here and there in the first half or the second half of a verse: see i. 7, 27; ii. 16, 32; iii. 38, 41, 43, 59; iv. 3, 25, 30, 40, 48*2, etc.

39. Sanskrit छाया renders मुकुलतमानि; that implies that the reading of the text might have been मउलदमाइ. But here we can conveniently take तेषां वक्त्राणि मलिनतमानि भवन्ति 'their faces become superlatively dark or faded'. मइल though usually equated with मलिन, may be traced back to a word like *मृदिल, मृद् f. dust etc. The figure of speech is दृष्टान्त.

40. णवरि अ is taken as अनन्तरं by the छाया. We have an उपमा here, and it is quite apt.

41. चाणूर and मुष्टिक were celebrated wrestlers in the service of कंस whose special favour they enjoyed. Being awake they protected (अवंति) the whole army. If we could read णिहिलमुवंति, the meaning would be 'they inspect the whole army'. We have an उत्प्रेक्षा here.

42. कैटभ and मधु were terrible demons. It is said that they tried to kill Brahman seated on the lotus springing from विष्णु's naval. विष्णु-कृष्ण killed them, and hence he gets the names कैटभ or मधु-सूदन (see also ii. 7, 32, 34).

43. चाणूर thinks that he would tickle कृष्ण's vanity and induce him to fight against a heavy champion by saying गोवालो etc. भूत्रालो is apparently king कंस. Note the alliteration effected throughout the verse. Here the figure of speech is अर्थान्तरन्यास.

44. Compare भाग० 10. 43. 32–40. Daityas are a race of demons or giants who fought against gods and molested the sacrifices. Often they are associated with दानवs.

45. नाम appears to be used here simply as an explative. If they fight, the Bhoja king will be able to know who is superior or inferior in the strength of arms

46. णेण=अणेण चाणूरेण. कृष्ण enters into a duel with चाणूर and बलराम with मुष्टिक.

47. The doubling of प in प्परुस appears to be euphonic. Or should we read पिब्बोलं परुस etc. ? बाहुजंतं refers to the armlocks adopted in wrestling. Are we to read खुब्भंतं तिहुवण etc. ? आसि and आसी, both the forms are current.

48. Compare with this and the following verse भाग० 10. 44. 1 10.

51. जोइरिंगणोहा would have been a normal reading. Here the figure of speech is दृष्टान्त. Cf. भाग० 10. 44. 28–31 etc. with this and the following verse.

53. Here the figure of speech is श्लेषोपमा. Naturally some words, which are to be construed both with कृष्ण and गरुड and both with कंस and serpent, are to be understood with a twofold meaning. विसमहिअं=विषमहृदयं or -धियं and विषमधिकम्. विणअत्ति= विनत+अर्ति and विनता+अर्ति. गरुड is a mythical bird-man on which विष्णु rides. कश्यप was his father and विनता his mother. विनता was not on good terms with her cowife and superior कद्रु, the mother of serpents, and was treated by her almost like a slave. गरुड wanted to rescue विनता from this slavery, but the serpents demanded अमृत as a price for विनता's freedom. अमृत or nectar was obtained, and in addition गरुड got a boon that all the serpents would be his food. गरुड gave अमृत to the serpents and rescued his mother; but इन्द्र, with whom गरुड had already entered into conspiracy, outwitted the serpents and carried the pot of nectar Cf. भाग० 10. 44. 36–तं खड्गपाणिं विचरन्तमाशु श्येनं यथा दक्षिणसव्य-मम्बरे। समग्रहीदुर्विषह्योग्रतेजा यथोरगं तार्क्ष्यसुतः प्रसह्य ॥ On the next verse cf. ibid. 10. 44. 34–35.

55. प्पवडिअ–प्रपत्य, Gerund of प्रपत्. The word वत्थि perhaps stands for वशा or fat. If it is to be traced back पत्थी, a देशी word for पात्री, then it refers to the bony socket of the heart. I have taken कुणइ=कृणोति from कृ 5 U, to injure, to hurt.

56. गरुड is the conveyance of विष्णु, but he is allowed to sit on the roof when विष्णु is driving in a chariot; so विष्णु–कृष्ण gets the title गरुडध्वज. Here the figure of speech is अर्थान्तरन्यास.

57–8. Compare भाग० 10. 44. 42; also कंसवधम् of शेषकृष्ण vi. 46. Such descriptions are quite common in Indian literature in such contexts. Note the alliteration here and there.

59. कंस had eight brothers कङ्क, न्यग्रोधक etc. See भाग० 10.44. 40–1. The second letter is the same in all the four lines. Though the brothers were wicked, they went to heaven because they were killed by कृष्ण who is an incarnation of God.

60. We have alliteration here and there in this verse, and the figure of speech is परंपरितरूपक.

In this canto verses 1–56 are composed in प्रहर्षिणी metre which is four times – – – | ⏑ ⏑ ⏑ | ⏑ – ⏑ | – ⏑ – | –, and is thus defined: मनौ जरौ गुरुर्यत्र गुणैर्दिग्भिः प्रहर्षिणी । (वृ० वा० २७); verse No. 57 is in पृथ्वी metre which is four times ⏑ – ⏑ | ⏑ ⏑ – | ⏑ – ⏑ | ⏑ ⏑ – | ⏑ – – | ⏑ – ||, and is thus defined: वसुग्रहयतिः पृथ्वी जसौ जसयला गुरुः (वृ० वा० ३४); verse No. 58 is शार्दूलविक्रीडितम् (see p. 190 above); verse No. 59 is in स्वागता metre which is four times – ⏑ – | ⏑ ⏑ ⏑ | – ⏑ ⏑ | – – ||, and is thus defined: रनभा गुरुयुग्मं च स्वागतेति निगद्यते (वृ० वा० १७); and verse No. 60 is in हरिणी metre which is four times ⏑ ⏑ ⏑ | ⏑ ⏑ – | – – – | – ⏑ – | ⏑ ⏑ – | ⏑ – ||, and is thus defined: रसोपायहयैश्छिन्ना नसौ मरसला गुरुः । हरिणी (वृ० वा० ३५).

CANTO FOUR

1. The world was oppressed by the tyranny of कंस, so कृष्ण brought relief to all the beings by slaying कंस. Here the figure of speech is रूपक.

2. प्रसादलक्ष्मी is compared with हंसराजि and other items are to be construed similarly. The figure of speech is उपमा.

3. कुलपालिकाः or even कुलबालिकाः. Formerly they were afraid of moving about lest the king कंस might molest their chastity.

4. There is यमक at the close of *a* & *b* and *c* & *d*. In the second line अणंतराअं is taken as अनन्तरागम् by the छाया. Can we not take it as अनन्तरात्रम् and interpret thus: 'youths that desire to sport with (their) beloveds over endless nights without any hindrance'? They were sorry because the night comes to end; they wished that it was endless. Cf. the sentiment expressed by the king in विक्रमोर्वशीयम् iii. 22–अनुपनतमनोरथस्य पूर्वं शतगुणितेव गता मम त्रियामा। यदि तु तव समागमे तथैव प्रसरति सुभ्रु ततः कृती भवेयम् ॥

5. विढत्त, usually translated as अर्जित, is rendered by the छाया as विधृत. The first three adjectives are to be construed with विलासदिढ्ढी as well as खग्गलट्ठी. The figure of speech is परिसंख्या. With the death of कंस there has been a good deal of change in the circumstances: people are happy (No. 2); ladies can move freely (No. 3); youths have no hindrance in their sports (No. 4); and lastly, as stated in this verse, voluptuaries too get much liberty.

6. Bhojas and Andhakas are the clan-names of the descendents of Bhoja and Andhaka. उग्रसेन is the father of कंस, and कंस had wrested the crown by deposing him. So कृष्ण, after killing कंस, restored उग्रसेन to the throne. माआपिदरे i. e., the parents of कृष्ण who were imprisoned by कंस (see i. 12 above).

7. वृष्णि is a clan-name derived from वृष्णि, a descendent of यदु. कृष्णं belongs to this branch of lunar race. णे=माआपिदरे Acc. pl.

8. The meaning of चिरस्स is partly covered by दिग्घाउणो. आनकदुन्दुभि and देवकी are the parents of कृष्ण. The former is वसुदेव himself, and he is so called because the drums of heaven resounded at his birth.

9. The first is the description of the chest of बलराम and the second is that of कृष्ण; this distinction is due to their natural bodily colours.

10. The occasion and context are not quite fitting, still the author makes अक्रूर narrate the various events in the lives of बलराम and कृष्ण. At any rate the poet wants to narrate the other events of कृष्ण's life in this poem. All these events are referred to in भाग० at places more than one. They are collectively stated at भाग० 10. 26. 1–15. This narration of events reminds us of the praise poured on कृष्ण by भीष्म in शिशुपाल० xiv. 54 etc.

12. The छाया renders संस्मररात्रिमध्ये, on that memorable night', taking संस्मर=संस्मरणीय. I have however taken शम्बररात्रिमध्ये 'on a cloudy night'. The cther part I have thus consurued: कलिंदअण्णा तुज्झं जंघाण लंघीअ (=लंघ्या). On this and the next verse, cf. भाग० 10. 3 closing verses, espically No. 51 which runs thus: मघोनि वर्षत्यसकृद्यमानुजा गम्भीरतोयाघजवोर्मिफेनिला। भयानकावर्तशताकुला नदी मार्गं ददौ सिन्धुरिव श्रियः पतेः॥ I have translated 12 & 13 as independent verses apparently taking तं for जं. As they stand 11–13 would be taken together.

13. शौरिः a patronymic of वसुदेव. In exchanging कृष्ण with a cowherd girl Vasudeva was a loser; but the gravity of the occasion demanded it, because कृष्ण's life was in danger. The figure of speech is अर्थान्तरन्यास. तुए=त्वया, quite usual in dramas.

14. See भाग० 10. 6. पूतना was a female demon, a daughter of बलि. She attempted to kill the infant कृष्ण by suckling him, but instead of her milk कृष्ण sucked her life and reduced her to death. She goes to better worlds as she meets her end at the hands of divine कृष्ण whom she tried to suckle.

15. घरेसएण is an अलुक् compound. तृणावर्त was a demon in the service of कंस who sent him to destroy कृष्ण. He assumed the form of a whirlwind (चक्रवातः), covered the area of गोकुल with dust and sand, and in that turmoil carried off the infant कृष्ण, but was overpowered by the weight of the child and was consequently killed. जिणा=येन (Pischel § 427–28). चक्कवाअ (=चक्रवात) was reduced to the position of चक्कवाअ (=चक्रवाक bird) in the lake of the यमलोक, i. e., he was killed. See भाग० 10. 7. 20. etc.

16. The word गव्व stands for both गन्य and गर्व as shown in the translation.

17. There is pun on the word माआ. कृष्ण rescues people who are bound by माआ (=माया), but he himself is bound to a mortar by माआ (=माता or मातृ). Note माआए is Inst. sg. from माआ=मातृ. कृष्ण was ever mischevous. Once he broke the pot of curds which enraged his mother यशोदा who consequently tied him down to a mortar. After a good deal of effort she could manage to get a sufficiently long rope to fasten round his body (भाग० 10. 9. 14 etc.)

18. By way of revenge परशुराम destroyed कार्तवीर्य-अर्जुन who was known as सहस्रबाहु and who, according to another tradition, had thousand arms. The back-ground of the event of कृष्ण's breaking a pair of अर्जुन trees is like this. Two यक्षs, नलकूबर and मणिग्रीव, were once sporting with ladies in the river Ganges. They were excessively drunk and completely nude. नारद was passing by that way. At the sight of the sage नारद the ladies clothed themselves, but the two brothers were too drunk to mind their nudity. नारद was offended by their behaviour, felt that they did not deserve to be men, and cursed them that they might be turned into trees for a period of one hundred years. They would be relieved, however, by the contact of कृष्ण. For his mischief, we have seen above, कृष्ण was tied to a mortar, but divine as his power was, he pulled the mortar through the interspace between the pair of अर्जुन trees (viz., the two यक्षs converted into trees) in the veranda. His pull was so forcible that both the trees were uprooted; and consequently the यक्षs were released from the form of trees. Cf शिशुपाल० xiv. 80 with this verse.

19. बकासुर was a demon in the service of कंस Once he assumed the form of a crane and tried to swallow कृष्ण who was playing with his companions. His mouth and throat were burnt and consequently कृष्ण was vomitted. Just on the spot कृष्ण finished him to death when he further attacked him with the beek (भाग॰ 10. 11. 48 etc.). णिअगोसआइं पआरअंतं can be construed both with णं=तं कृष्णं and सहस्समोहं=सहस्रमयूखम्; accordingly गो can mean 'cow' as well as 'ray of light.'

20. अघासुर was a demon in the service of कंस who despatched him to destroy कृष्ण. He came to गोकुल and assumed the form of a huge boa-constrictor. The cowherds entered its mouth mistaking it for a mountain cavern. कृष्ण also entered its mouth with a view to rescue others, and enlarged himself to such an extent that the serpent was burst to death (See भाग॰ 10. 12. 13 onwards). The छाया reads कर्मदोषात् perhaps with a reading कम्मदोसा in view.

21. In this verse the author has the following incident in view. ब्रह्मदेव made the cows, cowherds etc. invisible for a period of one year, and thus tested the power of कृष्ण who could outwit ब्रह्मन् by his all-pervasive ability. Cf. भाग॰ 10. 13, especially verse 15. Verse 44 runs thus –एवं संमोहयन् विष्णुं विमोहं विश्वमोहनम्। स्वयैव मायययाजोऽपि स्वयमेव विमोहितः॥ ब्रह्मन् realizes that he was outwitted, seeks shelter of कृष्ण's feet, and then offers a long prayer (see भाग॰ 10. 13. 60 etc. and 10. 14 also which chapter is called ब्रह्मस्तुति). Better read कवलडूपाणिं for कवलद्ध–, which is apparently a name of कृष्ण who, as a typical cowherd, carries a bunch of grass in his hand. The adjective सपाणिकवल for कृष्ण is often used in भाग॰, see 10. 13. 14. 61; 10. 14. 1 etc.

22. Compare भाग॰ 10. 11. 36 etc. where various sports are described. Verse No. 36 runs thus: वृन्दावनं गोवर्धनं यमुनापुलिनानि च। वीक्ष्यासीदुत्तमा प्रीती राममाधवयोर्नृप॥

23. On this verse see भाग० 10. 15. 21 etc. धेनुक was a demon who lived in a palm-grove from which the cowherds once wanted to enjoy the fruits. धेनुक assumed the form of an ass and began to attack बलराम who was shaking the trees. बलराम seized the ass by its legs, whirled it round till it was dead, and threw its body on the top of trees which were thereby thoroughly shaken as if by a whirlwind. All the trees fell down as much as the enemies therein like धेनुक. Thereafter people could enter that forest freely, and the cows also could graze happily there. Thus people were made happy and the burden of the wicked was removed from the earth.

24. अङ्ग is a term of address, a particle implying attention, assent or desire etc. It is constantly used in भाग० in these contexts. वीससिमो a direct corruption of the Sk. form. The word धेनुक is used with two different meanings, and hence the apparent contradiction.

25. Note the यमक at the opening of *a* & *b* and *c* & *d*. कालिआहि=कालिय+अहि and कालिकाभिः. कालिय was a serpent king with five hoods. Being afraid of गरुड whom he had offended, he came and dwelt in a deep pool of यमुना, and thus proved a bane to the living world all around. The child कृष्ण once jumped into the pool, and when he was entwined by the snakes he overpowered them. He simply danced with dignity on the hoods of कालिय who had to pray for कृष्ण's mercy. कृष्ण spared others but forced कालिय and his attendants to go to the ocean. We have here उपमा. This and the following verse describe the above event. Cf. भाग० 10. 16. 3 etc.

26–7. दामोदर is a name given to कृष्ण due to a rope going round his belly when he pulled the mortar between a pair of अर्जुन

trees noted above. The author depicts here the scene of boy कृष्ण stepping and dancing on the hoods of कालिय. The language flows quite in tune with the ideas of the author. Cf. भाग० 10. 16. 24 etc. In 26 the figure of speech is उपमा, and in 27 स्वभावोक्ति.

28. कालिय had his vanity completely smashed by कृष्ण whose mercy he implored. कृष्ण blessed कालिय with protection from सुपर्ण गरुड on account of whose fear he had migrated to यमुना. Cf. भाग० 10. 16. 63 and also 10. 17. 1–10 etc. The figures of speech here are अर्थान्तरन्यास and पर्याय.

29. This incident refers to the context when he was praised by नागपत्नीs, cf. भाग० 10. 16. 33 ff., also 10. 17. 13. Are we to take second णाअ=नाक, heavenly, in the light of दिव्यस्रग्गन्धवाससम् in भाग० 10. 17. 13? The figure of speech is उपमा

30. Once a forest-fire was spreading in the forest on the banks of यमुना. Every one sought the shelter of कृष्ण who consequently swallowed the flames. Cf. भाग० 10. 17. 21–25: इत्थं स्वजनवैक्लव्यं निरीक्ष्य जगदीश्वरः । तमग्निमपिबत्तीव्रमनन्तोऽनन्तशक्तिधृक् ॥ २५ ॥. Another similar event is described in भाग० 10. 19, and that chapter is called दावाग्निपान. The figure of speech in this verse is अर्थान्तरन्यास.

31. About प्रलम्ब see Notes on i. 21 above. The destruction of प्रलम्ब is described in भाग० 10. 18. गोवाअंतं is an adjective of प्रलम्ब who had assumed the form of a गोप. Note the sound effect in the last line.

32. Cf. भाग० 10. 22, which is called गोपीवस्त्रापहारः, especially verses 8–9 etc.

33. Once the hungry गोपs were sent by कृष्ण to a sacrifice that was being celebrated in a forest, but the priests turned them off without giving them food with no regard for कृष्ण who sent them. Then कृष्ण advised them to beg food from their wives who, despite the objection raised by their beloveds etc., showed their respect for कृष्ण and offered food to the गोपs (see भाग० 10. 23). कृष्ण blesses them thus: तन्मनो मयि युञ्जाना अचिरान्मामवाप्स्यथ ॥ ३२ ॥'

34. The pastoral people of व्रज, नन्द and others were once out to perform a sacrifice in honour of Indra who bestows rain etc., but कृष्ण induced them to stop it and worship the mountain गोवर्धन (see भाग० 10. 24). Here the figure of speech is उपमा.

35. When his worship was stopped by कृष्ण, Indra felt offended, was quickly enraged, and poured down a fatal deluge of rain with a view to wash away the गोवर्धन mountain and all the people of that area; but कृष्ण lifted up the mountain गोवर्धन on his finger, held it for seven days like an umbrella, and thus prepared a solid shelter for the people of वृन्दावन. Indra was outwitted, and at last he paid homage to कृष्ण. Cf. भाग० 10. 25, especially verse 19 etc. This verse is a fine illustration of the author's confident handling of the language.

36. पर्वतवैरिन् is Indra who had cut off the wings of mountains that were boisterously flying causing a great anxiety to the world. When कृष्ण protected all people from the rains, Indra was humiliated, and he offered glowing praise at the feet of कृष्ण. At that moment, the heavenly cow sprinkled him with milk and thus coronated him like Indra. Just as Indra is the Indra of the Devas कृष्ण is the Indra of Gopas: the former is देवेन्द्र and the latter गोपेन्द्र. गोविन्द is only a Prākrit form of गोपेन्द्र. भाग० explains गोविन्द by saying गवामिन्द्रतां गत: (10. 27. 23*1). The form पओहि is a direct corruption of पयोभिः.

37. अभ्रमुवल्लभः is ऐरावत, the elephant of Indra. Cf. with this and on the last verse भाग॰ 10. 27, especially verse 22: एवं कृष्णमुपामन्त्र्य सुरभिः पयसात्मनः। जलैराकाशगङ्गाया ऐरावतकरोद्धृतैः॥ etc. Note the syllabic repetition in the last line.

38. प्रचेतस् is the name of वरुण. As Nanda once entered the waters of यमुना out of time (or as भाग॰ puts it अविज्ञायासुरीं वेलां), he was carried away by an असुर in the service of वरुण; but कृष्ण saw वरुण, got respects from him, and brought his foster-father back to the joy of all the गोपs. (see भाग॰ 10. 28).

39. Pischel postulates a word * तूर्थ to explain the etymology of तूह which is usually equated with तीर्थ (§ 58). For the description of रासक्रीडा see भाग॰ 10. 29 etc.

40. Are we to read पवंचिअविवंचिअं ? Cf. भाग॰ 10. 29–33.

41. अक्रूर is addressing these verses to वसुदेव (and देवकी), and hence दे णंदणो (=तव नन्दनः कृष्णः). Note the form दिक्खु from Sk. दिक्षु Loc. sg. The figure of speech is रूपक. See भाग॰ 10. 29 etc. and 10. 15. 9 etc.

42. Once a certain गोपी, for whom कृष्ण had shown some special attachment, was puffed with pride. She requested कृष्ण to carry her as she was not able to walk. कृष्ण asked her to mount his shoulders but disappeared all of a sudden. She repented for her vanity and began to lament (भाग॰ 10. 30. 34 etc.). कृष्ण is not accessible to men in whom तमोगुण predominates. Here we have विरोध and उपमा. Note the form दक्खणिज्ज, perhaps a compromise between दर्शनीय and प्रेक्षणीय.

43. On the disappearance of कृष्ण, गोपीs felt very sorry; when their vanity melted away, कृष्ण again appeared before them in full glory; and their sports became all the more attractive (see भाग॰ 10. 31–32). Here the figure of speech is दृष्टान्त.

44. शङ्खचूड was a servant of कुवेर. In his attempt to kidnap some गोपीs he was killed by कृष्ण; and the jewel from his crown was passed over to बलराम (भाग॰ 10. 34. 25 ff). अरिष्ट was a दैत्य sent by कंस to destroy कृष्ण. He assumed the form of a savage bull and attacked कृष्ण. कृष्ण twisted its neck, pulled out its horn and thrashed it thereby so much that it vomited blood and died on the spot (भाग॰ 10. 36. 1–15). The name of the दैत्य is अरिष्ट so च+अरिष्टः=चरिट्ठो; this Sandhi unusual. Should we read किं गरिट्ठो अरिट्ठो? As to केशिन् see Notes on i. 21 above (भाग॰ 10. 37). व्योम was an असुर, a descendent of मय. He put on the dress of a cowherd, and playing with the cowherd boys closetted them in a cave the mouth of which he closed with a slab of stone. कृष्ण came to their rescue and destroyed व्योम (भाग॰ 10. 32. 26 etc.) Here the author hurriedly refers to three events in one and the same verse.

45. कंस invited कृष्ण with the pretext of the bow-festival and with the aim of killing him; but the arrival of कृष्ण resulted into the destruction of कंस himself. In fine, his plan turned against himself. The illustration given by the author is quite significant.

46. माया or योगमाया is really the daughter of नन्द and यशोदा, but she was exchanged with child कृष्ण and brought to the bed of देवकी in मथुरा. कंस wanted to smash that female child on a stone, but it slipped from his hands and flashed forth in the sky like lightening (भाग॰ 10. 4). Thus she is the sister of कृष्ण who is therefore मायाग्रज.

47. This verse expresses the blessings of the parents to **राम** and **कृष्ण.**

48. **कं पि लच्छिं=कामपि अवर्णनीयां लक्ष्मीम्.** The author concludes the last verse with the word **लक्ष्मी**, as he began the first verse with **श्री (= लक्ष्मी).**

48*1. This verse explains why the author wrote this poem. He claims that it is a new poem and that its study would introduce one confidently into the extensive field of Prākrit literature; and he wishes that all should read it. **रूह** I have taken as **रोधस्**, a dam. It is not unlikely if it is a wrong reading for **तूह=तीर्थ**, a ford, a road.

48*2. For his protection he invokes god **विष्णु** who is saluted by all other gods including **ब्रह्मन्.** This verse is in Sanskrit, and the second letter is the same in all the lines.

In this canto the author has used a large number of **वृत्त**s. Verses Nos. 1, 2, 6, 8, 9, 11 and 13–18 are composed in **उपजाति** metre which is a combination of stanzas of lines of **इन्द्रवज्रा** and **उपेन्द्रवज्रा.** According to our author there are fourteen varieties of it (**वृ॰ वा॰ १४**). Nos. 3–5, 7, 10, 19 and 20 are composed in **उपेन्द्रवज्रा** which is four times ⏑ – ⏑ | – – ⏑ | ⏑ – ⏑ | – – || and is thus defined : **उपेन्द्रवज्रा कथिता जतजेभ्यो गुरुद्वयम्** (**वृ॰ वा. १२**). Verse No. 12 is composed in **इन्द्रवज्रा** metre which is four times – – ⏑ | – – ⏑ | ⏑ – ⏑ | – – || and is thus defined : **ततजेभ्यो गुरुद्वन्द्वमिन्द्रवज्राभिधीयते** (**वृ॰ वा॰ १३**). Nos. 21, 22, 34, 36, 42, 45 and 48*1 are composed in **वसन्ततिलक** which is four times – – ⏑ | – ⏑ ⏑ | ⏑ – ⏑ | ⏑ – ⏑ | – – || and is thus defined : **शक्वर्यां तभजा जो गौ वसन्ततिलकं मतम्** (**वृ॰ वा॰ ३०**). Nos. 23, 26, 46 and 47 are composed in शार्दूलविक्रीडित. (see p. 190 above). Nos. 24 and 32 are composed in वसन्तमालिका (see p. 179 above). Nos. 25 and 38 are composed in स्वागता metre (see p. 200 above). Nos. 27 and 40 are composed in पृथ्वी metre (see p. 200 above). Nos. 28, 43 and 48*2 are composed in मञ्जुभाषिणी which is four times ᴗ ᴗ – | ᴗ – ᴗ | ᴗ ᴗ – | ᴗ – ᴗ | – || and is defined thus : सजौ सजौ गुरुर्यत्र सा भवेन्मञ्जुभाषिणी (वृ० वा० ३०). Verse No. 29 is written in रथोद्धता metre which is four times – ᴗ – | ᴗ ᴗ ᴗ | – ᴗ – | ᴗ – || and is defined thus रेफो नकारो रेफश्च लगौ चेयं रथोद्धता (वृ० वा० १७). Verse Nos. 30 and 31 are composed in शालिनी metre which is four times – – – | – – ᴗ | – – ᴗ | – – || and is thus difined शालिनी मतभ्यो गौ विरतिर्युगवाजिभिः (वृ० वा० १६). Verse No. 33 is written in मन्दाक्रान्ता metre which is four times – – – | – ᴗ ᴗ | ᴗ ᴗ ᴗ | – – ᴗ | – – ᴗ | – – || and which is defined thus: उपायैश्च नयैरश्वैर्विरामो यत्र विद्यते । मन्दाक्रान्ता तु सा ज्ञेया मभौ नततगा गुरुः ॥ (वृ० वा० ३६). Verse Nos. 35, 39, 41 and 44 are composed in स्रग्धरा metre (see p. 190 above). No. 37 is written in द्रुतविलम्बित metre which is four times ᴗ ᴗ ᴗ | – ᴗ ᴗ | – ᴗ ᴗ | – ᴗ – ||, and it is thus defined: नभाभ्यां च भराभ्यां च युक्तं द्रुतविलम्बितम् (वृ० वा० २०). And No 48 is composed in मालिनी metre (see p. 179 above).

INDEX

(of Proper Names in the Text)

N.B.-The dark numbers indicate that some biographical information is given in the Notes at those places.